WITHDRAWN FROM
THE LIBRARY

KT-146-712

WINCHESTER

KA 0423510 X

NEW HORIZONS IN CRIMINOLOGY

CONVICT CRIMINOLOGY
Inside and out

Rod Earle

UNIVERSITY OF WINCHESTER
LIBRARY

For my mother and father

UNIVERSITY OF WINCHESTER

0423510X

First published in Great Britain in 2016 by

Policy Press
University of Bristol
1-9 Old Park Hill
Bristol
BS2 8BB
UK
t: +44 (0)117 954 5940
pp-info@bristol.ac.uk
www.policypress.co.uk

North America office:
Policy Press
c/o The University of Chicago Press
1427 East 60th Street
Chicago, IL 60637, USA
t: +1 773 702 7700
f: +1 773-702-9756
sales@press.uchicago.edu
www.press.uchicago.edu

© Policy Press 2016

British Library Cataloguing in Publication Data
A catalogue record for this book is available from the British Library

Library of Congress Cataloging-in-Publication Data
A catalog record for this book has been requested

ISBN 978-1-4473-2364-8 hardcover
ISBN 978-1-4473-2368-6 ePub
ISBN 978-1-4473-2369-3 Mobi

The right of Rod Earle to be identified as author of this work has been asserted by him in accordance with the Copyright, Designs and Patents Act 1988.

All rights reserved: no part of this publication may be reproduced, stored in a retrieval system, or transmitted in any form or by any means, electronic, mechanical, photocopying, recording, or otherwise without the prior permission of Policy Press.

The statements and opinions contained within this publication are solely those of the author and not of the University of Bristol or Policy Press. The University of Bristol and Policy Press disclaim responsibility for any injury to persons or property resulting from any material published in this publication.

Policy Press works to counter discrimination on grounds of gender, race, disability, age and sexuality.

Cover design by Policy Press
Front cover image: istock
Printed and bound in Great Britain by CPI Group (UK) Ltd,
Croydon, CR0 4YY
Policy Press uses environmentally responsible print partners

MIX
Paper from
responsible sources
FSC® C013604

Contents

Acknowledgments

Way back in 2000, Tim Newburn gave me an academic job when I really needed one and kept me in work until I found my feet. He, along with Mike Shiner who welcomed me at Goldsmiths College and steered me through my first research project, provided a warm and embracing introduction to the realm of research and academic practice. Tim has been an inspiration and model of intellectual generosity. His enthusiasm for ideas and research, for collaboration and rigour in method and writing, along with his tireless energy and sparkling humour are, thankfully, infectious but almost entirely harmless.

Before that, John Lea, Jock Young, Roger Matthews and Jayne Mooney, my tutors on the MA Criminology at Middlesex, found and fed a hunger for criminology I did not know I had. Jock's gentle coaxing and genial good humour was light and casual but irresistibly memorable. His premature death is a huge loss to criminology. John recently disclosed to me his own time inside – a month on bail spent in Brixton prison in the mid sixties after his arrest protesting against the military seizure of power in Greece. He was an inspiring and generous teacher.

Coretta Phillips at the LSE is the reason I am able to write this book. She has encouraged and inspired me with patience, insight and thoughtful reflection. She included me in the ESRC project on Ethnicity, Identity and Social Relations in Prison in 2006 and as a result I was able to complete a PhD by Publication. Coretta warned me, at the outset, that many otherwise productive academic relationships have come apart over messy disputes on the distribution of authorship of a project's findings. Having agreed these in advance and as we proceeded to develop publications, we avoided such an outcome and continue to profit, in the best senses of the word, from a productive relationship. That Coretta waded through a complete draft of this book and made helpful and encouraging comments on each chapter, indicates how exceptionally lucky I have been to work with an academic who combines generosity and intellectual openness with systematic organisational thoroughness. Though we still disagree about pre-formatting text in Microsoft Word documents, working with Coretta has never been anything less than a pleasure.

It was through Coretta that I met Andreas Aresti and between us, and the able support of Sacha Darke, we hatched the idea of a British Convict Criminology group. With Andy and Sacha and the enthusiastic encouragement of many members of the British Society

UNIVERSITY OF WINCHESTER LIBRARY

of Criminology the group has grown to include other ex-prisoner scholars, such as Bill Davies and Dave Honeywell. Bill's close and supportive reading of various chapter drafts was particularly welcome. They have all been a supportive presence during the preparation of this book, and the future of Convict Criminology in Britain is in good hands with them.

Jeffrey Ian Ross and Stephen C Richards of the US Convict Criminology group have been a source of inspiration through their invention and organisation of Convict Criminology, with other ex-convict scholars in the US. Both have provided generous encouragement and guidance in completing this book.

At the Open University I am grateful to my colleagues in the Department of Health and Social Care, particularly Richard Hester, Wayne Taylor and Carol Johnson for providing a stimulating and supportive academic environment. My Head of Department, Mary Twomey has never been anything less than supportive and has helped focus my efforts and interests. OU Colleagues in Social Policy and Criminology, particularly my PhD supervisors Deb Drake and Steve Tombs show how it should be done, with integrity, originality and without compromise.

At Policy Press Victoria Pittman has steered the project to completion with a minimum of fuss and bother. I am particularly grateful to Andrew Millie, the Series Editor, for inviting me to take this project on, and prompting me to write about convict criminology.

My children, Chloe, Joe and Hannah, have kept my feet on the ground and my heart bursting with pride. Charlotte has put up with me for the best part of 30 years. Her love and support throughout the various criminological projects I've worked on are a helpful reminder that when all is said and done, borrowing slightly from Rilke,[1] loving each other and keeping our family well is the work for which all other work is merely preparation.

I am very lucky to have two wise older sisters and a smart younger brother who provide me with constant intellectual traffic and emotional warmth. This book is dedicated, with love, to my mother and father. With children of my own I now know more of what I've put them through. Even though theirs was a generation given much more to hope and faith in the future than the anxious misgiving that grips

---

[1] 'For one human being to love another: that is perhaps the most difficult of all our tasks, the ultimate, the last test and proof, the work for which all other work is but preparation.' Rainer Maria Rilke, Letters To A Young Poet

my own, the distress I must have caused at various times, alluded to herein, cannot have been easy to bear. For that, I am sorry. They have expected nothing and been willing, it always seemed to me, to give everything, so this is for them.

NEW HORIZONS IN CRIMINOLOGY

Series editor: Professor Andrew Millie, Department of Law and Criminology, Edge Hill University, UK

Preface

The Policy Press *New Horizons in Criminology* book series provides concise authoritative texts which reflect cutting edge thought and theoretical developments in criminology and have an international scope. Divided into eight chapters, these short accessible texts explain principles and developments clearly before going deeper into the subject, and are written so that the non-specialist academic, student or practitioner can understand them. Written by leading authors in their fields, the series aims to become essential reading for all academics and students (and practitioners) interested in where criminology is heading.

When I first proposed a series on 'New Horizons' one criminologist suggested that criminology does not need any more criminologies. The subject of criminology has expanded so much over recent years that perhaps it should have time to draw breath – growing from 'a smallish cottage industry' (Loader and Sparks, 2012, 4) to the extent that most universities now offer criminology and/or criminal justice at undergraduate or postgraduate levels. Yet, my reply was that without exploring new areas of enquiry the subject could stagnate. If criminologists had not been willing to explore new horizons there would not have been the expansion from conventional crime and justice issues into important research on, for example, state crimes, social harms, green issues or cultural identity, as reflected in 'new' criminologies such as green criminology and cultural criminology. For any discipline to remain vibrant it needs to explore new areas and, where relevant, to draw on other disciplines and investigate innovative methodologies. This does not mean the past is cast aside. Instead, by exploring new horizons light might be reflected back onto criminology's traditional core. The criminological imagination (compare Young, 2011) continues to expand with new approaches being adopted by criminologists and criminological approaches being relevant to new areas of study. This book series aims to reveal to a wider audience these cutting edge developments.

From day one I wanted a book on convict criminology to be included in the series. I was thrilled when Rod Earle accepted my invitation. His writing is both highly readable and insightful. I first came across Rod's work in this area at the annual conferences of the British Society of Criminology where he has been on various panels (alongside Sacha Darke, Andreas Aresti, Jeffrey Ian Ross and others) discussing the scope of a convict criminology. 'Born in the USA', convict criminology has spread to other shores and taken on new meanings and possibilities. These conference panels have always provided exciting and animated discussions and a challenge to the conventional approach when studying criminal justice, of the outsider looking in. In this important new book Rod unpacks the job of a convict criminologist, and considers 'the possibilities of insider perspectives, of ex-prisoner scholars contributing to criminological knowledge'. The book comes highly recommended.

Foreword by Shadd Maruna

In praise of an unusual and obvious idea

So, I am waiting for a lift in a soulless American hotel during yet another criminology conference. It is 1999, I am certain, but I do not remember where we are. Also waiting is a famous American criminologist and two younger conference-goers whom I assume are his PhD students as they appear to hang on his every word and laugh nervously at his fairly pedestrian jokes. One of the students asks him, "Have you heard of this convict criminology thing?" He hadn't. "I guess they are ex-prisoners who are now criminologists and writing about prisons," she says. Sceptically, the professor asks, "So, the argument is, what, that you can't really understand imprisonment unless you've been locked up yourself?" He pauses for a moment, contorts his face and looks down at his shoes while he digests this unusual idea for the first time. Then he lifts his eyebrows, holds out his arms, palms up and shrugs, "Well... they're probably right." The two students (and I) gasp to ourselves. Really!? Then, the criminologist follows this up, "But, I mean, what are we supposed to do with that? Go out and commit a crime? I think you two best stick to your secondary data analysis." And, with a sharp exhale of breath, the three of them have another laugh at the professor's wit. Most likely, none of the three of them will give convict criminology another thought.[1]

The same is certainly not the case with me. I would go on to think about convict criminology a lot over the next 15 years. I was there at one of the first ASC panels on the subject. (I thought it was *the* first, but then maybe it was just *my* first.) It might have been 1997. The room was nearly empty, so someone suggested we put our chairs in a circle. To break the awkwardness, the inimitable Chuck Terry quipped, "I feel like we're at an AA meeting, 'My name is Chuck and I'm a positivist.'" Since then, I've been to maybe close to a dozen panel sessions that were almost always filled to capacity, and always the most free-wheeling and enjoyable discussions at any criminology meeting. As well, I have been lucky enough to sit in on some of the first UK convict criminology panels at British Society of Criminology conferences. I regularly read and assign convict criminology research to

---

[1] Please forgive the anecdote, but you will see I am trying to keep with the style for this remarkably literate and wonderfully readable book.

my students, occasionally help out at the *Journal of Prisoners on Prisons*, and have taught criminology inside prisons. What is most important is that I have had the great honour and privilege to mentor a number of formerly incarcerated students in undergraduate and graduate courses, and I have learned an enormous amount from collaborating with them on research projects over the years.

At the same time, I actually have a lot of sympathy for that famous professor in the lift. Yes, there is something absolutely common-sensical about the animating concept of convict criminology, but at the same time it was never completely clear to me whether I could myself ever 'do' convict criminology and as such 'what to do with it' as an idea. Until now, I admit that I did not fully appreciate just what convict criminology meant for all of us non-cons who study crime or what its impact has been on the wider field. I get it now. You will too when you finish this remarkable book. Indeed, this is the book that the concept of convict criminology has always needed and deserved, articulating the movement's core epistemology and raison d'être in a way that I have not read before.

I see it like this. David Garland describes two approaches to the study of crime: Criminology of the Self and Criminology of the Other. Whereas the latter can justify draconian penal expansion and practices such as the death penalty and solitary confinement, the former is the route to understanding and therefore addressing criminal behaviour. Convict criminology is, of course, an ideal example of a Criminology of the Self. The professor who announces to the class that she has herself been to prison automatically challenges the objectification that is an omnipresent risk in the study of crime. Likewise, in published work, the convict criminologist can literally use the pronoun 'we', not 'they', when discussing the lives of ex-prisoners or those who have been processed through the criminal justice system.

Yet, it is more than this. Without convict criminology, the Criminology of the Self may not even be a possibility. A parallel would be to imagine the subject of African American studies with no African American scholars or teachers, or LGBTQ studies consisting exclusively of heterosexuals about gay desires and identities. Such a thing would seem an absurdity today, but of course, both existed not that long ago in modern universities. African American lives were the sole property of white anthropology until the transformative contributions of WEB Du Bois (whose spirit infuses Earle's book from start to finish, appropriately enough), just as the essence of gay and lesbian identity was the property of heterosexual psychiatry until even more recent works by Foucault and others. This is not to say, if there is any doubt, that non-African American scholars cannot contribute to African American studies or that straight people cannot research gay lives. There are incredibly strong examples of both. The point is only that without such first-person voices and perspectives, a field of study can be reduced to the worst sort of othering, leading to disastrous policy consequences as predicted by Garland (and, surely, some subfields of criminology, largely untouched by convict criminology, such as risk assessment and biopsychosocial research, illustrate this hypothesis rather nicely).

The question, then, is not so much 'What are we supposed to do with convict criminology?' Rather, 'What is convict criminology supposed to do for criminology?' After reading this book, my sense is that we might just owe it our fundamental legitimacy as a field of study.

Shadd Maruna
Dean of the School of Criminal Justice
Rutgers University–Newark, USA

'**Though the fruits of crime are bitter, the roots are tender**'

Albert Camus, *The Rebel*

ONE

A personal introduction

A RING OF GREEN SLIME

I had only been in prison one day. It was time to go out into the exercise yard and I was anxious because it was clearly a kind of informal and vaguely social occasion.

The exercise yard? It sounded like a prison cliché. As I emerged through the door into a high walled compound I could see the walking circle of prisoners forming, and couldn't quite believe my eyes. It was just like in the movies, except they weren't wearing striped uniforms, just shabby grey trousers and jumpers. Walking round and round in a circle, going nowhere, like in the cliché. It seemed an unreal stereotype of meaninglessness. Prison life. Do I go with the flow or what? I didn't know what else to do, so I wandered slowly toward the circulating straggle of men, and fell into step.

It was 1982. I was 24. Now, I have crowded fragments of indistinct memories about the occasion, but one that has always stayed with me is the awful ring of green slime that had formed on the inside of the circle as the men spat gobbits of phlegm to one side. A string of men walking slowly round and round in a circle, three times a day, and like some kind of human-formed seaweed on the tarmac, the accumulated expectorations of 200 men disfigured the exercise yard with passively malign intent. Prison. Men. All in it together.

Early one morning some 25 years later I was in another prison, and another exercise yard. This time I wasn't a prisoner. I was on the other side of a wire mesh fence, looking in toward the men walking slowly round and round. Observing, not participating this time. I didn't want or need the exercise because I hadn't been locked in a small cell since 7pm the previous evening. I'd walk the dog when I got home. I caught myself thinking about the ring of green slime, though. No sign of it in this prison. What else was different? The knot of nerves in my stomach and the tightness as I felt myself wrestling with it were not so different to those I had felt 25 years earlier, familiar now as an anxiety about being in the wrong place, not fitting in, feeling vulnerable, but in a transitory way I could handle. This was research not a prison sentence.

I was learning how I might conduct research among these men, to learn about the way race, ethnicities and masculinities shape prison life, and are shaped by prison experience.

This book is not about that research (see Earle, 2009; 2011a; 2011b; 2011c; 2012; 2013; 2014; Earle and Phillips, 2012; 2013; 2015; Phillips and Earle, 2010; 2011; Phillips, 2012) but it is about the experience of being twice inside prison, on different sides of the wire and the walls. My memories of once being in a prison, and the activity of researching another prison came together repeatedly over the months of that research project. Having two types of experiences of prison to draw from became gradually more significant as the ethnography developed momentum and I started to write about it for a PhD thesis. In this book I examine what these contrasting points of view might mean for something called 'criminology' and people who call themselves 'criminologists'. The book explores whether and how having personal experience of being in prison makes any kind of difference to studying or researching crime and punishment, or teaching criminology. It asks if 'doing time' can contribute something distinctive to 'doing criminology', and whether 'convict criminology' is an apt enough description of this 'something'.

For men, doing prison time is usually the product of serious violence, fairly sustained involvement in criminalised activities, persistent bad luck or particularly poor judgement, in various and innumerable combinations.[1] In my case, the last three out of those four apply. For the moment, that is all I am going to say about my convictions. Disclosure of crimes and convictions are a sensitive topic within convict criminology involving complex questions of privacy, stigma, self-management, shame, pride and professional respect. For the time being, I ask you to ask yourself if, how and why (not) knowing what is involved in those convictions affects your reading of this text.

[1] Only about 5 per cent of the prison population is composed of women and women's pathways into prison, and out, are very different to men's. They are more likely than men to receive a prison sentence for a first offence. The offences they are likely to commit, the circumstances implicated in its commission, the sentence they receive and their prospects afterwards, are also likely to be differ significantly from men's (Home Office, 2007).

Acquiring convictions and qualifications

To get sent to prison means being arrested, going on trial and being convicted, usually more than once. 'Doing time' in prison can precede trial but after conviction the amount of time behind bars is settled. In my case, a thankfully brief, typically unnecessary, three-month sentence was handed out to me by a judge in a bright red robe and a white horsehair wig. That he garnished the sentence with his personal evaluation that I was 'more of a knave than a rogue' suggests that he wasn't just dressed for the part but relished his place in the court's reputation for being a world apart, and out of time.

Those various experiences of arrest, police detention and questioning, remand on bail and convoluted legal procedure, prosecution, trial and conviction that culminated in a prison sentence are the staple diet of conventional criminology. It is sometimes said that criminology is all about the three Cs: cops, courts and corrections, but I have been quite surprised by how few criminologists appear to have any direct, first-hand experience of these three key stages. Perhaps they are not telling, and that is entirely their prerogative, but with one in four men in the UK acquiring a criminal conviction by the age of 30, and increasingly being required to disclose it in employment selection procedures (Henley, 2014; Stacey, 2015) the lack of first-hand experience of criminal justice among criminal justice academics is, at least, suggestive of some kind of selection bias. Aside from the possibility that criminologists are more prone to virtue, and less liable to temptation, than the ordinary person in the street, it says something revealing about middle-class and working-class career trajectories and the different social architecture they encounter as they progress through the age/crime curve. A further possibility is that increasingly, criminologists in the UK are women, and thus far less likely to acquire a criminal conviction. Or that criminologists are very smart people and don't get caught. As any well trained social scientist is likely to point out, all the above apply, in various combinations.

In recent decades, becoming a criminologist is likely to involve leaving school with some decent exam results, graduating from university with a degree, possibly in criminology, then several more years at university doing a post-graduate qualification in criminology, social research methods or some combination thereof. For the most part and for most people, the two ways of doing the three Cs, doing time for crimes and doing criminology, are mutually exclusive. But, as I came to the end of my prison research project in 2009, I met someone else who was doing similar sort of work to me, who had also been to prison and was concerned by the connections involved. Dr Andreas Aresti had escaped the self-evident perils of nominative determinism (your name determines what you become), secured a social science PhD and was involved in a series of campaigns concerned with the predicaments of prisoners and ex-prisoners. By word of mouth, and with the supportive encouragement of various academic colleagues, such as Sacha Darke and Dave Manlow at the University of Westminster, we discovered that there were a few more people around studying for their PhD, and interested in an academic career. A few of us got together and discussed the formation of a group like the convict criminology group that had been established in the 1990s in the USA. This book emerges from those contacts and examines what kinds of relationships might exist, or we might create, between criminal convictions and academic qualifications as sources of knowledge about crime, criminal justice and criminology. It is a book that asks if procedures of criminal conviction and academic qualification, like those described above, combined, amount to a way of doing criminology that could be called 'convict criminology'.

Troubling 'the convict': doubtful convictions, colonial misgivings

An immediate difficulty arises in the word 'convict' which is loaded with a variety of unhelpful connotations. At one level it is relatively simple and familiar: a term for people in prison, criminals. But, on the English side of the Atlantic it isn't a word commonly used in either conversation or academic analysis. In the UK, the term has either a transatlantic or an archaic resonance. It brings to mind images of the fugitive convict, Abel Magwitch, made famous in the films and illustrations of Charles Dicken's novel, *Great Expectations*: a chain-dragging wretch, dressed in stripes and on the run from the notorious convict ships moored on the Thames estuary.

The term 'convict' also evokes a fixed condition and unbending ideas: convictions are both solid opinions and enduring labels. In this respect, it suggests a creative tension and unsettling ambivalence with one of the great animating traditions of radical criminology, the labelling perspective. As Howard Becker (1963, 9) remarked: 'The deviant is one to whom that label has been successfully applied; deviant behavior is behavior that people so label.' A criminal conviction is the archetype of labels in criminology, the stickiest of them all, and the most defining of its purpose. It is the eponymous source code of the discipline.

'The Convict' has nagging gothic connotations of horror and stigma that are unhelpfully hard to shake loose. The convict system is a historical reality that carries with it violent images of terror, slavery, forced labour, exile and banishment that make it a difficult term to embrace positively. It is always and already implicated in the systematisation of punishment from flamboyant, expressive cruelty to 'the mechanical apportioning of strictly metered punishments designed to wear each prisoner down into bovine acceptance' (Hughes, 2003, 404; Foucault, 1979). The convict is the abject figure of enlightened humanity, presenting to the moral reformists of the late nineteenth and early twentieth century all the necessary criteria for their programmes of moral uplift and improvement, with all their attendant perversities and horrors (Ignatieff, 1978).

The convict is inextricably tied up with the idea, the realities and the project of the penal colony. The deportation of convicts from Britain, first to the Americas, and then to Australia and Tasmania, in the eighteenth and nineteenth centuries is no simple coincidence alongside the trade in people from Africa as slaves. Ideas about human difference, hierarchy, social order and social control, fell heavily on the criminalised white populations subject to penal transportation but the full force of racialisation was directed at indigenous populations and most cripplingly on Africans. Penal colonies, such as Australia, were used, as the name implies, to punish people as well as establish colonial objectives. Populated by white convicts and ruled by white military officers they became places where the colonial powers rehearsed and refined programmes of categorisation, law, control and segregation on reluctant and resistant populations (Cuneen et al, 2013).

Cuneen et al (2013) describe how the deliberate exclusion of black and indigenous people from the progressive reform of the most excessively brutal aspects of penal servitude in the colonies served to attach an exclusive and 'intrinsic' whiteness to the liberties and democratic rights proclaimed by the Enlightenment. Punishments of particular brutality and violence were gradually phased out, or graduated to lesser intensity and severity, for white convicts but maintained for slaves, black and indigenous convicts in the colonies (Moore, 2014). As such, the treatment of convicts and penal reform was heavily implicated in the racialisation and manufacture of whiteness at a critical stage in the establishment of British and other European Empires. As one of the first and greatest of US sociologists, WEB Du Bois (1903) notes, 'whiteness' operates not just in the capacity to deliver material advantage to poor white people, it instills a profound psychological dividend. Abject as their conditions were, ordinary white

UNIVERSITY OF WINCHESTER LIBRARY

men and women of the colonies and penal camps were privileged with inclusion in humanity by their differential treatment, at the expense of the exclusion and degradation of black and indigenous people. Their eligibility to be subjects of progressive penal reform was predicated on their being white. It was a gift from above and as such it was a poisoned chalice that cemented the racial hierarchy on which colonialism, and their own subordination to its needs, depended. These 'rules of engagement' between race and criminal justice set up a process of mutual construction that is both ongoing, self-perpetuating and cyclical (Spivakovsky, 2013)

Specific colonial and patriarchal understandings of humanity, personal and social life shaped both the figure of the convict and penal practice in the colonies and 'at home', in the British metropole (Moore, 2014; Hall, 1996). These reveal the convict as a figure that links penality and punishment with strategies of imperial expansion, colonisation and racialisation. Accompanying the emergence of the convict is always their capacity for labour, a human latency to which they are frequently reduced. The association between slave labour and convict labour provides the principal rationale for their rehabilitation in as much that it promises to return the convict to conventional social relations through the dubious dignity of wage labour.

Culture, conscience and convictions

'Convict', then, is a word with a long and troubled history. And words matter because, as Raymond Williams (2014) insists, they are the material of struggle, reflecting changing relations of social force and influence. 'Convict' is a label that resists social inversion or reclamation, as has happened with pejorative terms like 'queer' and 'dyke'. In the hands of gay liberation movements these words were turned from terms of abuse and disparagement to ones of empowerment and belonging. Black people's struggles have reclaimed many such words, forcing language and vocabulary into contested territory and out of the grasp of white power. 'Convict' is an unlikely candidate for such recuperation. Simply put, there is rarely anything for anyone to celebrate in a conviction. It is applied as much by law as by prejudice, and in that sense, can only be effectively undone by law. A conviction can be 'quashed' in court but until then it carries a degree of acquiescence and legitimacy, both in the intended stigmatic effect of the labelling and the process of its application through a court of law. A conviction also carries some measure of resolution for victims and though they may have been rendered marginal by judicial procedure (Christie,

1977), they are entitled to remain a significant party to any process of redefinition.

In some aspects of popular culture a convict is regarded simply as a habituated criminal, a fixed category of being and 'a person...for whom institutional confinement has become a way of life' (Empey, 1970, 13). The anchorage of the term 'convict' in formal legality places it somewhat beyond the moulding and reshaping tendencies of popular culture: convictions may be overturned through 'due process' of law rather than reclaimed or destabilised by cultural struggle. Indeed, perhaps the most radical, organised and educated cohort of prisoners to have emerged from British prisons in recent times are those Irish republicans who explicitly and strategically resisted the imposition of criminal status on their imprisonment – they refused to be convicts. For Irish republican prisoners and ex-prisoners in the 1970s and 1980s, who used their incarceration as both a political tool and an opportunity to develop their politics, convict status was resisted and rejected in principle and practice (Beresford, 1987). In criminalisation Irish republicans recognised not a sociological perspective but a British political strategy to fragment and isolate their resistance to the partition of Ireland by rendering their struggle a mere criminal conspiracy. Irish republicans' orientation to prison and political struggle in the 1970s and 1980s was one in which 'higher education' was part of an emancipatory continuum that drew from Paulo Freire's ideas about conscientisation (Freire, 1970; 1985). It was sociological critique developed as an intellectual mobilisation toward a specific political objective: a 32-county socialist republic.

Freire's work may be less familiar to twenty-first century students in the west than it was to my generation who entered university campuses in the late 1970s when they still hummed with activities sparked by the women's liberation and anti-war movements, Black nationalism, Pan-Africanism, militant socialists, anarchists and anti-apartheid activism. Freire may have been pre-occupied with relations between 'the Third World' and 'the First World', and his ideas taken up mainly in revolutionary Latin America, anti-colonial struggles in Ireland and the liberation movements of Africa, but his concern to re-contextualise familiar words (such as *favela*, the Portuguese word for slum) and re-examine their implications, is consistent with the project of convict criminology. His work has been about finding voices otherwise silenced in relations between the powerful and those over whom they wield power. That is something any prisoner knows about.

Convicts, as a category of people, have a relationship to criminology that is similar to, perhaps analogous with, the 'Third World's' relationship to the 'First World'. On a rather basic level, they are a source of raw materials. For Freire, concepts and words must be rooted in the social framework in which those learning about them exist. Developing this conceptual dialogue between experience and epistemology (the study of how we know what we know) presents unique possibilities for critical analysis. This is not a question of semantics or solipsism, says Freire, but a form of cultural action, a process of *conscientisation*: '[a] process in which men [sic], not as recipients, but as knowing subjects, achieve a deepening awareness both of the socio-cultural reality which shapes their lives and of their capacity to transform that reality' (Freire, 1970, 51). In this sense, convict criminology is a project to produce a distinctive transformative form of knowledge about crime and about criminology. Within criminology, Harcourt (2011) argues that reshaping the public imagination of 'the convict' is one of the cornerstones of the struggle to de-legitimatise mass incarceration. Convict criminology takes up that question and offers the public imagination a new challenge, another way of seeing convicts that unsettles familiar meanings and images.

Convict criminology is thus an epistemological project, rather than an organisation composed of a minority, oppressed or excluded group. It is a listening project without guarantees of success, which also amplifies the voices of those for whom criminology has provided a connection to parts of their lives stained by crime and experiences of criminal justice. It doesn't mean that having criminal convictions automatically qualifies you as an expert on crime, or to become a criminologist, just as having a heart attack doesn't qualify you to become a heart surgeon. It does mean, however, attending to the murmurs of the heart, the feelings that accompany the movement from prison convict to university teacher.

Troubling and staggering: the boom in criminology

> History is the raw material for nationalist or ethnic or fundamentalist ideologies, as poppies are the raw material for heroin addiction. The past is an essential element, perhaps the essential element in these ideologies. If there is no suitable past it can always be invented...I used to think that the profession of history, unlike that of, say, nuclear physics, could at least do no harm. Now I know it can. Our studies can turn into bomb factories. This state of affairs affects us in two ways. We have a responsibility to historical facts in general and for criticising the politico-ideological abuse of history in particular. (Hobsbawm, 1993, 63)

Eric Hobsbawm's concern about the abuse of history for political purposes tells of the way a seemingly disinterested academic discipline may be implicated, complicit or even instrumental, in terrible harms. Not many criminologists are prepared to admit as much about criminology, though the danger of 'our studies being turned into bomb factories' is probably just as real if prisons were the equivalent, criminology's own improvised enclosing device. If anything, for criminology, an academic discipline whose growth from the 1980s uncomfortably coincides with a shift in government policy and rhetoric from a war on poverty to a war on drugs, the analogy of the poppy flowering into heroin addiction is too close for comfort. In criminology the conversion from the delicate flower of deviance to the delicious narcotic of crime is industrial in both scale and effect.

In 1994 when, as an unqualified social worker, I started evening classes for a Certificate in Crime and Deviance at Birkbeck College in central London, criminology was a relatively obscure subject, still in the early stages of the explosive growth that would characterise the next two decades. I was looking for ways of making sense of the wave of hostility, suspicion and anxiety that seemed to be gathering around young people's offending behaviour at the time, and my own role in constantly re-structured social services for young people.

Towards the end of my studies I came across an article by Mary Tuck (1994, 65), Head of Research at the Home Office from 1984 until her retirement in 1990. This is how she began her article:

> I am a criminologist. The other day I ran into an economist friend, just after the Home Secretary [Michael Howard] had made his famous tub-thumping conference speech about the need for more punishment, more custody as the answer to rising crime rates. 'Why is it, Mary,' he said 'that in your field, Ministers can stand up and say things that everyone in social science knows to be nonsense? We economists may disagree. We may give the Treasury different advice. But no Minister can stand up and say things which every academic economist in the country knows to be just plain wrong. What are your lot of social science advisors doing? Why are they not getting their message across?

Those economist friends did not exactly cover themselves in glory in the years preceding the 2007/8 banking crisis that crashed the global economy into a brick wall. Since then, economists that once ridiculed the idea of printing money to get out of the fiscal crises of the mid-1970s have not been slow to endorse 'quantitative easing' as a suitable tonic for the deflating global economy, even when most of that money has been simply sucked out of taxpayer's pockets into banks and tax havens.

Sociologists in the 1980s and 1990s scanning the unfolding horizons of modernity pointed toward an increasingly secular, if somewhat disenchanted, world but somehow failed to notice the emergence of radical Islam and its capacity to mobilise popular sentiment and aggressive defences of the weak (Sayyid, 1997). Criminology and social science more generally, it seems, is less exceptional in its failures than Mary Tuck's economist friend imagines.

When I started studying for a Master's degree in 1995, British criminology was a relatively small discipline that appeared to be tearing itself to pieces over its failure to account for the meteoric rise in crime rates in the preceding three and a half decades. The principal argument was whether crime had any 'ontological reality' or was merely a distracting confection generated by the predations of rampant capitalism. As 'Administrative', 'Left Realist', 'Left Idealist' and 'Abolitionist' criminologists slugged it out in the pages of journals and book compilations (Young and Matthews, 1992; 1993) it is now reasonably clear that crime rates stopped rising in most western countries, and certainly in Britain, around this time in the mid-1990s. Then they began to fall, significantly and consistently (Blumstein and Wallman, 2006; Tseloni et al, 2010).

Criminology is still a refreshingly argumentative field but rather short of answers about why crime rates appear to have gone into reverse, and are continuing to do so, against expectation, prediction and historical precedent, during the steepest and most sustained economic decline of modern times. A decline that is the result of the 2008 banking crisis which the economists engineered by neglect or failed to predict, according to preference. In the midst of this decline criminology has started asking itself how it can become more 'public' and why its research messages are so regularly misunderstood or misinterpreted, especially when it comes to the efficacy of prison (compare Loader and Sparks, 2010). Even as criminology grows 'like Topsy' as an academic discipline, colonising the social science departments of an expanded and reconstituted higher education sector, the discipline is revisiting its existential crisis – 'What is it all for?'

The trouble starts, as Mary Tuck points out in her article, because no one pretends, or even wants, to understand economics, much less, the person-in-the-street, while the reverse is true of crime. Everyone, it seems, has a pet theory about crime and is often keen to share it.

Can you imagine casual conversations at the bus stop, or in the café or the pub about the real meaning of debt, price elasticity or the role of the bond market?

This is not just a case of economics fulfilling its reputation as 'the dismal science', or criminology the excitingly flamboyant and deviant one. As the French philosopher and anthropologist Bruno Latour (2014) points out, it is because 'the economy' (aka capitalism) has largely replaced both religion and nature as the mystic guiding force to which humanity is fatalistically and intuitively subordinate. The resurfacing of fundamentalist religions is a symptom of the struggle to reclaim some sense of agency over the relationship, but the economy calls the shots. The message it delivers is that it is not a metaphysical God who works in mysterious ways, but the singular reality of The Market. As a result thinking about, and feelings about, economics tends to leave people feeling very helpless, impotent in the face of 'market forces' because they operate according to a natural mystic, over their heads and beyond their ken, out of reach of even professional economists.

If the economy escapes people's comprehension because it has come to be understood as a force over which no-one and no institution has any control, governments have discovered they can much more easily demonstrate their potency when it comes to crime. Crime is a very human activity, something we all do and are all involved in that provides a compelling moral register to a variety of behaviours. According to Jonathan Simon (2007) we are now 'governed through crime' because it is an urgently experienced policy issue that quickly delivers political returns, more or less regardless of the policy outcome. As a result, talking tough on crime and promising more law and order became the political mantra of western Anglophone governments for the last quarter of the twentieth century. The outcome in the USA, Simon's exemplar, is terrifying, and, if you are black, increasingly fatal.

In the face of the new vitality of criminal justice systems, and the relative, possibly related, decline of social justice movements, critical criminologists appear to have had almost no impact on the popular myth that the best way to control crime is to arrest offenders and put them behind bars. Criminologists, for all their expansive eclecticism and expert knowledge about the complex causes of crime, the uncertain consequences of punishment and the very limited effects of policing and prison on crime rates, have completely failed to dislodge the widely held belief that the police control the level of crime in society and that imprisonment needs to be the primary response (Rock, 2014). This obstinate and inconvenient feature of the criminological landscape should remind us of the proposition that 'a popular conviction often has the same energy as material force' (Gramsci, 1971, 377). Criminology, in its broadest sense, is thus implicated in ideological struggles and the formation of a certain kind of capitalist hegemony. This hegemony fosters a narrow kind of 'realism' that defines itself as universal, inevitable and without alternatives (Fisher, 2012).

Michel Foucault's (1979) acute diagnosis of the way prison systems expand paradoxically because of their limitations and misplaced faith in their elusive, always just out of reach, efficacy prompted his famously dismissive assessment of criminology (Foucault, 1980, 47):

> Have you ever read any criminological texts? They are staggering. And I say this out of astonishment, not aggressiveness, because I fail to comprehend how the discourse of criminology has been able to go on at this level. One has the impression that it is of such utility, is needed so urgently and rendered so vital for the working of the system, that it does not even seek a theoretical justification for itself, or even simply a coherent framework. It is entirely utilitarian.

Criminology has since gone on to other levels, in scale and theoretical complexity, and it would be unfair, unwise and inaccurate to characterise it now as so narrowly or simply utilitarian. But there's no arguing with its vitality. In the last 20 years the number of taught criminology modules available for study in UK higher education institutions has more than trebled and it has never been easier to study the subject. From being a specialist subject confined to a few post-graduate degrees, it is now being introduced to school students as an A-Level. The proliferating number of academic journals that service this growing field of study is testimony to the rude health in which it finds itself (Bosworth and Hoyle, 2012).

The journey into convict criminology

The next two chapters consider the emergence in the United States of convict criminology where it all began in the 1990s as a distinctive perspective and particular response to the American experience of crime and punishment. Chapter Two starts by considering the contributions of Frank Tannenbaum to criminology and their relationship to the prison sentence he served as a young political activist with the International Workers of the World. Tannenbaum's work around US racism is explored and I speculate on the extent of his relationship with the pioneering black scholar, WEB Du Bois. The personal experiences of both scholars appear to have a relationship to the academic analysis of crime and criminal justice that has largely escaped scrutiny but may have some bearing on their work. The chapter concludes with a discussion of the life of Saul Alinskey, a reluctant academic who eventually devoted himself to community and political activism. Alinskey's unconventional style and approach to criminological research drew deeply from his working-class roots and conflicts with police. Imprisoned on several occasions, Alinskey held most criminologists in contempt, and would resist any attempt to label himself as one, let alone a convict criminologist, but his life and work provide lessons and insights for those who do.

Chapter Three introduces the pivotal figure of American convict criminology, John Irwin. Irwin's life and times are contrasted with those of another man who fashioned links between his life in crime and prison, and his wider social horizons but who did not survive to study them at university. George Jackson's death at the hands of prison guards and John Irwin's pioneering academic work with prisoners form the basis for a discussion of the emergence of convict criminology as a distinctive voice in the US and beyond. The chapter examines contemporary US convict criminology through the collections edited by, among others, Jeffrey Ian Ross and Steve C Richards. It discusses the contribution of the *Journal of Prisoners on Prison* and engages with the developing body of academic work and activism that characterises US convict criminology.

Chapter Four identifies the Russian anarchist, Peter Kropotkin, as the original convict criminologist through a detailed consideration of his study, *In Russian and French Prisons*. A highly respected and influential social scientist, Kropotkin served five years in Russian and French prisons and established new methods of research and writing informed by his unusual experience on both sides of the prison wall. Convict criminology did not emerge from this neglected work, but the chapter goes on to consider the ways in which various European intellectuals have experienced prison life at first hand. It traces some of the histories of collaborative work with prisoners by criminologists and other academics in Europe. It includes discussion of Michel Foucault's work with *Groupe D'Information Sur Prison* (GIP) in France, Antony Negri in Italy, and the unique alliances formed with prisoners through the contributions of Thomas Mathiesen and Louk Hulsman, among others, in the formation of KROM (the Norwegian Association for Penal Reform). In the UK Mike Fitzgerald's, and others', work during the 1970s and 1980s in England with the Protect the Rights of Prisoners (PROP) group locates the current emergence of British convict criminology in a political and historical context of the work of prisoners and ex-prisoners and their supporters in the UK.

Chapter Five switches perspectives from the historical to the contemporary and examines how the stigma of a criminal conviction has been animated in popular culture in the UK through the operation of the Criminal Records Bureau. These developments are contrasted with the changing fortunes of the Rehabilitation of Offenders Act 1974, and its attempts to limit and repair the damage that criminal convictions impose. The cultural and social profile of criminal convictions condition the wider environment in which convict criminology operates, and the chapter concludes by reviewing international policy around the handling and dissemination of criminal convictions.

Chapter Six interrogates the racialising dynamics of prisons from a perspective that promotes critical analysis of gender, class, race and ethnicity. The work of Stuart Hall and Loïc Wacquant are discussed and a critical debate about 'whiteness' is introduced as a way of combating the marginalisation of anti-racism in contemporary criminology. With the people involved in convict criminology, both in the UK and the USA, being mostly men and mostly white, developing analysis that challenges the stark racial disparities of criminal justice, and its masculinist tendencies, is an urgent priority. It presents theoretical and methodological challenges that are outlined in this chapter as a way of furthering critical discussion within convict criminology, and beyond.

Chapter Seven looks at how the experience of being in prison may be epistemologically important to criminology. The chapter asks of convict criminologists what it is they can bring to the criminological table that few others can do. The chapter explores the role of biography, auto-ethnography and reflexivity in writing creatively about prison and criminology. The masculine and existential characteristics of prison life are explored, with some concluding thoughts on the philosophical ramifications of writing from a convict criminology perspective.

Chapter Eight, the final chapter, situates the predicaments of contemporary criminology in a post-colonial context and examines further how convict criminology perspectives can enrich the critical potential of the discipline. Questions about the utility of 'coming out' as a convict criminologist are explored with a suggestion that the issue is more about 'stepping up' than 'coming out'. Some indications of the future outputs and agendas of convict criminology in Britain are previewed, before concluding with a discussion about the ethics of vulnerability as a viable analytical framework for developing further convict criminology work.

Using our imagination

Throughout the chapters the argument emerges that convict criminologists have much to offer students and wider publics on how we understand crime, prison, people and society.

The intellectual dilemmas of developing this account of my own prison experiences and demonstrating how they are intrinsic to the project of convict criminology, has not been entirely straightforward. They are an exemplary archetype of the dilemmas analysed by Robert Merton (1972) in which different kinds of knowledge are generated in research contexts by the relative positions of an 'insider' and an 'outsider'. Predictably and unavoidably prison, as a research context, sharpens that boundary.

My response in this book is to open each chapter with a short autobiographical vignette based on some aspect of prison life as I remember it or feel for its further consequences in my life and work. This provides the basis for an experiment in sociological autobiography along the lines recommended by Merton (1988, 18): 'a narrative text that purports to tell one's own history within the larger history of one's times'. However, autobiography, as the novelist Muriel Spark (1981) has one of her characters point out, is littered with the pitfalls of 'nostalgia, paranoia and a transparent craving to be liked'. There are undoubtedly aspects of all these vices in what follows but the vignettes and narrative are presented in the spirit of C Wright Mills (1959) who urged that the connections between personal biography, social structures and history belong firmly in the sociological imagination.

Personal narrative is a valuable if not entirely unproblematic phenomenological methodology. On one level it is a reflexive effort to avoid too much theoretical abstraction, and on another it is a reminder that the 'particular subjectivities of authors are crucial and should be textually embodied rather than effaced' (Hesse, 2003, 239). This aspect of critical autobiography provides a way of both knowing and revealing that we all have certain predispositions to see and feel things in particular ways, and that these shape our understanding and intuitions. Working with Coretta Philips (Phillips and Earle, 2010) on the epistemological significance of masculine, ethnic and racialised differences helped me to develop this approach in relation to whiteness, gender and class. In relation to convict criminology the connections are at least as relevant, if not as self-evident: I wouldn't be writing this book if I hadn't spent some time in prison, so those experiences need to be in the book somewhere.

The pattern of providing each chapter of a sociological text with an affective or lyrical opening was pioneered by WEB Du Bois (1903) in 'The souls of black folk'. I wouldn't have thought of doing so had this not been drawn to my attention by Les Back's relentless championing of this inspiring book. Presenting biographical vignettes is a form of 'creative nonfiction' that has become a rhetorical strategy in some strands of critical race and whiteness studies (Ryden and Marshall, 2012). It is a strategy reasonably familiar to convict criminologists who may have been obliged to ritually 'confess' or 'come out' in ways that Michel Foucault (Foucault, 1978) might not have entirely approved of and would certainly have tangled with critically (see Chapter Eight). Whatever the confessional imperatives, the personal narratives implicit to convict criminology helpfully connect it to a wider set of sociological perspectives, craftwork and methods. It is my hope in deploying them here that the traffic becomes two-way, heavier and mutually enriching.

TWO

Born in the USA: early origins of convict criminology

GROSS MORAL TURPITUDE

When Oscar Wilde first went to the USA in 1882 he was asked at customs if he had anything to declare and he allegedly replied 'Nothing but my genius.' It wouldn't be quite as simple as that for a convict criminologist, even if they were to be as extraordinarily wonderful as Wilde. Several months before my first trip to the USA to attend the American Society of Criminology annual conference in Atlanta, Georgia, I submitted my application for a visa to the US Embassy in London. It was July 2007. Not content with the usual Criminal Records Bureau (CRB) enhanced disclosure form, the embassy required me to pay for its own independent procedure commissioned through the Metropolitan Police. I duly complied and the completed documentation earned me an invitation to an interview at the Embassy. For other members of the British contingent of criminologists who travel to the USA for such an occasion, the procedure is relatively straightforward. The visa waiver agreement allows them to sweep through customs, passport in hand, declaring their genius only if they see fit.

I fretted about the interview at the embassy, and fantasised gloomily about the bright lights that would be shone in my face, the traps and trick questions I might stumble into. What was the test? How could I pass? I recalled the story told to me by a friend, a political activist, who had travelled to Los Angeles in the early 1980s for a conference, only to be stopped at customs after she obligingly told them that she worked for the London Underground. She was held for several hours while they searched their database of subversive organisations with that recklessly frank piece of information. They had associated London's subway system with a rare species of left wing revolutionary organisation in the US, The Weather Underground, sometimes referred to as The Weathermen, to confuse British customs presumably.

The US Embassy is an imposing building, and at the time of my visit, ringed with concrete, anti-attack bollards. Like at an airport, there were complex electronic screens to pass through, involving the removal of shoes, belts and all electronica. After two hours sitting in a large and orderly waiting hall, my number was called and I approached a booth expecting to be taken down a corridor and into the room where the bright lights and men in suits would be waiting. A small, inoffensively dressed woman smiled at me through a glass grill and greeted me politely, confirmed my details and asked if I still took drugs. 'No, of course not' I dissembled weakly, suppressing the impulse to wink or elaborate criminologically. 'I see,' she said, 'you've got various convictions but they are all a long time ago, so I don't think that it should be a problem, but all this information will be passed back to the Department of Homeland Security. They will make the decision, and your passport will be returned with the visa, if appropriate.' She didn't exactly say 'Thank you. Have a Nice day', and neither did I but it was all very civil.

I waited, and waited, and at the beginning of October, three weeks before I was due to fly out my passport was returned to me with a visa and letter saying that despite my conviction for 'crimes of gross moral turpitude' I was welcome to visit the USA. I had to look up 'turpitude' in the dictionary. 'Depravity.' 'Vileness.' That's laying it on a bit thick, I thought. These Americans!

Disembarking into Atlanta airport's arrival hall my partners in criminology went one way, the visa waiver way, and I went another, and it was quite a revelation. On my own, I was escorted to a large waiting room and the atmosphere chilled as I sat among a motley collection of the distressed, the displaced and the anxious waiting for my number to be called by the man in uniform at the counter. A young woman was involved in a lengthy argumentative discussion with one of the officers about the expired dates in her paperwork. I was tired, and nervous but I didn't seem to be in as bad shape as most of the people in the room. The uncertainty, the insecurity, was palpable and I felt it catching at me. What if my papers weren't in order and they take me away? What does that even mean? How have I never been in a situation where I've asked myself that question? Another heated discussion broke out further down the counter. It occurred to me that this was what French migration and human rights activists refer to as the condition of 'les sans papier' – to be 'without papers' is to be, at any moment, without status, a nobody with nowhere to go. Utterly contingent. Ontological insecurity, I realise, can be a lot more than that awful feeling I get the night after I've had too much to drink. It's structural not chemical.

My number is called and I feel nervous even as I try to act confident and relaxed. The man at the counter is not so nice. 'What's this conference then?' he asks. 'The American Society of Criminology' I say, hoping he doesn't ask more questions, 'why' questions. 'Uhuh', he looks at me, pauses for dramatic effect, and says 'Ok, all done here.' I rejoin my British criminology colleagues who have been waiting patiently for me to reappear. I am in the USA, land of the free, home of the brave and convict criminology.

The next year I make the mistake of thinking of returning to the American Society of Criminology conference and that my application will be more straightforward. Nonetheless I complete the paperwork earlier, in June. For reasons I cannot fathom and for which am not entitled to an explanation, the process is far more protracted though I am told quickly enough that I will not need to be interviewed. My passport with obligingly agreed visa is returned in the first week of December, a month after the conference, and long after I have cancelled flights, registrations and accommodation.

It's seriously small beer compared to the profound and devastating insecurities endured by the 'sans papiers', migrant labourers and refugees. There is no equivalence with their experiences but the experience is educational nonetheless. My passport is not quite up to the mark. Those criminal convictions never fully erased. I think as a young man my recklessness was at least in part a testing of my various privileges; just how durable could they be? The sociologist in me tells me one thing. My PhD says she's right. My convictions have another story. One I try to tell.

Convict criminology, like Bruce Springsteen, was born in the USA. It is a product of the extraordinary configurations of crime and punishment that characterise the world's richest nation. As is well known among criminologists, the USA generates nearly one quarter of the world's prison population from a mere 5 per cent of its population. The rate of incarceration is five to ten times higher than rates in western Europe and results in a society where nearly one out of every 100 adults is in prison or jail (NRC, 2014). In the USA there are more people under correctional supervision than there were in the Soviet Gulags at the height of Stalin's reign of terror. There are more black men in prison, jail or on parole than were enslaved in 1850. If you are a black person in the USA you are seven times more likely to be sent to prison than if you are a white person. More than half of all black men without a high-school diploma go to prison at some time in their lives, and in many US states ex-convicts cannot vote (Gopink, 2012; Osterwell, 2015).

The USA is also home to the largest, the most numerous and the most prolific criminology programmes in the world. Collectively, they 'prepare students to deal with criminals, understand the justice system and work to prevent crime' (US News, 2014). The juxtaposition of such exceptional rates of differential criminalisation and penalisation and the exceptional scholarly resources of the US higher education system, begs a number of questions about the functional correspondence between universities and prisons that are only just beginning to attract critical attention.

Evidence for the sheer scale of crime, imprisonment and criminology in the USA is not hard to find but its impact can be fiendishly difficult to interpret. In this chapter, the pre-history of convict criminology in the USA is examined by looking closely at the lives of two scholar-activists who are retrospectively identified as exemplar convict criminologists before the term had been coined. The next chapter considers the emergence in the 1990s of the self-declared New School of Convict Criminology as a distinctive and organised critique of conventional US criminology.

A 'Wobblie' start – Frank Tannenbaum: agitator, convict and criminologist

According to Sumner (1994), the history of twentieth century US criminology might be understood as the process by which ideas about various wayward behaviours were manoeuvred through concepts of compulsive deviance to pathological criminality. A key figure in this transition is Frank Tannenbaum, who has been posthumously identified as the first convict criminologist.

Born into the Jewish community of Galicia in southern Poland in 1893, Frank Tannenbaum followed his father and went to the United States with the rest of his family in 1904. The Tannenbaum's were among the two and half million east European Jews who fled from pogroms and the dying shtetl between 1880 and 1914 to settle in the United States. Soon after they arrived, he left his parent's farm in Massachusetts to find an education for himself in New York, and in 1909 secured his 'naturalisation' as an American citizen (Yeager, 2011). In New York he became active in radical politics, and joined the International Workers of the World (IWW), one of America's few durable and distinguished gifts to the international socialist and labour movement.

The Wobblies, as they were sometimes affectionately known, were founded in 1905 in Chicago and rapidly became one of the preeminent US labour movement organisations of the time. More radical and less compromising than many of its contemporaries, it was strongly influenced by anarchist thinkers and ideas. Among its leading lights in New York at the time was the celebrated anarchist and feminist, Emma Goldman, and Frank Tannenbaum is mentioned in her memoir, *Living*

My Life (Goldman, 1931). He was a regular presence in the office of the magazine Goldman edited with Alexander Berkman. *Mother Earth* was a journal that described itself as 'A Monthly Magazine Devoted to Social Science and Literature'. The subtitle of the magazine serves as a timely reminder of how close the relationship of social science was to revolutionary politics at the turn of the nineteenth century. Max Weber, for example, on the other side of the Atlantic, was spurred by the 1918 revolution in Germany to draft his lecturers on 'Politics as a Vocation' (Breiner, 1996). The distance between political action, sociological inquiry and social transformation was considerably narrower, and perhaps more easily bridged, than currently appears to be the case.

In 1914, Tannenbaum, perhaps radicalised by his proximity to such a luminous and charismatic figure as Goldman, mobilised a group of unemployed and homeless men to occupy the Roman Catholic Church of St Alphonsus on Broadway. He was arrested and prosecuted for 'unlawful assembly' at the tender age of 21. At the end of his trial he stood convicted but defiant, declaring from the dock: 'that was my crime – telling the producers of bread to get a bit of it for themselves' (Yeager, 2011, 179). Tannenbaum was sentenced to one year of penal custody on Blackwell's Island, with a fine of $500, and the threat of a further six months if the fine was unpaid. Fortunately the fine was paid with the assistance of funds raised by his Wobblie comrades, but Tannenbaum's 12 months was not an easy ride.

Yeager's (2011) invaluable archive research reveals that Tannenbaum spent two months of his sentence in punitive solitary confinement for his agitation with other prisoners against prison conditions, mistreatment and neglect. In his subsequent articles, published in a Wobblie newspaper, *The Masses*, he describes the unsanitary conditions, such as men dying of tuberculosis being locked up with healthy prisoners, and numerous beatings by guards. He reports a riot occurring after the senior prison warden imposed a collective punishment on more than 100 prisoners because of the rowdy Fourth of July celebrations of another handful of prisoners. The riot was eventually supressed only by the firing of live rounds into the air, although protest actions continued to be organised with Tannenbaum a key figure in negotiations with the regime.

On his release Tannenbaum's articles about Blackwell's Island in *The Masses* were forwarded by a sympathiser to the editor of a more mainstream magazine, *The Atlantic Monthly*, and published to a wider readership. This led to a formal investigation by the State Commission on Prisons and, eventually, the resignation of the Blackwell's warden.

Tannenbaum was encouraged by his success in drawing attention to prison conditions and the positive reception of his articles to consider an application to study at university. He was accepted by Columbia University in 1916 and completed a degree in economics and history. While studying he maintained his interest in prison reform and in 1917 he testified before the New York State Prison Commission about degrading and brutal prison conditions (Yeager, 2011).

Tannenbaum's first-hand experience of the gap between public rhetoric on the benefits of prison as a form of rehabilitative punishment, and its grim realities come across strongly in his early writing.

His first article in *The Atlantic Monthly* is titled 'Prison Cruelty' and in it he remarks that 'cruelty has always marked prison administration. We have records of brutality in prisons stretching over all written history, and including practically every nation of which we have written records' (cited in Yeager, 2011, 182). He describes the regime he endured at Blackwell's Island, which still retained elements of the notorious 'silent system' pioneered in Auburn prison in the late nineteenth century. Tannenbaum details the ways in which the imposition of such a strict and petty regime involves the generation of hundreds of minor infractions against prison order by prisoners, and their obsessive but arbitrary policing by prison warders. His personal accounts of being deprived of pencils, paper and thread, and the accompanying punishments of being denied food, light and warmth are compelling for being so directly experienced.

A distinctive feature of his early writing on prison is his characterisation of it as a system that generates and exacerbates differences among people by debasing them and marking them out from their community. According to Tannenbaum, the main difference between 'the average Joe' in the community and those in prison is simply having 'been caught and the rest are still to be caught' (cited in Yeager, 2011, 182). Prison regime's petty authoritarianism, like the one he experienced, set prisoners up in 'a vicious circle leading on to greater isolation and to more cruelty and more isolation' (cited in Yeager, 2011, 182).

Crucially though, Tannenbaum was not content to generalise only from his own experiences and was drawn to the empirical methods that characterise social science. As part of a role he secured for himself with the National Committee on Prisons and Prison Labor he toured 70 prisons in the summer of 1920. His interests were driven by a synthesis of his anarchist politics, his concern for prisoner's conditions and the possibility of reform. This found expression in his desire to promote self-government among prisoners, the need for education and for prison warders to adopt different ways of working with prisoners. His tour, however, confirmed his worst fears about the innate tendency of prisons to crush the human spirit: 'There is no spiritual life in the average American prison. There is no hope, no inspiration, no stimulus, no compulsion of the soul to better things. It is hard, cold, frozen, dead' (cited in Yeager, 2011, 182).

The prisons Tannenbaum visited fell a long way short of his already lowered expectations. The influence of the Auburn[1] model was waning all too slowly and no viable replacement model could be identified on his tour. Instead he found prisons full of enforced idleness, torpor and ill-health. Prison wardens, he suggested, were largely incompetent and poorly trained. His remedy was to recommend the reorientation of provision toward education rather than punishment: 'the function of the state should be not to punish but to educate. The place of the penal department ought to be taken by a new bureau, dedicated to health education and industry – entrusted to experts in these respective fields' (cited in Yeager, 2011, 184).

A key feature of Tannenbaum's critique, that draws from his experiences of the IWW's syndicalism,[2] was to foreground the need to create *prisoner* welfare leagues within each penitentiary. These, he insisted, would provide prisoners with the capacity and motivation for greater authority over their own affairs, and the resulting self-government would contribute not only to their welfare but improved discipline and constructive rehabilitation. These prescient analytical insights are entirely consistent with contemporary theories of desistance (Maruna, 1997; 2001) and prefigure many of the concerns of what is now called convict criminology.

Indications of the strength of Tannenbaum's identification with, and reading of, social science are provided in his monograph, *Darker Phases of the South* (1924). This examination of the labour relations of slavery analysed the chain-gang system, prison-farms and the convict-

[1] The Auburn Model was a system of custodial punishment that emphasised rehabilitation through strictly disciplined work routines during the day and enforced silence at night. It was designed to break and rebuild prisoner's sense of self. It takes its name from the Auburn Prison, New York.

[2] The form of anarchism advocated by the Wobblies is described thus: 'Plain folk running society for their own benefit without bosses, without politicians, without a coercive state, army, navy, airforce or marines, but without hatred or suspicion of foreigners, or the frequently all-encompassing guilt that because we're rich, someone wants to take our riches away from us. The belief in freedom and internationalism makes the Wobblies just about the most American ideal possible' (Buhle and Schulman, 2005).

lease system used by the coal mining industry. Clearly influenced by work of the great African American sociologist WEB Du Bois (1903) he calls attention to the 'the colour line' drawn through the penal system. He also refers to 'the veil', a key term in Du Bois's sociology that refers to the generation among black people of a distinctive 'double consciousness' arising from the denial of their humanity by white society. Du Bois and Tannenbaum corresponded regularly as Tannenbaum (1946) developed his second major publication *Slave and Citizen: The Negro in the Americas*. This, and his first book, earned Tannenbaum a place in what became known as the Harlem Renaissance (see Wintz and Finkelman, 2004). This was the name given to a period between the end of the First World War and the 1930s when African Americans asserted their own, militant and distinctive cultural presence in American life.

Although Tannenbaum's writings on race in the USA are even less well recognised than his criminological writing, they include themes that resonate strongly with current concerns. For example, his comparative approach in *Slave and Citizen* (1946) draws out the contrasting experience of racialisation in Brazil and the USA, a theme picked up by Paul Gilroy (1993) in *The Black Atlantic*. A key distinction Tannenbaum identifies in the US slave system that differentiates it from Brazilian experience is the denial of humanity to black people in the US, their complete exclusion from human hierarchy, rather than a place at its base. The consequences of this key difference were likely to be profound he predicted, and should not be underestimated. Recognising different racisms and the form this differentiation takes is a central feature of contemporary critical race theory, and Tannenbaum had already provided an empirical account of their presence and implications.

In *Darker Phases of the South* Tannenbaum included the experience of poor white people's reaction to the advancing struggle for black emancipation and the potency of the violence associated with reaction against it. This, he insisted, produced a dehumanisation of both the victim and the perpetrator and he linked this to the conditions of white workers in the company-owned mill towns where every aspect of their lives was controlled by the employer. In these circumstances, Tannenbaum suggested, poor whites found a sense of agency and power, hope and excitement in the arcane ritualism of the Klu-Klux Klan. Violence and aggression against black people offered them temporary escape from the grinding poverty and dull hardships of white working-class life. They were sustained by an 'underlying apprehension that the South will be outstripped in the population by the coloured as against the white. It is fear of losing grip upon the world, of losing caste, of losing control' (Tannenbaum, 1924, cited in Wintz and Finkelman, 2004, 1159). These themes of anxiety, resentment and mobilised reaction in white working-class communities also resonate powerfully with contemporary research on race in the UK and the USA (Nayak, 2005; Roedigger, 2007; Ware and Black, 2002).

Some indication of Du Bois's influence and the extent of Tannenbaum's collaboration with him is contained in letters that suggest that Du Bois helped Tannenbaum to meet with black research respondents in Texas. He is warned 'Remember, however, that in Texas it is a rather risky business for a colored man to entertain a white man in any way, or be seen with him' (Du Bois, Letter, 7 November, 1924). Du Bois also comments on Tannenbaum's 'excellent conception of the paradox in the Negro problem', the theme that it damages the material prospects of working-class white people: 'I think you can prove that either whatever is denied the Negroes is also denied the whites; or in such cases where this is not true, the monopoly of whites brings them either no advantage or not nearly as great advantage as they imagine' (Du Bois, Letter, 22 May, 1923). This correspondence alludes to another of Du Bois's key concepts: the subjective sense of benefit that white workers find in distinguishing themselves from black people. Du Bois (1935, 700–1) called it a 'psychological wage' that afforded them a sense of access to the protection of the courts, the police, to the rights of citizenship denied to black people.

Suitable public enemies: fear of a red planet

Tannenbaum's trajectory from radical political activism to academic inquiry was probably accelerated by two further political events, one in New York, the other in Mexico. The first was the 'Palmer raids' in which the US Attorney General, A Mitchell Palmer, recruited John Edgar Hoover as his special assistant and proceeded to launch a vicious witch hunt against American radicals. On 7 November 1919 over 10,000 suspected communists, anarchists and labour movement organisers were rounded up using powers of detention in the 1917 Espionage Act and the 1918 Sedition Act. The vast majority were subsequently released but Tannenbaum's political guiding star, Emma Goldman and 247 others were peremptorily deported to Russia.

The USA was in the grip of its first 'Red scare'. Palmer was convinced that the recent proletarian revolution in Russia, led by Lenin's Bolshevik party, was about to surface on America's East coast. Palmer claimed that communist agents, directed by their Russian 'puppet masters', were on the verge of organising an uprising the like of which had toppled the Czars. On 2 January 1920 a further 6,000 people were arrested and held without trial when Palmer announced that there was a communist conspiracy to seize power on 1 May that year. In New York five elected socialists were expelled from the legislature, and although no evidence of the conspiracy was ever discovered, the raids established socialism as an overseas political threat from which the US has never fully recovered. Many of those held without trial, and most of those deported, were members of the IWW and Tannenbaum cannot but have been affected by the raids.

Tannenbaum continued to work around prison reform but, like many US radicals, his interests in labour relations were drawn toward another revolution occurring closer to home on America's southern border. The revolution in Mexico in 1910 heralded a dramatic programme of progressive land reform that captured Tannenbaum's imagination, and propelled his doctorate thesis on *The Mexican Agricultural System*. He completed his studies in 1927 and published his thesis as *The Mexican Agrarian Revolution* in 1929.

On completion of his PhD, Tannenbaum made one further foray into penal reform by taking up a position as Reporter to the Wickersham Commission on Penal Institutions, Probation and Parole. He launched a scathing attack on the timidity and vacillation of the final report at its launch, deriding it as 'a mild, friendly document when it ought to be a severe and unrelenting indictment of the present penal system and all its doings' (cited in Yeager, 2011, 186). This, as much as anything he subsequently wrote, captures the tone of what was to become convict criminology in the USA. As Yeager (2011, 186) remarks. '[It was vintage Tannenbaum, the Tannenbaum of his youth when he was a member of the IWW.' His speech to the gathered ranks of the American Prison Association receiving the flawed report is worth quoting at length:

> "I am saying nothing new here, but merely repeating what has been said a thousand times before by people of all degree and in a thousand places, that imprisonment makes people worse rather than better. Not only should no man be sent to prison except as a last resort, but no man ought to be kept in prison a day longer than is absolutely essential for the safety of society. And the prison which stands between the convicted man and his ultimate return to society ought to be an institution that is dedicated to the reconstruction of individual character."

He insisted on inserting changes to the document that itemised the various riots that routinely occurred across the penal estate but were missing from the report. He described the fire that killed 317 prisoners in Ohio prison, also missing from the report. He provided an account of the torture inflicted on prisoners in the segregation unit of the prison in Clifton, New York, and the beatings of 75 prisoners in the state prison in Missouri. Vintage Tannenbaum, classic convict criminology.

In 1935 he took up a lecturer position at Columbia University, returning to the subject of his PhD as a specialist in Latin American history. In 1945 he was made a full professor in the History department, but not before he had made his most lasting and insightful contribution to criminological theory.

Tannenbaum's (1938) *Crime and the Community* is a radical and intellectually innovative analysis of crime that prefigures many ideas that were later to become mainstream. Although he is now regarded as the progenitor of labelling theory, *Crime and the Community* is a complex and original synthesis of numerous criminological themes that form part of the orthodoxy of symbolic interactionism.

Tannenbaum's identification with the wave of social activism and political reform that gripped the USA between 1890 and 1920 pulled him toward what has come to be known as the Progressive movement. Progressives recognised the new challenges to ways of being social in the cities bursting into life across the country. For Progressives, urbanisation heralded a new role for the state at local and national level. They argued that new forms of sociality, buzzing with the diversity of immigrant populations, could not depend on stable families, the church or traditional community ties to regulate social life. Furthermore, capitalism itself was becoming recognised as manifestly fallible, as demonstrated by the Stock Market crash, the Great Depression, and the experience of the Dustbowl agricultural crisis. In Franklin Delano Roosevelt the Progressives found a figurehead who was prepared to declare, in 1937, that 'the inherent right to work is one of the elemental privileges of a free people' (cited in Kunkel, 2014, 92). Not many presidents of the USA have been as forthcoming since. The State, Progressives urged, would need to be more assertive in its functions; law making and courts would need to be modernised; new forms of knowledge about social intervention needed to be developed on the basis of 'social science'.

The Progressives were heavily influenced by European positivist traditions of sociology, particularly its ambition to bring scientific methods to bear on human and social issues. Accompanying the political ferment that had drawn the young Tannenbaum to the

Wobblies' activism, was a new academic interest in 'deviance' as a form of disruption to the dynamics of social progress. The twin themes of culture and community were prominent in this academic interest, as were the politics of race and pathology. African Americans were not only far more vulnerable to the human suffering which the Progressives identified in urbanisation, they were all too often defined as its cause. Du Bois's (1903) sociological masterpiece, *The Souls of Black Folk*, captures this tragedy in a single, piercing epigram that haunts criminology to this day: 'How does it feel to be a problem?' As Gabbidon (2007) demonstrates, Du Bois's research anticipated many themes that would become central to the theorisation of crime in western criminology, but he is rarely attended to in conventional criminological scholarship.

Tannenbaum had been helped by Du Bois and their correspondence indicates mutual respect and support for their respective projects. Du Bois may have shared his own experiences of a brush with the law. As a schoolboy he was caught stealing grapes from the orchard of a prominent local landowner and only narrowly escaped being packed off to a reform school. He was saved by the intervention of his school master who advocated on his behalf. According to Biko Agonizo (2007) the experience had a profound effect on him, not least because the older he got and further he travelled into academic life, the more he would have become aware of the potentially disastrous consequences he had so narrowly avoided. Then, as now, young black lives pivoted one way or another on the sharp edges of criminal justice interventions. Fortunately for Du Bois the threat was avoided, and sociology is the richer for it.

As with much of Tannenbaum's work, his reference to the extent of black imprisonment, its role in the US labour process and the existence of 'the colour line' woven through American political, economic and cultural life, evokes comparison with contemporary concerns, but *Crime and the Community* also borrows implicitly from another of Du Bois's threads: affinity with the oppressed, sensitivity to their suffering and the significance of personal experience voiced so effectively in the opening vignette of *The Souls of Black Folk*.

> Between me and the other world there is ever an unasked question: unasked by some through feelings of delicacy; by others through the difficulty of rightly framing it. All, nevertheless, flutter round it. They approach me in a half-hesitant sort of way, eye me curiously or compassionately, and then, instead of saying directly, 'How does it feel to be

a problem?' they say, 'I know an excellent colored man in my town'; or, 'I fought at Mechanicsville'; or, 'Do not these Southern outrages make your blood boil?' At these I smile, or am interested, or reduce the boiling to a simmer, as the occasion may require. To the real question, 'How does it feel to be a problem?' I answer seldom a word.

The failure to refuse

At the heart of Tannenbaum's (1938, 18–20) analysis of crime is the nature of social conflict, reaction and social interaction. His work with young men and boys involved in gangs had revealed to him how potent their reaction was to being seen as problematically different. He identifies both the moral loading and glamourous appeal that the descriptive vocabulary of crime carries with it and the forceful authority with which it is applied to the young person:

> The verbalisation of the conflict in terms of evil, delinquency, incorrigibility, badness, arrest, force, punishment, stupidity, lack of intelligence, truancy, criminality, gives the innocent divergence of the child from the straight road a meaning that it did not have in the beginning and makes its continuance in these same terms so much more inevitable. (Tannenbaum, 1938, 18)

Tannenbaum alludes here to Thrasher's (1927) influential notion of the 'criminal career' but unsettles it with his implication that for the child concerned the originating conflict may have had no forward momentum, but for it being provided to them by 'the community'.

As he goes on, he outlines what in the 1960s would be re-theorised as 'secondary deviance' and 'deviancy amplification':

> The process of making the criminal, therefore, is a process of tagging, defining, segregating, describing, emphasising, making conscious and self-conscious; it becomes a way of stimulating, suggesting, emphasising and evoking the very traits that are complained of. If the theory of relation of response to stimulus has any meaning, the entire process of dealing with the young delinquent is mischievous in so far as it identifies him to himself or to the environment as a delinquent person. (Tannenbaum, 1938, 20)

'Mischievous' is a generously mild understatement of the harmful potentials he identifies. In language that has only become more evocative as it has become more conventional, Tannenbaum presents the basic principles of labelling theory: 'The person becomes the thing he is described as being...the emphasis is upon the conduct that is disapproved of...The harder they work to reform evil, the greater the evil grows under their hands...The way out is through a refusal to dramatise the evil' (Tannenbaum, 1938, 20).

Colin Sumner's (1994) assessment of Tannenbaum is that he has been drastically underestimated and neglected. The more prominent figures of Becker (1963), Lemert (1967) and Matza (1964; 1969) and their justly famous contributions to criminological theory are all pre-figured in Tannenbaum's book but loom much larger in criminology's reading room. Even Stan Cohen's (1980) ideas about folk devils are anchored in the refusal to heed Tannenbaum's advice: 'evil' is dramatised with relish and abandon, folk devils are inflated and moral panics catch like fire in the cycle of deviancy amplification.

Crime, according to Tannenbaum, is not the result of pathology but manufacture. I cannot help but feel his analysis is rooted in his politics, and his politics in his experience. He had experience of complex entanglement in social conflicts involving New York's hungry and homeless workers. He had seen them 'tagged' and their behaviour reduced to the criminal coda of 'unlawful assembly'. In prison he subsequently found himself among even less fortunate men and felt the gyroscopic thrust of its revolving door. He was in a position to triangulate his theory around what he saw and felt inside prison, and what he knew of how it was perceived by those outside, and how it was presented by those invested in its workings. He knew that when it comes to prison what it said on the box was not what you found inside. His familiarity with Du Bois may have encouraged him to work these experiences into his analysis. He had been behind the veil of outward appearances so his time as a convict, his experiences of poverty, inequality, injustice and criminal justice provided his metier as a criminologist. Frank Tannenbaum provides a neat originating mould for convict criminology.

Saul Alinsky: Community organising with convictions, criminology without conviction

Saul Alinsky may not fit the convict criminologist mould exactly, but his story shares many features of Tannenbaum's. Born in 1909, he was slightly younger than Tannenbaum, and the son of Jewish immigrants from Russia rather than Poland. He grew up in the Chicago slums that were to become the focus of his life and work. His biographical trajectory reverses Tannenbaum's in that he started out as a research sociologist attached to Clifford Shaw's Institute for Juvenile Research (IJR) at the University of Chicago, but ended up abandoning sociology for political activism, although in truth the two were never distant forms of activity for Alinsky.

Alinsky's parents were conservative orthodox Jews who divorced when he was 13, resulting in a trans-American adolescence split between his father in California and his mother in Chicago. He was first arrested as a teenager after seeking to avenge an anti-Semitic attack on a friend by some local Poles. The Jewish context of both his subsequent activism and his Chicago neighbourhood is well captured in an interview Alinsky conducted with *Playboy* magazine in 1972, shortly before his death. His maverick tendencies, wit and unique style are self-evident:

> [Anti-Semitism] was all around us in those days. But it was so pervasive you didn't really even think about it; you just accepted it as a fact of life. The worst hostility was the Poles, and back in 1918 and 1919, when I was growing up, it amounted to a regular war. We had territorial boundaries between our neighborhoods, and if a Jewish girl strayed across the border, she'd be raped right on the street. Every once in a while, it would explode into full-scale rioting, and I remember when hundreds of Poles would come storming into our neighborhood and we'd get up on the roofs with piles of bricks and pans of boiling water and slingshots, just like a medieval siege. I had an air rifle myself. There'd be a bloody battle for blocks around and some people on both sides had real guns, so sometimes there'd be fatalities. It wasn't called an urban crisis then; it was just two groups of people trying to kill each other. Finally the cops would come on horses and in their clanging paddy wagons and break it up. They were all Irish and they hated both sides, so they'd crack Polish and Jewish heads equally. The melting pot in action. You don't have that hostility in Chicago anymore; now Italians, Poles, Jews and Irish have all joined up and buried the hatchet – in the Blacks. But in those days, every ethnic group was at each other's throat.

Alinsky studied sociology under the legendary names of the first Chicago School, such as Robert Park and Clifford Shaw but was disdainful of academic routines. He graduated with an Archaeology major but declared the discipline to be 'as dead as its subject matter' (cited in Bennett, 1981, 212). His assessment of Chicago School sociology belies its reputation as a cutting edge carving a trail through the Ivory Tower tradition of academic social research:

> As an undergraduate, I took a lot of courses in sociology, and I was astounded by all the horse manure they were handing out about poverty and slums, playing down the suffering and deprivation, glossing over the misery and despair. I mean, Christ, I'd lived in a slum, I could see through all their complacent academic jargon to the realities. It was at that time that I developed a deep suspicion of academicians in general and sociologists in particular, with a few notable exceptions.

In his *Playboy* interview Alinsky is candid about indulging his skills and intelligence in avoiding paying for necessities like food and meals. Ever the innovator, he opted to share his scheme for avoiding the cash registers at a local chain of cafeterias with his fellow students. As he tells it 'we got the system down to a science, and for six months all of us were eating for free'. Challenged by his interviewer about whether he had any moral qualms about his 'life of crime' Alinsky is quick to put him right in characteristic style:

> 'Crime? That wasn't crime – it was survival. Oh, sure, I suffered all the agonies of the damned: sleepless nights, desperate soul-searching, a tormented conscience that riddled me with guilt – Are you kidding? I wouldn't have justified, say, conning free gin from a liquor store just so I could have a martini before dinner, but when you're hungry, anything goes – There's a priority of rights, and the right to eat takes precedence over the right to make a profit.'

Echoes there of the criminal trial of Tannenbaum the convicted Wobblie!

After graduating in 1930 he accepted a fellowship in criminology at the University of Chicago where his graduate assignment was to secure insights into the increasingly prominent gangs that were establishing themselves in the city, including the Capone gang. In this capacity he began to establish a feel for researching 'from the inside' that is a characteristic of convict criminology. After some difficulty he won the confidence of senior members of the gang, proving himself to be a good listener to their stories, and a keen observer of their habits of mind and action. Nevertheless, he did not warm to the work and opted instead to join the Institute of Juvenile Research (IJR) so that he could work more closely with a group of 'delinquent' Italian boys he had befriended on the Near West Side of Chicago.

Alinsky was influenced by Shaw's life history approach and encouraged the young men to share their stories with him with a view to producing a book, 'Companions In Crime', that would present their accounts in their own words and on their own terms (Bennett, 1981, 213). Although the book was never completed some of the work involved bears close resemblance to the kind of work undertaken now by convict criminologists in the USA.

Declining to be house trained

The period from 1933 to 1936 is occupied by his professional attachment to the state prison as a staff criminologist and coincides with his first published article, 'A sociological technique in Clinical Criminology' (cited in Bennett, 1981, 214). In this article he describes two principles that guide his practice and inform his 'technique'. The first principle is 'To know your community is to know your delinquent.' Alinsky recounts that being able to connect with a prisoner by demonstrating intimate knowledge of their neighbourhood usually elicits 'an excited flow of conversation'. The second, linked, principle is to be able to use the kind of language with which they are familiar. As ever, no-one can tell it like Alinskey:

> The usage of delinquent vocabularies characteristic of the inmate's community is of great value in the establishing of a close rapport. To illustrate, if the question 'Have you ever been chased by the police while you are in a stolen car and have the police shoot at you?' is phrased 'Have you ever been in a hot short and got lammed by the local heat and have them toss slugs at you?', a warmer and more responsive answer usually results. (Cited in Bennett, 1981, 215)

Alinskey found little satisfaction in his work, either as a researcher at the IJR or as a 'house criminologist' at the State prison. With typical insight he felt the process was hardening his sensibilities and that he was becoming, in his own words, 'institutionalised – callous. I would be interviewing an inmate and I no longer had any real curiosity as to why this particular guy did what he did. I knew it was time for me to get out' (Bennett, 1981, 215).

To the *Playboy* interviewer he elaborated further:

> There were a lot of factors involved. For one thing, most of the people I was working with – other criminologists, wardens, parole officers – were all anaesthetized from the neck up. God, I've never in my life come across such an assemblage of morons…I was revolted by the brutalization, the dehumanization, the institutionalized cruelty of the prison system. I saw it happening to me, too, which was another important motivation for me to get out. When I first went up to Joliet [the prison], I'd take a genuine personal interest in the prisoners I'd interview; I'd get involved with their problems, try to help them. But the trouble with working in an institution, any institution, is that you get institutionalized yourself.

Alinsky's allegiance to conventional criminology and social science was becoming progressively weaker. Even his alliance with the pioneering Chicago Area Projects was tested by wider global events. Beyond the plight of share-cropper farmers in the southern states, and the evictions and rent strikes of the northern cities lay the growing shadow of fascism in Europe, and its sympathisers in the US. Raising funds for the International Brigades to fight fascism in Spain became a priority. 'Wherever you turned you saw injustice' he remarked in his interviews, and therein lies the problem of criminology. Where Alinsky saw injustice, his fellow sociologists and criminologists saw social disorganisation, or worse, individual pathology. For Alinsky it was a question of politics not social science, and it was to politics, both conventional and unconventional, that he devoted most of his life.

As far as Alinsky was concerned disseminating academic papers, Shaw's 'small time confessions' and life histories, was a well-intentioned but monumental waste of time. He was not content with social science's rear view mirror that promises to make perfect sense of the past. He didn't want to 'march backwards into the future' as Marshall McLuhan (1964) puts it. His ambition extended beyond the civil service that many academics seem to think is the apogee of aspiration. In Weber's (1919) terms he lived 'for politics' not 'off politics'. It was his vocation and one he filled with charisma and vision. His political activism became legendary and he was repeatedly arrested and thrown into jail, serving a series of short sentences for a variety of convictions associated with his political agitation.

The titles of Alinsky's books, *Reveille for Radicals* (1946) and *Rules for Radicals* (1971) tell their own story about his priorities and eventual trajectory away from academic life and into politics. Stan Cohen refers approvingly to his approach in the final 'What is To Be Done?' chapter of *Visions of Social Control*. In Alinsky's methods and priorities there is much common ground with the approach which convict criminology advocates.

Both Frank Tannenbaum and Saul Alinsky belong to a generation and a time in the USA when criminology and sociology more generally were struggling with the relative potentials of rhetoric as opposed to the positive promise of science (Bennett, 1981). They took different paths forward but each deserve recognition and provide illuminations that lit the way for convict criminology to emerge from another wave of political ferment and another period of academic efflorescence. In the next chapter John Irwin is introduced as the archetype and originator of convict criminology, a criminologist who moved from convicted robber to criminology professor in the space of 30 years from the 1960s to the 1990s.

THREE

US convict criminology comes of age

SHARING A CELL AND SOMETHING MORE

My prospective cell mates don't look pleased to see me as I'm led into their cell. That makes three of us in a cell designed for one. There's a bunk and a single bed. The top bunk is mine they tell me. It's a tight squeeze, three beds, three people, a small wooden cupboard, a desk and two chairs. A bucket, with a lid, to piss in at night if you have to. The cell is probably about 9 feet wide and 15 feet long. The single bed fits across the door end, the bunk down the long side.

After the screw has gone they lighten up. It's not my fault they have to accommodate me, deal with the disruption to their pattern of sharing space. And time. In 1982 prison overcrowding is another symptom of a system in crisis. With capacity for approximately 24,000 people in 1982, there are over 40,000 people in the prison system and I am one of them. 'Two's company, three's a crowd' never felt more true. Dave and Steve are a few years older than me but still young. They are from the northwest but ended up here in HMP Norwich after going on the run from a trial they couldn't face. They robbed a few places, they tell me, and take a few drugs now and then. They tried to rob a petrol station and got caught, knowing they would eventually, but not really caring. They are relaxed and easy going. They are settled into their sentence, a couple of years. Not their first, but the worst yet. Perhaps their last as they seem to want leave the wildness behind them, and settle down, but aren't sure how. We get on ok. They are amused because I get books and a newspaper sent in. One of my sisters has organised for the *Guardian* to be delivered. The other sends me a book she picked up in America with a title that makes them laugh: *I Know Why The Caged Bird Sings*. 'Is she taking the piss?' they ask of my sister's gift. Dave doesn't read it but he does offer to bind it for me in hardback covers. Dave and Steve both have 'jobs' in the bookbinding workshop, and urge me to get a transfer there as soon as I can. 'Tell them about how you were a printer', they tell me, 'It's the best job in the prison'.

I start in the basic unskilled workshop pasting strips of reinforcing paper down the spine of brown Social Security folders, the ones that hold all the paperwork when you go and 'sign on' for unemployment benefit or social security payments, your UB40 as it's called, after the Birmingham based reggae band of that name.[1] I feed a strip of brown paper through metal glue rollers and fold a card pocket into place, then pass the folder on down the assembly line to the next prisoner. We each have stacks to work through. So this is prison labour, I reflect, assembling the paperwork for the administration of the unemployed. Nice touch. The tempo is slack, the ambient boredom flat, acceptably dull.

After a couple of weeks I get a transfer to the bookbinding workshop where paperback books for prison library stock are carefully parted from their covers, then reassembled with the covers replaced on cloth covered hardback board. They last longer like that. The week before I leave, Dave gives me my re-bound copy of Maya Angelou's book. It's not quite the only souvenir I take with me from HMP Norwich, but it is the only one I still have. It was as much of an eye opener to me as the prison. It tells me about an America I don't know, and about the power of writing with a force I've never felt.

Robbery and reading in Los Angeles: John Irwin

If there is a mould for convict criminology into which I have tried to retro-fit Frank Tannenbaum and Saul Alinskey, it is a mould shaped around the figure of John Irwin. Reading John Irwin's (1980) description of the paradoxical 'ragged edged vitality' of prison life and the 'stupefaction' of doing time I felt a spark of recognition. This phrasing captures some essential characteristics of men's prison life with rare economy and precision. Irwin knows what he is talking about because in 1952 he robbed a petrol station in Los Angeles and was sentenced to five years in prison. During some of that time he started to study through a university provided extension programme where he accumulated enough credits to apply for a full time degree. On release he began an undergraduate degree in physics at the University of California, Los Angeles (UCLA), before being persuaded, by the eminent US criminologist Donald Cressey, to switch to sociology, with

---

[1] This is a joke. The band took the name from the government Social Security form as a political gesture toward the issue of mass unemployment, before it became normalised.

a major in criminology. If it was a meeting of minds, it was not an entirely friendly encounter with the existing sociology of prison life:

> I was introduced to the sociology of the prison, particularly to some of the new theories about the inmate social system. I considered the theories, tested them against information that I could dig out of my memory, and discovered they did not fit. Extended discussions with Professor Cressey eventually led us to interview many ex-convicts and revise the current theories. (Irwin, 1980, xxi)

Thus conceived is the project of convict criminology in a nutshell: how does direct, first-hand experience of imprisonment correspond with its theorisation and academic representation in criminology. It led to the development of a conceptual model of prisoner's social relations, the importation model, which has become a mainstay of penal theory (Irwin and Cressey, 1962). Rather than the prevailing model suggested from Sykes (1958) notions of a single prisoner society bonded through solidarity, Irwin and Cressey showed how prisoners bring their many cultural habits and social bonds into the prison instead of leaving them at the gate as Sykes proposed.

Irwin's subsequent academic career consolidated his activism around prison issues. The eventual result was a mode of practice that validated the combination of personal prison experience and critical academic scholarship. In 1961, less than ten years after his conviction, Irwin graduated from UCLA and a few years later he enrolled onto the doctoral programme at the University of California, Berkeley. He was recruited to a research project on parole and the ensuing thesis, completed in 1968, was published as *The Felon* in 1970. Although the dispassionate prose and detached narrative of *The Felon* reveals the impact of his social science training at Berkeley (Platt, 1980), in later life Irwin became progressively more candid about the relationship between his academic work and his prison experiences: 'My prison experiences, five years at Soledad, a medium-security California prison, after several years of living the life of a thief and drug addict, as well as my post-prison years not only determined my academic career path but also shaped my sociological perspective in definite and profound ways' (Irwin, 2005, ix).

Similar convictions, deadly differences: George Jackson

In 1960, a few years after Irwin was convicted, another young man robbed a petrol station in Los Angeles and also ended up in Soledad prison. Aged 18, George Jackson was accused of stealing $70, and like Irwin he had previous convictions so he also took the advice of his court-appointed lawyer that a quick guilty plea would be rewarded with a lighter sentence. He got an indeterminate sentence of one year to life. In San Quentin State Prison, then Soledad, for the next ten years of his life, he became an autodidact, transforming himself into a leading thinker and activist of the emerging prisoner's movement and an eloquent spokesperson for Black Nationalism. His letters to friends and political allies on the outside are collected in *Soledad Brother* (Jackson, 1971) and *Blood in My Eye* where I found another evocation of prison life that I think reveals a very personal understanding of its form: 'The ultimate expression of law is not order, it's prison' (Jackson, 1972, 119).

Jackson's book of prison letters, *Soledad Brother*, was published with a Preface from an ex-prisoner, the celebrated French literary maverick, Jean Genet. Genet was a graduate of the Mettray Penal Colony in France that, in an earlier manifestation, features so famously in Foucault's *Discipline and Punish*. Genet alludes to the ways in which prison interiors are known to prisoners:

> I have lived too long in prisons not to recognize, as soon as the very first pages were translated for me in San Francisco, the special odour and texture of what was written in a cell, behind walls, guards, envenomed by hatred, for what I did not yet know so intensely was the hatred of the white American for the black, a hatred so deep that I wonder if every white man in this country, when he plants a tree, doesn't see Negroes hanging from its branches. (In Jackson, 1971, 23–4)

Jackson died in, rather than graduated from, prison as Irwin did and their two stories tell of the divergent paths available to bright young men, white and black, in the 1960s and 1970s.

In Soledad, Jackson's friend and Black Panther Party comrade, WL Nolen was shot dead, along with two other black prisoners, by a white prison guard during a yard riot involving members of the Aryan Brotherhood, a neo-fascist, white, racist prison gang. Three days later it was announced over the prison radio that the coroner had ruled that the killings were 'justifiable homicide' and no one would be prosecuted.

As tensions grew in the prison that evening a guard was attacked and killed on one of the Soledad landings and Jackson, along with two other men, was charged with his murder. The publisher's Preface to *Soledad Brother* remarks 'Three unarmed prisoners are provoked and shot dead by a white guard who is completely exonerated; one white guard is subsequently killed and three black prisoners face the gas chamber' (Jackson, 1971, 12). At his trial, in August 1970, at Marin County courthouse George's younger brother, Jonathan, burst into the courthouse with an automatic weapon in a desperate attempt to free the accused men. In the ensuing melee, three jurors were taken hostage, and Jonathan Jackson and the judge were among those killed before the siege ended.

The circumstances leading up to and surrounding the killing of George Jackson at San Quentin prison the following year, 1971, are contested (Yee, 1973). Some years later a jury convened by a civil rights action into the shooting of the three black prisoners found that eight white prison officers had 'willfully and unjustifiably' conspired to kill the three prisoners. They had set up the confrontation between the two groups of black and white prisoners, and prepared the armed response that led to the fatalities among the group of black prisoners (Yee, 1973).

Some claim that Jackson's success in securing the support of radical lawyers in San Francisco to challenge his murder charge, and the gathering of wider radical support resulted in his assassination. He had become a key figure in the Black Panther Party, and his capacity for exposing and resisting racism in the prison system had begun to attract vocal international support. The authorities claim that he had been provided with a gun by his comrades and was shot while attempting to escape. Ten years on from his conviction for a $70 robbery he was dead.

One final twist that links George Jackson's story to that of convict criminology is that Angela Davis, another member of the Black Panther Party, was subsequently accused of providing the weapons for the Marin County episode, arrested and jailed. She was later acquitted of all the charges she faced, including conspiracy, kidnap and murder. Professor Angela Davis (1971; 1983; 2003; 2005) is now an emeritus (retired) professor of the University of California, whose work on racism, feminism and, most recently, the US prison–industrial complex is widely published and internationally acclaimed. In 1971 while awaiting trial in prison she edited, with Bettina Aptheker, *If They Come In The Morning*, an anthology of writing about political prisoners. Though not convicted, Davis's experience of imprisonment on remand and awaiting trial provide her with all the necessary requirements of a convict criminologist.

I do not want to labour the connections between John Irwin's life and George Jackson's death but given what has occurred in US prisons, race relations and the criminal justice system since 1970, their respective trajectories are more than merely coincidental. The colour line presented to Tannenbaum, and US social science more broadly, by Du Bois cannot be washed away by writing it out of the story. Disconnecting race from US criminal justice and criminology affords them a relative autonomy that the empirical evidence rarely supports (Gabbidon, 2014). They are always in it together but in ways that a predominantly white academy seems to find harder to identify consistently than the few black prison scholars available to write on the topic (see Alexander, 2012; Murakawa, 2014).

Ideal prisons in turmoil

Irwin's (1980) account of the volatile environment within and around US prisons in the 1970s has become a widely acclaimed classic of prison sociology. In the final sections of the book Irwin sets out his attempts to mobilise and organise prisoners around the establishment of the Prisoners' Union. As Tony Platt explains in a combative review of the book, it shows Irwin as 'deeply committed to praxis'. Irwin's work illuminates the basic precepts of what was to become convict criminology: 'to translate conceptual knowledge into political action, to use theory as a weapon of practice and to infuse theory with the lessons of direct experience' (Platt, 1980, 70). Prior to its publication Irwin had been involved in drafting the influential report of the American Friends Service Committee, *Struggle for Justice* (AFSC, 1971). This report was unusual in bringing together notable criminal justice scholars and those who had been on the receiving end of criminal justice. It presented anecdotal evidence and personal testimony from prisoners to develop a radical critique of punishment and a stinging riposte to the prevailing models of rehabilitation.

Stephen C Richards, one of the founding cohort of convict criminology recalls Irwin's reservations about the way the policy recommendations of *Struggle for Justice* were subsequently used to support the imposition of longer prison sentences in the US. In an early example of the unintended consequences that litter the history of criminal justice reform, Irwin and the other authors of *Struggle for Justice* demonstrated how white prisoners tended to benefit from indeterminate sentences by being more likely than black prisoners to secure early release on parole. As a result they argued for determinate sentences. When these were introduced in many US states during the 1980s the result was a dramatic increase in sentence length, which led to prisoners doing more time and prison populations increasing. In 1970 the US total 'jail plus prison' population was no more than 300,000 men and women, by 2015 it had grown to over 2.4 million (Richards, 2015a). Irwin's well intentioned recommendations on sentence reform in *Struggle for Justice* are implicated in this growth. *Prisons in Turmoil* was published ten years later and its title is something of an understatement of the intervening period.

Soledad Prison where both Irwin and Jackson did time was built in 1946 on the crest of progressive, post-war optimism. It was purpose built to embody all the best things that a prison could be as the California Department of Corrections aligned itself firmly with the spirit of liberal reform and the new social science propelling it through government. Soledad prison was 'a collage of floral walkways, baseball diamonds, gymnasiums, movie theatres, classrooms and private cells' as Yee (1973, 10) puts it in his aptly titled *Melancholy History* of the prison. The humanitarianism of its founding ideals emphasised treatment, persuasion and rehabilitation but, as the subtitle of Yee's book reveals it was soon to be a case of 'a Utopian Scheme Turns Bedlam'.

Prison rehabilitation schemes always imagine much more than they deliver (Carlen, 2008), and as the models failed in the USA they became more intrusive, more intense and increasingly penal (see Richards, 2015b for an account of prisoners' resistance to these trends). Soledad promoted the idea of a therapeutic prison, a place for healing and care rather than punishment and containment. It was an idea of gently administered correctional guidance delivered to grateful and compliant felons who would disappear on release to lives of quiet invisibility. This image of docile compliance, manageable and teachable prisoners, is the prison's most persistently cherished delusion.

In the progressive alternative to the punitive vision, prisons in the post-war USA would become unrecognisable before ultimately disappearing. Looking forward from the 1940s, ambitious and optimistic criminologists predicted prisons would not survive their punitive limitations, their many alternatives and the exposure of their repeatedly false promises. Hermann Mannheim declared in 1942 'The days of the prison as a method for the mass treatment of law breakers are largely over' (cited in Tonry, 2004, 3). In the mid-1960s Norval Morris (1965, 12) was still buoyantly upbeat: 'It is confidently predicted that before the end of the century the prison in its present form will become extinct.' The view backwards from the second decade of the twenty-first century shows how wrong they were. Recidivism, revolving doors, riots, increasing brutalism and unremitting growth was the fate of US prisons from the 1970s onwards; prisons in turmoil indeed.

As a prisoner Irwin caught the trailing edge of Soledad's optimism but he is no apologist for its dream. The critique of rehabilitation crafted in *The Struggle for Justice*, returns in *Prisons in Turmoil* with the force of his own experience and 10 years of riots, repression, neglect and violence that swept through California's prison system in the 1970s. A footnote in the final pages (Irwin, 1980, 247) reveals why.

Irwin, having concluded his account of the troubled Prisoner's Union and its associated activists, notes that '[O]ne of the important obstacles that must be removed is the public conception of the prisoner.' The footnote elaborates:

> A few days after writing this sentence I was reading an article by Eve Pell. One of the prison movement activists during the late 1960s and early 1970s, she had written the following statement: 'But fashions change; the public grows bored, and today the image of the man behind bars is no longer that of a social protester such as George Jackson, but rather of a mass murderer such as Son of Sam.'

As Irwin declares '[T]hese extraordinary cases distort the reality. Most prisoners are still in prison for relatively petty crimes...What we need is a new theory of crime and penology, one that is quite simple. It is based on the assumption that prisoners are human beings and not a different species from free citizens.' If prisons are to be used, they must be used sparingly, he suggests, so that those inside are treated as human. Once inside, prisoners should be provided with resources 'to achieve self-determination, dignity and self-respect' (Irwin, 1980, 247–8).

Here, surely, is a telling echo of Tannenbaum's critical insights from 1938: because of the 'verbalisation of the conflict in terms of evil...The person becomes the thing he is described as being...The harder they work to reform evil, the greater the evil grows under their hands... The way out is through a refusal to dramatise the evil' (Tannenbaum, 1938). Irwin's emphasis on, and dedication to, ensuring prisoners have a voice and are given dominion over their own affairs as much as possible within the prison, recalls Tannenbaum's advocacy of self-managed Prisoner Welfare Leagues within each prison. Both men had witnessed and experienced the degradation of social and personal autonomy that accompanies imprisonment. They had felt its corrupting force and resisted its insidious hierarchies.

In theoretical terms Irwin and Tannenbaum appear to recognise autonomy as a continuous accomplishment of the prisoner rather than something simply given or withdrawn by the prison. Autonomy in this sense is an existential accomplishment predicated on interaction with others. This autonomy is thus always implicated in care for the predicaments of others as similar to one's own, in human affinity (Tronto, 1995). Experientially, it is based on the certain knowledge that 'convicts are human like us' (Irwin, 1980, 248) and a refusal to allow them to be rendered otherwise. Both men are 'vulnerable', in the positive sense of possessing a heightened sensitivity (Gilson, 2014) to such perspectives because of their direct experience of imprisonment. Irwin (1980, 248) is sanguine but steadfast about 'pushing' such an empathetic approach: 'I admit that many prisoners, like many free citizens, act like monsters. But they are not monsters'. He refuses to dramatise evil.

1997: here come the cons...

Towards the end of the 1990s, Irwin's long-standing commitment to prisoners' and ex-prisoners' education laid the groundwork for the emergence of 'convict criminology' workshops at successive American Society of Criminology (ASC) conferences. Irwin (2003) describes a simple telephone call from a PhD student eager to meet him because of their similar experience of being convicted and writing about prison. Chuck Terry and John Irwin became 'instant friends' and Chuck introduced John to some of the growing number of postgraduate criminology students who were also former prisoners, people like Alan Mobley, Richard S Jones and Stephen C Richards, among others. Out of the talk and the meetings emerged the idea of setting up a session at the 1997 American Society of Criminology annual conference with the title 'convict criminology'. The time was ripe. Prison research appeared to be in decline. Irwin (2003) noted that the largest and most widely read US academic journal, *Criminology*, had barely covered the issue of prison in the previous two years, despite vigorous growth in prison numbers, variable prison conditions and sharpening patterns of racial conflict.

Chuck Terry and Alan Mobley were telling Irwin about their frustration with criminology courses they had studied and how they were now starting to teach at university. Like Irwin had felt in the 1960s when he arrived on criminology's doorstep fresh from the prison gate, Terry and Mobley reported their sense of a discipline obsessed with intrinsic criminal difference: 'many criminologists...

UNIVERSITY OF WINCHESTER LIBRARY

see [criminals] as less than human, as inferior or evil deviants' (Irwin, 2003, xix). Alongside an anthropological fascination with 'exotic specimens', criminology in the booming and restructured US university education sector seemed to 'tolerate or participate in the inhumane and counterproductive treatment' of prisoners by fostering an ideology of pathological difference (Irwin, 2013, xix). The toxic message Terry and Mobley were getting from criminology was 'Prison is where monsters are kept away from ordinary folk and trained to be less monstrous.' What they knew as ex-convicts, that most prisoners were people quite like themselves who had done stupid things, too many times, counted for less than nothing. They felt themselves compromised, in more ways than one, by having to teach an approach to crime they didn't believe in or recognise from their own experience. Having been through a variety of criminal justice procedures, culminating in imprisonment their knowledge of 'its shortcomings, injustices and idiocies' should be welcomed by the discipline, not rejected, said Irwin, and between them the panel at the 1997 ASC was organised.

'Convicts Critique Criminology: The Last Seminar' was the first time a group of self-declared ex-criminals, ex-prisoners or ex-convicts presented themselves as academic criminologists with something distinctive to say about the discipline. An alliance with supportive non-convict criminologists, such as, among others, Jeffrey Ian Ross, William S Treaga and Barbara Owen, emerged from the ASC panel. In 1998 Ross and Richards sent invitations to the panel's academics and students suggesting an edited book compiling the accounts of ex-convict academics which was duly published in 2003, the first anthology of explicitly articulated convict criminology (Ross and Richards, 2003). This foundational collection established the academic viability of the model and the credentials for its originality. Ross and Richards subsequently guided convict criminology along two principle forms of activity: collective publishing projects and teaching or mentoring ex-con graduate students into professional positions. Along with other core members of the group, such as Rick Jones and Greg Newbold, Ross and Richards have devoted substantial resources to correspondence, teaching, support and co-ordination. As a direct result of their work, convict criminology in the US has grown and flourished, supporting around 30 ex-con academics, and some 300 members of the broader network. A lot of their work is invisible and much of it does not register in conventional metrics of academic performance but without it there would be no convict criminology.

Ross and Richards (2003, 6) locate distinctive convict criminology perspectives in the conjunction of the persistent failure of US prisons, the importance of prisoners' rights movements, insider perspectives and the centrality of prison ethnography. 'Convict scholars' they declare 'are able to...merge their past with their present and provide a provocative approach to the academic study of criminology, criminal justice and corrections.' They set out the convict criminology enterprise as a collaborative, lateral, collective project. It includes students and professors, researchers and teachers. Significantly, Ross and Richards note the inclusion of academics without criminal convictions, and those who prefer not to disclose their convictions. The reasons for non-disclosure are complex and include 'a reluctance to revisit a painful time in life', a desire to move on unencumbered by stigma and to let the past remain buried behind them (Ross and Richards, 2003). Being open to scholars without criminal convictions extends the range of criminological experience available to support the development of the group, and reinforces its commitment to collaboration and dialogue.

Convict Criminology identifies the challenge posed by Harcourt (2001) on what it will take to reshape the image of the convict in the public imagination: convicts *can* become professors, convicts *can* teach, convicts *can* be public intellectuals, authors, researchers, students, and, of course vice versa. Since 1997 convict criminology in the US has made its presence felt in each of the subsequent annual gatherings of the American Society of Criminology by organising panels and roundtable discussions. Until his death in 2010, John Irwin provided moral support, academic inspiration and scholarly guidance to the group, always making time to meet and encourage new ex-convict graduate students. By force of example he pushed the door open into criminology for ex-convict scholars. He made sure it didn't close behind him and personally greeted many as they crossed the threshold (Richards, 2010).

Convincing misfits or the new criminology?

The 17 chapters of *Convict Criminology* introduced several new scholars to criminological publishing and an academic readership, and many, though not all, contributors were ex-convicts. The range of ex-convict academic experience extends from full professor to graduate students. Divided into three sections, the book provides critical summaries of criminological knowledge, convict criminology methods and its diverse perspectives. It ends with 'an invitation to join us' in the identified task of 'changing corrections'. The invitation is addressed to 'those who are still in the closet, ex-cons with PhDs who don't want to reveal their status, or ex-convict graduate students, or members of the criminology/ criminal justice community'.

The convict criminology website (www.convictcriminology.org) was set up and populated with resources to facilitate engagement with the project of establishing the 'New School of Convict Criminology', as set out in the book. It presents the agreed definition of convict criminology: 'the work of convicts or ex-convicts, in possession of a PhD or on their way to completing one, or enlightened academics and practitioners, who contribute to a new conversation about crime and corrections'. This suitably catholic definition specifies the key penal characteristics required to contribute to the development of the school, and its eagerness to include 'fellow travellers' without experience of imprisonment.

The website goes on to declare its 'use of "New" is mirrored on Taylor, Walton, and Young's (1973) seminal work *The New Criminology*'. This ambitiously locates convict criminology in a project that systematically unpacked the theoretical and ideological prescriptions of criminology using the tools of radical socialism and New Left Marxism. This sets a high bar for the 'New School of Convict Criminology'. As Alvin Gouldner remarks in his foreword to *The New Criminology*, Taylor, Walton and Young presented 'perhaps the first truly comprehensive critique…of the totality, of past and contemporary, of European and American, studies of "crime" and "deviance"'. Rather than aspiring to this paradigm-bending benchmark of theoretical and analytical sophistication, the scholars of the New School of Convict Criminology may be better placed to simply compensate for what Gouldner (1973, xiii) describes as the traditional Marxist's 'limited insight into, and stunted compassion for, the lowly'.

Convict Criminology is probably closer to the 'misfit sociology' described by Geoff Pearson in Taylor, Walton and Young's (1975) follow-up volume, *Critical Criminology*: 'misfit sociology enabled individuals to solve the problem of the relationship of their lives as social scientists and their lives as men and women; it allowed them to put together in their lives *politics, social science* and *compassion*' (Pearson, 1975, 163, emphasis in original).

Pearson's sanguine assessment, even back then in the early 1970s, that the political optimism that facilitates two-way traffic between activism and scholarship was declining and rendering the journey 'more tortuous' is a cautionary remark, noteworthy for its salience to the present decade (see for example Belknap, 2015). Drawing from the vibrant countercultures of the 1960s and 1970s 'misfit sociology' prospered in the absence of 'a clear unifying tendency', usually provided, at the time, by explicit left-wing commitment according to Pearson. Although 'the theoretical air' of misfit sociology was 'thin' it allowed 'a number of conflicting orientations to exist side by side' (1975, 148), and so it is with convict criminology in even leaner times.

Over a decade has passed since the publication of Ross and Richards (2003) *Convict Criminology* collection. In 2012 the proliferation and diversity of US convict criminology was reflected in a special double issue of the *Journal of Prisoners on Prison* (*JPP*) co-edited by Stephen C Richards and Michael Lenza. The journal is itself an exemplary form of the sentiments and actions that propel convict criminology, although it remains distinct from the US group. Published in Canada, the *JPP* was established in 1988 to help amplify prisoner's perspectives in the International Conference on Penal Abolition (ICOPA). This bi-annual gathering of activists, academics, journalists and assorted others, organises for the abolition of imprisonment, penal systems, carceral controls and the prison-industrial complex.

The journal encourages submissions from serving and ex-prisoners, and fosters collaborative writing projects between established prison academics, prisoners and ex-prisoners. As the managing editors Larsen and Piche (2012, 1) note that the journal emerged 'in response to the under-representation of the voices of the criminalised in criminological and public discourse on punishment'. By bringing these voices forward the journal expands the resources for criminological theorising and generates challenging pedagogical and methodological perspectives for criminologists. Produced in Canada under the imprint of the University of Ottawa Press, the journal is not easily found in UK academic collections but deserves wider readership among penologists and prison research communities (www.jpp.org.uk). In an era when academic publishing seems to excel in circulating roughly the same ideas to roughly the same people, and functions most effectively as an accelerator in career progression, *JPP* is a breath of fresh air: inspiration, literally. Convict criminologists have supported *JPP* by contributing and reviewing articles, sitting on the editorial board and promoting readership of its perspectives among students and other scholars.

Exemplars and dilemmas of convict criminology

In one article of the *JPP* special issue, Alan Mobley, an experienced convict criminologist academic, writes with another less experienced author, Richard Hendricksen (Hendricksen and Mobley, 2012). Hendricksen reflects on the contrasting paths available and taken by himself and another prisoner on their release from the same prison.

It is a fine example of the auto-ethnographic potential that is often central to convict criminology, and exemplifies the efficacy of thorough peer mentoring that lies at the heart of the organisation. 'A Tale of Two Convicts: A Reentry Story About the Impacts of Ethnicity and Class' reveals in compelling personal detail the trajectories that racism and class hierarchy prepare for prisoners on release. Richard, a white American, and compares his experience to that of Josh, a Mexican American he shared prison time with and with whom he was released.

Richard is embraced by his recently reconstituted family, provided with meals, shelter and connections to the world of work. Josh is consigned to a Temporary Living Placement, his mother already struggling to cope with the return of another son from another prison. The two keep in touch, mainly by phone. Richard gets a job, low-paid but 'with an honest paycheck' and is supported by his family onto a college course. Josh slides into debt, relies on food bank handouts and struggles to find work. By the start of their second year of release Richard is on his way to a college degree, Josh is on his way back to prison for breaching the licence terms of his release.

The poignant closing remarks of the article reflect on how typical the differences in their two stories are. They are worth quoting at length:

> The difference in the outcomes for Josh and me was not that I worked harder and struggled to succeed more valiantly than he did. The opposite is much closer to the truth. Without resources Josh faced difficulties every day securing a roof over his head and food to keep himself alive. Yet, he did not steal, cheat or commit crimes. He kept trying. When we regularly talked on the phone and he would tell me what was happening in his life, I often felt a mixture of unearned security and guilt for simply having a room, a roof over my head, food in the kitchen, or that my mother could lend me ten or twenty dollars when I needed it from her tips she brought home from work until I found a job. (Hendricksen and Mobley, 2012, 115)

The authors go on to rage against the absurdity with which they are confronted:

> Around $30,000 a year is spent to further stigmatise and punish Josh. That is more than it costs me to get my four year degree at a university. It makes no sense to me. The American public is being taken for a ride through the

politics of fear and difference. (Hendricksen and Mobley, 2012, 115)

In their introduction to the article the authors present the reader with the convict criminologist's invitation to 'become involved in the emotional information conveyed in these accounts'. By their presence on the page they remind us that 'These are real people...If prisons harm, which they most surely do, these are the people they hurt.' These are Richard and Josh's personal problems made public issues, biography connected to social structure, and history made present, in the best traditions of sociological craftwork (Mills, 1959).

The 17 articles gathered for the anniversary special issue of *JPP* reveal the changing contours and expanded horizons of convict criminology. The editors include an article that presents convict criminology with some of its most troubling dilemmas. One of the contributing authors to the *JPP* special issue reveals himself as someone who served six years and three months in prison in the 1990s for non-violent sex offences committed against minors when he was a young man.

Within most western prisons, men sentenced for sexual offences are often regarded as pariahs. Violence against women, although commonly practised by men, is paradoxically regarded as a dishonourable form of masculinity. Men's use of violence is valued most highly by other men as a threat rather than an actuality, and the public exposure of having used it against 'the weaker sex' usually confers little prestige, and frequently the reverse. As with many forms of power, it is often most potent when it is least visible. Men convicted of abuse or sexual exploitation of children are held in even greater contempt than those with convictions for rape and the abuse of women. They represent to conventional heterosexual masculinity the ultimate violation of its codes.

Writing on his own,[2] the author presents an argument that attempts a lot but achieves less. Although the ambition is intended to explore the stigma attached to the form of offending behaviour, sanction and punishment he discusses, it does not succeed as well as the collaboration

---

[2] The author is not identified in this critical discussion in deference to the sensitivities of the issues raised and to limit his exposure to the possibility of unfair secondary criticism remote from any engagement with the full article in the *JPP* special issue. Richards (2015a) reports on the author's experience of extensive and unwarranted discrimination, violent victimisation and personal courage in completing his PhD.

between Hendricksen and Mobely because there is less evidence of sociological craft and imagination at work. Whereas Hendricksen, in partnership with an experienced author and convict criminologists, discusses the social structures of race and class that frame his personal experience, the corresponding matrix of gender and power is absent from this account. Although the author raises important issues about the false securities and vicious animosities that the extra-punitive legislation against sex offending mobilise (for a critical overview see Wacquant, 2009a, chapter 7), the chapter struggles to move beyond a sometimes plaintive account of personal injustice. I do not want to dismiss the significance of this experience, or the additional hardships and victimisation that frequently accompany such convictions. The author's inside account of being subject to particular, pernicious and extended punitive supervision can surely contribute to broader struggles against injustice, misogyny, exploitation and abuse, but by deploying, for example, the terminology of a 'war against sex offenders' he implies a misplaced equivalence to black people's experience of 'the war on drugs' and other criminal justice policies.

Surveillance and notification procedures imposed on people convicted of sexual offences in the US have become excessive and extraordinary, but the context for their imposition requires more extensive critical interrogation than the author provides. Some of this might address the widespread extent of men's sexual violence against women and children, and the abject failures of criminal justice systems to police it or provide redress to women and children subject to abuse by men. The article closes with an appeal for a convict criminology perspective on sex offenders and the author raises some important issues about the right to move on (see Chapter 5) and be considered free from the stigma that accompanies all convictions, and specifically convictions for sexual offences against women or children.

Ex-cons and sex cons: solidarity, collusions and evasions

As Crewe and Ievins (2015) note there are signs of 'a quiet revolution' in prison research of which the *JPP* is a prime example. It is a revolution in which researchers pride themselves 'on giving voice to the voiceless' and bending their efforts toward 'the marginalised, exploited or dominated groups' (Jewkes, 2012, 65). However, Crewe and Ievins also identify some familiar exclusions from the conventional list of worthy causes, pointing out that 'some prisoners have always been valued more than others' (Crewe and Ievins, 2015, 135). 'Sex offenders' often tend to disappear from view and are as shunned by mainstream ethnographic prison researchers as they are threatened by other prisoners.

Although there is a growing body of research on men who commit sexual offences, much of it remains conventionally structured by the reformative, correctional and diagnostic priorities so thoroughly rejected by the new generation of 'quiet revolutionaries'. A rare exception to this 'regrettable bias' (O'Donnell, 2004, 253) against people who have committed sexual offences can be found in the work of James Waldram (2007; 2009; 2012; 2015).

Waldram deliberately extends ethnographic intentions of listening to sex offenders, hearing their personal stories and appreciating cultures of adaptation and accommodation with prison life because 'the only way to eliminate the problem and protect ourselves is to understand it as fully as possible' (Waldram, 2007, 969). He reports (Waldram, 2015) that it has been far from easy to conduct his research but even more difficult to publish his accounts in the form he has been accustomed to when working with and writing about other prisoners.

The ethical quandaries posed by writing or researching with or about men who have committed sexual offences arise from the way their offending is understood to be both exceptionally harmful and exceptionally pathological. In these circumstances the solidarity of the 'sympathy-of-obligation' for prisoners' predicaments is cancelled, and replaced by a 'sympathy-as-problem' package that generates intense discomfort (Crewe and Ievins, 2015; Moolman, 2015). When it comes to men who have committed sexual offences, there is an implication that empathy in some way conveys endorsement, or at least fails to convey sufficient distancing. Cowburn (2013, 190), for instance, draws from his extensive experience of working with men who have committed sexual and other violent offences to insist that any rapport must be tempered by mindfulness 'of the person who was hurt by the violence'.

Crewe and Ievins (2015) identifies how these problematic experiences and dilemmas pose particular challenges to men, and particularly to men who align themselves with feminist practice and politics. Men, as prisoners and as researchers, are presented with other men who often fail to comply with the monstrous object their offences might suggest they should appear to be. Their ordinariness can be profoundly challenging rather than comfortingly engaging as it is with other prisoners (Moolman, 2015). Suspending judgement and embracing the humanity of the imprisoned man carries the twin perils of identification and collusion. Separating the offence from the offender, so effortlessly accomplished with other prisoners, becomes a task now heavily stressed with personal, social and methodological implications.

Convict criminology has nothing to gain by reproducing the conventional penal hierarchy of disdain that places sex-offenders as the lowest of the low, the ultimate of beasts among beasts and a class apart. Confronting and challenging prison's capacity to dehumanise is central to the personal accounts that populate convict criminology publications. As Irwin argues, men do monstrous things, but they are not monsters. That is as true for those who are convicted of sexual offences as for any other kind of offence.

An example of what convict criminology can bring to the critical analysis of sex crime is provided in another article in the *JPP* special issue. In it, an ex-con academic member of convict criminology writes with another established academic. Williams and Burnett (2012) provide the wider discussion that was missing from the other, sole authored, account, situating the various discourses on sexual offending and the policing of sexualities in historical and theoretical context. They explicitly identify the role of convict criminology in helping to bring forward silent voices and hidden perspectives, those of the convicted. These voices, they argue, can be part of the solution, their absence part of the problem. They urge that their inclusion is accomplished with due and explicit respect to others similarly silenced and devalued, such as the families of perpetrators, and for the accounts to value the perspective of victims and their families.

Although closely juxtaposed in the journal, the two contrasting articles suggest how hard it can be to resolve the tensions around the exclusion or marginalisation of those convicted of sexual offences. Taken together, they contribute valuable insights toward a progressive and critical discussion of men's sexual violence in society. The difficult issues they raise about gender analysis in criminology, and men's crimes in particular are not issues that are exclusive to convict criminology. Lander et al's (2014) edited collection and Waldrum's (2015) discussion of his ethnographic work with men serving prison sentences for sexual offences in Canada are both instructive and illuminating of what is possible in this neglected area of criminology.

Taking criticism, moving on

Convict criminology in the USA is a loose and open organisation where people are united in their concern to develop the validity of prisoners' and ex-prisoners' contributions to an academic discipline in which they have had a hitherto passive presence. These contributions are necessarily diverse in quality and perspective, but the voices of middle-class white men prevail well beyond their representation in the general population, as they frequently do in most aspects of higher education. The contrast with prison populations is stark, to say the least.

Convict criminologists have struggled to include accounts from black or African American ex-prisoners in their collections, or to systematically analyse the astonishing racialised parameters of America's penal nightmare. The differential access African Americans have to both prison and higher education, so much higher in the former and lower in the latter, constrain their participation, but as Belknap (2015) suggests there may be voices to embrace or steps to be taken to ensure that African American perspectives thrive, white assumptions are challenged and masculinist practice questioned.

Feminist academics and activists have contributed to each of the main collections of convict criminology discussed above, but are absent from the group of convicted scholars that comprise convict criminology. This is not altogether surprising. Levels of women's imprisonment are far below those of men, and their sentences generally shorter according to the less serious, less violent characteristics of their less prevalent offending behaviour. Women's experience of incarceration and their potential contributions to convict criminology therefore draws from a smaller and more slowly growing pool of relevant experience. But where such experience and intention does exist convict criminology can raise its profile and encourage further developments.

Dr Kathy Boudin, for example, treads the route taken by Frank Tannenbaum by moving from the revolutionary politics of the 1970s Weather Underground, via incarceration for political activism to becoming Assistant Professor of Social Work at Columbia University. Twenty-two years in prison for driving the getaway car in a bank robbery is harsh time by anybody's count. Boudin's development of a prison programme for incarcerated mothers, while still a serving prisoner, and similarly published (Boudin, 1998) is an exemplary intervention that any convict criminologist would be proud to claim. According to Belknap (2015) her work and perspectives are sustained by her son, who was adopted as an infant by two comrades following his mother's conviction. He has himself published an analysis of the impact on children of their parent's incarceration that could also lay claim to being a kind of second-generation convict criminology by proxy (Boudin, 2011).

Despite the limitations and difficulties discussed in this chapter, convict criminology is no longer limited to the carceral shadows cast by America's monumental prison system. In the *JPP* special issue several contributors report on extensions emerging on the other side of the Atlantic, in the UK (Aresti, 2012) and Finland (Hytonen, 2012; Ekunwe and Jones, 2012). The next chapter considers aspects of the European penal experience that have provided the soil from which these new, green shoots of convict criminology emerge.

FOUR

European origins, perspectives and experiences of convict criminology

IN THE CELLS WITH JIMMY

The challenge of completing my short sentence in HMP Norwich without serious mishap was made immeasurably easier by Jimmy. On the outside, I knew Jimmy's ex-wife, and her best friend was one of mine. They were Scottish, refugees from the heroin epidemic that was taking hold in Scottish working-class districts in the late 1970s as narcotics followed the oil money into cities like Aberdeen. That's where Jimmy was from. Both Jimmy and his wife had been users of heroin but they moved south in an attempt to break the chains closing around them. She had been more successful than he had. Jimmy found me after a couple of days and introduced himself. We had met only a couple of times on the outside where he had quite a fierce reputation. He told me that as soon as one of his cell mates moved on, there'd be a space for me in his cell.

Jimmy would come to find me during exercise in the yard, and during association. He looked out for me as we went to collect meals from the servery, and generally made his presence felt. I could read at least some of the signs of prison hierarchy and while Jimmy was clearly not playing to the hierarchy, his convictions for robbery, violence and hard drugs carried visible status. He was small, wiry and Scottish and you 'didn'ae mess with him'. I could ask Jimmy stupid questions about the impenetrable procedures for collecting post or getting tobacco.

After a few weeks I moved in. My arrival meant the cell was back to being a threesome and by that time I realised what kind of sacrifice Jimmy was making on my behalf, but after a few days the third guy was shipped out. Sharing a cell with Jimmy was easy. He knew how he wanted to do his time – he had two more years of a four-year stretch to go. I was a passing distraction and a relatively welcome one. We talked. He told me a lot about what heroin had done to him, to his friends, his relationship with his wife and his children. There was nothing but heroin in heroin addiction he said. Nothing else mattered. Whatever you thought you loved, you always loved heroin more. He had seen how it made people lie, cheat and hurt the ones they loved most dearly in the world, their mothers, their children – anyone. Everyone. Years later as I watched the film *Trainspotting* I recognised Jimmy's account of heroin and high times in Irvine Welsh's. And Jimmy too, in the character and appearance of Begbie, played by the slightly less handsome Robert Carlyle.

Jimmy insisted on an exercise routine. He explained that prison would control your body and mind if you didn't. He said 'as prisoners we have nothing, and I'm happy wi' that. It means they can take nothing from us.' And that's how he wanted it to stay. 'If they give you something', he said, 'they can take it away.' Long before the Incentives and Earned Privileges scheme was introduced into HMPS in 1995, Jimmy recognised the lines of power and control in prison, and wanted none of it. It was his time and he was going to take it, rather than them. He set his face against the prison, as you might when faced with a mirror you can't look away from.

Jimmy asked me what I remembered from my childhood and we talked about that, here and there, and he told me he worked on his memories in prison, at least partly because he worried he would lose them and they were what he had that couldn't be taken. Even with my short sentence, I recognised the value of this work and found myself doing it. Erwin James (2013, 7), who served a long sentence for murder before becoming a writer in the closing years of his sentence, has said 'Whoever you are and however long your sentence, in prison you live inside your head.' I don't think you'll find many prisoners or ex-prisoners who disagree.

Jimmy died in 2014. His premature death is an injustice visited on him by virtue of being born working class and Scottish. As a result he was *twice as likely to die* before the age of 65 as a man from a professional background in southern England (ONS, 2014). That would be me, breathing still, and thriving. He died free and among friends in Norwich.

Peter Kropotkin and the first work of convict criminology

Between 1882 and 1886 the Russian anarchist and lapsed aristocrat, Peter Kropotkin, was confined in a model French Prison: 'one of the best in France, and as far as my information goes, in Europe' (Kropotkin, 1887, 21). Building on previous experience in a Russian prison between 1874 and 1876 awaiting trial, provides Kropotkin with 'an opportunity of obtaining a personal insight into the results achieved by detention' (Kropotkin, 1887, 21). Published in 1887 *In Russian and*

French Prisons is probably the first published work that could legitimately claim to be a form of convict criminology. It draws not only from Kropotkin's own experiences but also extensively from the personal testimony of prisoners and ex-prisoners through a careful analysis of their own writing, diaries or notes. It is a foundational document in Kropotkin's anarchism, and deserves wider criminological recognition. In it, his early experience as a young army officer unexpectedly sent to report on Siberian prison conditions are combined with his later experiences on the other side of the bars.

His approach is similar to that of Tannenbaum in that he is appalled by everything he sees and is determined to expose the bankruptcy of the ideas and institutions he encounters in his extensive survey. The scope of the book is astonishing. It stretches from the most barbaric conditions of Kharkoff Central Prison in Eastern Russia, which he says, chillingly, makes 'Siberia look like paradise' (Kropotkin, 1887, 71), to the new and enlightened French model he finds himself in as a prisoner in southern France. Just as Irwin and Jackson found themselves in 'designer' prisons, the latest available model of the penal vision, so it is with Kropotkin way back in the nineteenth century. His study compiles quantitative data on prison populations but emphasises the varying qualities and range of prisoners' experiences. Through the pervading inhumanity and horror he identifies resistance and community, hypocrisy and humour. It is a detailed and nuanced account and within it, even in 1887, are considerations of most of the prevailing questions you would find in a contemporary criminology textbook or prison research report:

> Why are rates of recidivism after prison so high? What are the causes of crime? Why do reforms of prison fail to deliver what they promise? Why are rates of suicide in prison so high? What can be done about overcrowding? How can prison be researched? How overlooked is the collateral damage on prisoners' families? What is the most suitable form of prison labour? How should it be paid for? What is a reasonable wage for prisoners? How can illegal drugs (tobacco) and contraband be regulated? What are the difficulties and limitations of comparative penal analysis? Even, how are prison camps implicated in colonial projects (in Siberia)?

Perhaps that last one might escape the mainstream of contemporary penal scholarship, but in every other respect the questions he posed then are more than recognisable now. Over 100 years later, the answers he provides from back in the nineteenth century are painfully familiar to the twenty-first century. Prisoners reoffend because they arrive from harsh environments into one that prides itself on being even harsher. The brutalism of prison conditions and the stigma attached to it condemns the condemned rather than redeems them. The causes of crime that prison so obviously neglects are complex; they are 'social', 'anthropological', though Kropotkin is no fan of his contemporary, Cesare Lombroso, and 'Cosmic' (Kropotkin, 1887, 255) – as in environmental.

Kropotkin even confesses that in the early stages of his research into Russian prisons he was too easily seduced by the imperfections he discovered. There was so much that was so obviously wrong with prison that he thought it would be a relatively straightforward task to list the faults, prescribe remedies and witness the reform. He quickly excuses his false pragmatism as youthful idealism: 'I was only twenty years old' (Kropotkin, 1887, 29). Then, as he discovers more of the perennial features of prison dysfunction he becomes more critically circumspect and radical in his analysis:

> From time to time, somebody acquainted with prisons starts an agitation against the bad state of jails and lock-ups. Society recognises that something ought to be done to remedy the evil…A few kind hearted and energetic men and women continue, of course, amidst the general indifference, to do their work of improving the condition of prisoners, or rather of mitigating the bad effects of prison on their inmates. But guided as they are by merely philanthropic feeling, they seldom venture to criticise the principles of penal institutions; still less do they search for the causes which every year bring millions of human beings within the enclosure of prison walls. (Kropotkin, 1887, 18)

In Russia he discovers prisons built for 200–300 people housing 700–800. Overcrowding is already normal, he discovers, anticipated and expected. But while the numbers and bare data on meagre prison budgets, casual sadism, routine undernourishment and fearful mortality rates are readily available to the avid and committed researcher, there is still a problem he knows he must wrestle with, an epistemological problem, a problem of method. By way of example he quotes from the prison memoir of an army officer condemned to hard labour but subsequently pardoned by the Tsar after a few years' detention.

'On one occasion' (the writer says) 'we were visited by an inspector of prisons. After casting a look down the scuttle, he asked us if our food was good, or was there anything of which we could complain? Not only did the inmates declare that they were completely satisfied, they even enumerated articles of diet which we had never so much as smelt. This sort of thing' (he adds) 'is only natural. If complaints were made, the inspector would lecture the governor a little and go away; while the prisoners who made them would remain behind and be paid for their temerity with the rod or the black-hole.' (Kropotkin, 1887, 66)

Prisoners are wise both to the conditions of their incarceration and the terms on which it is managed and reviewed. This inside knowledge is dangerous and not readily exposed or shared with inspectors or researchers. As Kropotkin is quick to point out, to see through the veils thrown over the darker parts of prison life, or to get around the obstructions placed in the researcher's path, there is a simple remedy, convict criminology, or as he puts it: 'To know the reality, one must oneself have been a prisoner' (Kropotkin, 1887, 63). This injunction is no simple, solipsistic reference to the relevance of his own prison experience, but a broader methodological one: 'Records of actual experience are few: but they exist' (Kropotkin, 1887, 63). And he then proceeds through the course of his remarkable book to make extensive use of prisoners' letters, diaries and memoirs. He contacts relatives to corroborate stories, or to provide further details, and quotes from their revelations or reflections. The account thus becomes rich, vivid and insightful. Highly personal.

Would another researcher so fully appreciate the significance of the fabric lining and double layered walls Kropotkin finds in Trubetskoi House of Preliminary Detention where he himself spent two years awaiting trial in Russia? Would anyone who has not spent time as a prisoner be so sensitive to the sounds and sensory register of cell life?

The floor of the cells are covered with a painted felt, and the walls are double, so to say; that is, they are covered also with felt, and, at a distance of five inches from the wall, there is an iron-wire net, covered with rough linen and with yellow painted paper. This arrangement is made to prevent the prisoners from speaking with one another by means of taps on the wall. The silence in these felt-covered cells is that of a grave. I know cells in other prisons. Outer life and the life of the prison reach one by thousands of sounds and words exchanged here and there. Although in a cell, one still feels oneself a part of the world. The fortress is a grave. You never hear a sound, excepting that of a sentry continually creeping like a hunter from one door to another, to look through the 'Judas' into the cells. You are never alone, as an eye is continually kept upon you, and still you are always alone. If you address a word to the warder who brings you your dress for walking in the yard, if you ask him 'What is the weather?', he never answers. The only human being with whom I exchanged a few words every morning was the Colonel who came to write down what I had to buy – tobacco or paper. But he never dared to enter into any conversation, as he himself was always watched by some of the warders. (Kropotkin, 1887, 82)

Never alone: always alone! Kropotkin unerringly finds the quintessential features of how a prisoner experiences prison. Anyone who has spent time in a cell will feel that connection to being reached by 'thousands of sounds…here and there' and your sensitivity to the prison's effort to suppress them to reinforce your isolation. *In Russian and French Prisons* is convict criminology avant la lettre – before its time and utterly compelling.

Kropotkin is perhaps the first, of many, to note with consternation 'how so many improvements in the penitentiary system, although made with excellent intentions of doing away with some evils, always create, in their turn, new evils, and become a source of pain for prisoners'. He is almost definitely the first to report his personal experience as a prisoner of such reform. These experiences of penal confinement and hardship also provide Kropotkin with his faith in human decency and provide evidence for his later thesis on innate human predispositions toward mutual aid (Kropotkin, 1902). Most surprisingly, he finds among all the institutional violence of prisons a perversely revealed affirmation of human sociality:

I never cease to wonder [that]…so few of those who grow up in absolute neglect declare open war against our social institutions. These good feelings, this aversion to violence, this resignation which makes them accept their fate without hatred growing in their hearts, are the only real barrier which prevents them from openly breaking all social bonds, not the deterring influence of prisons. (Kropotkin, 1902, 270)

Prisons are remarkable to Kropotkin not because they demonstrate the efficacy of deterrence – they don't – but the resilience of sociality they contain. Prisons themselves represent the antithesis of this sociality and he notes how prison 'kills all the qualities in a man which make him best adapted to community life' (Kropotkin, 1975, 45). And he is not just talking about prisoners. Prison guards are victims of its corrupting power as well: 'it is the institution which makes them what they are – petty, mean persecutors' (Kropotkin, 1975, 56).

Kropotkin is known more for his political philosophy, anarchism, than his criminology but he was an accomplished social scientist, declining the offer of a Chair in Geography at Cambridge University (Ferrell, 2010). His contributions to criminology after the completion of *In Russian and French Prisons* take the form of a piercing critique of law and authority, and their combination as the political architecture of the state. His political activism in the turmoil of the late nineteenth and early twentieth century justifiably overshadow his criminology but, like some other early social scientists of the time, he resisted the hollow pathologies it offered.

Kropotkin insists on the social construction of criminality, problematising the conjuring trick of a criminology that is forever presenting us with new criminals to be locked up and treated, or locked away and forgotten. He devoted much of his life to a wider political philosophy that focused on the harms of institutionalised authority and laws, and took for granted the implied necessity of prison abolition. This work has inspired political movements throughout the twentieth century, and survives into the twenty-first. Kropotkin's books and pamphlets would have been found in the offices of *Mother Earth* where Emma Goldman encouraged young Frank Tannenbaum to mobilise the homeless workers of New York. The principles of 'mutual aid' and lateral organisation Kropotkin pioneered helped to shape the syndicalist politics of the International Workers of the World, and stressed the need to address the political horizon as much as particular acts of particular people. His influence remains strong in European abolitionist criminologies (Van Swaanigen, 1997; see also, for US influence, Tifft and Sullivan, 1980) where there are less identifiable 'convict criminologists' but plenty of evidence of support for the 'complete transformation of the fundamental conditions' he advocated rather than piecemeal reform and perpetual rebuilding.

Political convictions, criminal distinctions: comrades and criminals in prison

Within post-war European criminology there is no equivalent figure to John Irwin as a pivotal, formative influence in establishing convict criminology perspectives. However, notwithstanding Kropotkin's early claim to retrospective eligibility as convict criminology's founding figure, Louk Hulsman is entitled to be seen as aiding and abetting the perspectives with which it is associated, and fulfilling the basic criteria of having been imprisoned. Although he is most widely recognised as a pre-eminent advocate of prison abolitionism, Hulsman's radical opposition to penal procedure was anchored in personal experience (Van Swaanigen, 2010).

Hulsman was 16 years old in 1939 when war was declared in Europe against Hitler's Germany. He was arrested by Dutch police for failing to comply with orders to work in the industries being mobilised to support the German war economy. He had already been nursing anti-authoritarian sentiments in his strict Catholic boarding school but was as appalled by the supine stance of the Dutch authorities to the Nazi occupation as he was by the invasion itself. The hypocrisy he sensed in his schooling and in the Dutch collaboration at this time were formative influences. State and institutional authority lost all moral credibility for him, and though he was interned in a concentration camp, he insists that his three months in the camp were less hard going than the years he did in boarding school. This modest appraisal also furnishes Hulsman with a telling insight for convict criminology:

> The political prisoner loses neither his self-respect nor the respect of his peers. He suffers in many different ways; but he remains a man who can look the world in the eye. He is not rejected. That experience has taught me how crucial the acceptance and rejection of stigma is in the experience of exclusion and violence. (Hulsman and Bernat de Celis, 1982, 16, cited in Van Swaanigen, 2010, 141)

This distinction between political internment and criminal incarceration is a significant one for convict criminology. Political statesmen from Winston Churchill to Nelson Mandela have suffered the indignities of imprisonment, and attest to its lasting influence. Winston Churchill is relatively well known for insisting that 'The mood and temper of the public in regard to the treatment of crime and criminals is one of the most unfailing tests of the civilisation of any country.' His regard for prison conditions is often attributed to his having spent some time interned in a Boer prisoner of war camp in Pretoria, South Africa, at the age of 25. Even though he was barely four weeks in captivity Churchill began to feel the subjective weight of prison time and recorded his impression with his characteristic flair for coining an evocative image: 'The minutes crawl by like constipated centipedes' (cited in Kurki and Morris, 2001, 401).

Irish political prisoners who have gone on to secure prestigious public profiles populate the long struggle against British rule in Ireland, often with prison sentences served in exceptionally harsh conditions. Men like the Fenian Michael Davitt, sentenced in 1870 to 15 years penal servitude in Dartmoor, who educated himself in the principles of socialism while in prison and went on to become a Member of Parliament for County Meath. His political writings shaped the thinking of other famous radicals, such as Mahatma Ghandi, and Davitt insisted that prison 'had been his only university' (cited in Paseta, 2013, 197). They were both advocates of the prison hunger strike, Ghandi because of its resonance with the Indian practice of 'sitting dharma', and Davitt because of its connection with the Celtic tradition of *Troscad* (fasting on or against a person) and *Cealachan* (achieving justice by starvation).[1] The Lord Mayor of Cork, Terence McSweeney, a poet, philosopher and Irish Republican died in Brixton prison in 1920 after 74 days on hunger strike. In the process he delivered an evocative statement of political defiance that echoes through generations of political struggles of all kinds: 'it is not those who can inflict the most, but those who can suffer the most who will conquer' (cited in Beresford, 1987, 19).

In Europe, political struggle and imprisonment are more intimately and explicitly connected in the second half of the twentieth century than appears to be the case in the USA (but see Rodriguez, 2006), notwithstanding the skew of the politics of race there. In Europe, the

---

[1] This practice is referred to by the Irish poet William Butler Yeats in his play *The King's Threshold*:

King: He has chosen death:
Refusing to eat or drink, that he may bring
Disgrace upon me; for there is a custom
An old and foolish custom, that if a man
Be wronged, or think that he is wronged, and starve
Upon another's threshold till he die,
The Common People, for all time to come,
Will raise a heavy cry against that threshold,
Even though it be the King's.

'imprisoned intellectual' might present a stronger case for sociological recognition than the 'convict criminologist', because several prominent social theorists have prison records with varying degrees of connection to their academic work. Often, they are a product of a time in the 1960s and 1970s when efforts to become a 'public sociologist' (Buroway, 2005) or a 'public criminologist' (Loader and Sparks, 2010) could lead as easily into prison as they could to a professorial Chair in sociology or a seat in the House of Lords.

Revolutionary cons: Gramsci and Serge

The Italian communist and social theorist, Antonio Gramsci, is famous for his posthumously published *Prison Notebooks*. Imprisoned by the Fascist government of Italy in 1926 and held almost continuously until his death in 1947, Gramsci is credited with reformulating the terms of Marxist struggle in modern Europe. He is perhaps the most famous of imprisoned intellectuals.

Victor Serge may be the next most iconic of the genre, another anarchist and a 'vagabond witness' (Gordon, 2013) to the political turmoil of the early twentieth century. *Men In Prison* (Serge, 1977) tells his own story, the story of other men in prison and of a society at war with itself. It isn't social science writing, it isn't journalism and it isn't fiction; it is all of that and more: 'Everything in this book is fictional and everything is true' as he writes in the book's dedication. For any social scientist studying prison there isn't a better place to start. Writing with ten years of 'various forms of captivity' behind him, Serge's writing evokes prison experience with peerless and sometimes dazzling insight. Prison is a 'gallery of lost souls' where he finds: 'Suffocation? Drowning? A torpor sneaks into your veins, between your temples: All of life takes on the faded–ocher hue of the cell. You can no more escape this torpor than you can escape these four walls. The rhythm of your inner life slows down' (Serge, 1977, 62).

And yet, like Kropotkin, he finds prison a source of hope. In the face of brutality and degradation, something triumphs to survive: 'A victory over jail is a great victory. At certain moments you feel astonishingly *free*' (Serge, 1977, 66). That isn't an easy thing to say. It isn't an easy or a common victory and the price Serge pays is a high one. He was sent to prison because he refused to give evidence against a group of wayward 'illegalist anarchists' who had mistaken robbery for revolution and been arrested for a series of armed 'appropriations' in Paris. Serge commended their activities in the newspaper he was editing, was arrested as an accessory and took the five years handed out to him rather than turn them in, but: 'it burdened me with an experience so heavy, so intolerable to endure, that long afterwards, when I resumed writing [it] amounted to an effort to free myself from this inward nightmare'.

Serge's book is littered with profound analytical observations that condense various aspects of penal experience, not least, because they draw from personal experience. He writes from this personal experience toward a generic experience, as is clearly implied by the plural in the title of his book, *Men in Prison*, this is not just about him. As stated on the flyleaf: 'I have attempted, through literary creation, to bring out the general meaning and human content of a personal experience.' Thus, the connection to convict criminology is clear. He suggests, for example, that 'Every man who is thrown into a cell immediately begins to live in the shadow of madness' (p 33), which probably sounds slightly hyperbolic to an empiricist who hasn't heard the sound of a key being turned, or a bolt being slid on the door of their cell. My favourite, a comment on lewd graffiti, tells of the peculiarly contorted masculine vitality that seethes through prison life, and the slightly mad loneliness of men living without women: 'It is as if the throngs of men thrown together by prison needed only thirty words and a phallic symbol to express the essence of their suffering' (p 29). In this desolate observation there is a vital hint at the masculine dimensions of prison life, the virility it suppresses and the currency of resistance it provokes. John Berger (1977) said that 'the truth for Serge was something to be undergone' and this is written through the pages of *Men in Prison*, a sentiment surely familiar to convict criminologists.

Post-modern cons: Negri and Stiegler

More recently in Italy, Antonio Negri, the social theorist whose book, *Empire*, co-authored with Michael Hardt, became an international best-seller in 2001, was forced to complete the 30-year prison sentence imposed on him by an Italian court in the 1970s. At the time of his conviction Negri was a professor of the philosophy of law at the University of Padua's Institute for Political Science, and his route to prison post-dates his academic career rather than precedes it.

Negri was involved in the radical politics that gripped Italy in the 1960s, forging links between striking factory workers and protesting students. In 1969 he helped to establish Autonomia Operaia, Workers' Autonomy, an organisation committed to unorthodox industrial action and protest. It operated on the fringes of the powerful political machinery of the influential Italian Communist party. As protest and activism multiplied through the early 1970s, Autonomia Operaia devolved itself into a looser network of organisations. These radical groups emerged from and endured beyond the climax of political protests represented elsewhere by the events in Paris in May 1968.

The 'long 1968' in Italy produced a wave of political mobilisation that lasted from 1968 to 1977. Millions of Italians became involved in a sustained and profound contestation of the established political order. Workers in the Alfa Romeo and Fiat car factories occupied their workshops and linked up with protesting university and school students. The agitation reached a high-point in 1977 in an attempt to initiate an 'armed struggle for communism'. This attempt to foment armed revolt was developed most aggressively by the Red Brigades and the Armed Proletarian Nuclei, leading to a disastrous and deadly kidnapping of the former Italian Prime Minister, Aldo Moro. The murder of Aldo Moro by the Red Brigades was a political atrocity and strategic disaster, not least because it unleashed a ferocious reaction from the Italian state and re-fuelled the already robust neo-fascist reaction.

In April 1979 Negri was arrested and charged with armed insurrection, chief suspect in the police search to find a 'mastermind' behind the Red Brigades and murder of Aldo Moro. For several years he was held on remand in a protracted legal battle contesting the charges on which he was held. He continued his academic writing in prison, finishing an influential study of Spinoza, *The Savage Anomaly* (Negri, 1999), and various academic papers. Recently published in English for the first time *Pipeline: Letters from Prison* (Negri, 2015) reveals how he sought to sustain his political analysis and activity while inside.

His confinement was far from typical of the kind of imprisonment experienced by 'criminals', as he himself concedes and describes:

> My life in prison isn't bad. There are about 3,000 comrades currently held in the Special Prisons (for 'terrorists'). There is therefore a very rich level of political discussion. Our strength, even in prison, is indisputable. So, our conditions of imprisonment are not the worst. They are without doubt better than those that the common prisoner had to undergo before the influx of comrades into prisons. (Negri, 2015, 4)

Negri's trial was repeatedly postponed as the charges against him multiplied and by 1981, after three years in prison, it became clear that he faced a further nine years on remand while the Italian prosecutors prepared their case. As part of the campaign for his release, he stood for parliament as an MP for the Radical Party. His election provided him with temporary immunity from prosecution, and he fled to France for 14 years where he picked up his academic career among the French post-structuralists, most notably with Felix Guattari. In 1997, aged 64, he returned to Italy and was sent back to prison. He was released in 2003 and continues to publish acute political analysis (Hardt and Negri, 2011; Negri, 2013). Although no longer a fugitive in Italy, an invitation by the University of Sydney for him to come and provide a keynote address to a conference in 2004 was hijacked by the Murdoch-controlled press who vilified him as an apologist for terrorism. Negri's appearance was cancelled under pressure from the mounting controversy, but in its place the Australian sociologist, Raewyn Connell, provided an eloquent tribute and summary of his contribution to social theory (Connell, 2012).

In France, Bernard Stiegler (1998; 2010; 2014) is one of a new generation of influential theorists, reinterpreting Marx and post-War French Marxism. Like the American John Irwin, though, he started out as an armed robber. Leaving school a prematurely disenchanted 15 year old, after a few years drifting, Stiegler was sentenced to five years for robbing a bank in 1978. He is completely candid that his life-long devotion to radical philosophy was conceived in prison, his life transformed and his thinking provoked as a reaction to its grinding disciplines. His account of this transformation is published as *Acting Out* (2008) and is discussed further in Chapter 7.

Paris '68, Foucault and Groupes D'Information sur Prisoners (GIP): convincing convictions

Michel Foucault is not best known as a convict criminologist, although he was convicted in a French court of breaching copyright law, and fined accordingly. Foucault had not fallen among plagiarists but he had, according to the Paris court, duplicated and distributed a leaflet without providing the address of the printing press. The offending leaflet was produced by the Groupes D'Information sur Prisoners (GIP) and it was run off on a cheap duplicator in Foucault's Paris apartment. For those unfamiliar with pre-digital, pre-Web agitational technologies, a duplicator is a crude, messy and labour intensive piece of printing equipment, slightly smaller than a dishwasher that leaks ink almost as effectively as it prints paper. It was an early act of public criminology, perhaps, but Foucault's other main claim to fame, beyond his published work, is that he is the only member of a particularly luminous generation of French philosophers to have his ribs broken by the French riot police (Macey, 1995).

In 1968 the world nearly turned upside down. Mass protests erupted across Europe, the United States and elsewhere. In January, North Vietnamese forces launched the Tet Offensive (Tet is the lunar New Year) against the occupying US army and South Vietnamese forces, demonstrating that far from being defeated in the face of overwhelming military force, a small, developing country could defy the largest and richest. In March, in London, thousands protested against US involvement in Vietnam, and blockaded the US Embassy where violent scuffles broke out with the police and 200 people were arrested. In May over a million people took to the streets of Paris, and popularly supported strikers joined forces with protesting students. The President, Charles De Gaulle, was temporarily evacuated as the French government felt its grip on the country slip away and Paris erupted in a carnival of creative protests. In April, it was my tenth birthday and I got my first bicycle. Enoch Powell gave his infamous 'rivers of blood' speech in Birmingham and in the USA Martin Luther King was assassinated, and then, in June, Robert Kennedy, the US Attorney General.

The moment passed. In Paris a deal was struck by the French Communist Party and the popular movement gave way to the power brokers, but in the aftermath some of the revolutionary groups formed Gauche Proletarianne (Proletarian Left) to continue the struggle. In 1970 the French government banned the group, arrested its leaders and closed down its newspaper. The imprisoned members formed themselves into the Organisation of Political Prisoners (OPP) and called on the support of their allies among the French Left and radical intelligentsia. The sudden influx of large numbers of political prisoners into the French penal system strained its resources. Militant, organised and articulate, the new prisoners were appalled at what they found. On the outside there was dawning realisation of how little was known about the plight of prisoners, and Foucault's connections with Gauche Proletarianne and other radical elements of French political life propelled him into action with GIP in 1970.

Foucault believed that in order to properly confront the injustices of the French prison system, they had to establish the realities of prison life from prisoners themselves. He and his supporters had begun to hear about the dire state of conditions inside prison through the activities of OPP and Foucault reasoned that information about prison from prisoners could equip them with a counter argument, another source of knowledge, to pursue their challenge against prison authorities. Clear in principle, in practice the task was far from simple. Access to prison and to prisoners was almost impossible, so GIP produced a survey that was smuggled into, and out of, the prison by relatives. As they gathered insights from inside the prison system, and from prisoners beyond their contacts in OPP, the campaign developed momentum, drawing support from some of France's greatest post-war intellectuals, such as Helene Cixous, Jean-Paul Sartre, Simone De Beauvoir and Gilles Deleuze. Jean Genet's involvement linked across the Atlantic to George Jackson's predicament and the publication of his Preface to *Soledad Brother* in 1970.

GIP developed as an alliance of progressive lawyers, magistrates, journalists, philosophers, ex-prisoners and their families. It enabled those that were without a voice, prisoners, to tell of their own experiences and to form critical perspectives of their own. In this respect, the principles that propelled GIP in France are similar to those that prompt convict criminology, though the early 1970s in France are very different from the late 1990s in the USA. For Foucault it provided an impetus for his work on different regimes of truth. Most significantly, Foucault's interest in prison, power and the lives of prisoners subsequently took shape in his celebrated 1979 study, *Discipline and Punish*.

Foucault's intellectual orientation was intensely sceptical of what some convict criminologist might claim as central to their role, that is, that they can provide access to some hidden truth about prison. His concern for subjugated forms of knowledge focuses on the conditions of its production rather than simple exposure. Foucault's approach is to problematise the very idea of revelation, and particularly a popular obsession with 'hidden truth' or secret powers that must be exposed. As Jonathan Rée (Macey and Rée, 2008, 206) states: 'I think Foucault hates that idea that some of us are in the truth and others of us are outside, and this idea of the philosophy of the secret, which says knowledge is what happens when you get the key and find out the secret.' Much of Foucault's contribution to social theory, to penal studies and to criminology operates against this narrow understanding of how knowledge, human practice and social relations work.

Revolting British prisons: PROP not Profs

Convict criminology in the USA emerged out of the turmoil of the 1970s so vividly described by Irwin (1980), and the subsequent explosion in prison populations that occurred through the 1990s. In Europe with more modest penal growth, no single bridging figure like John Irwin has emerged as a graduate of both prison and university to develop and consolidate prisoners' perspectives on incarceration.

Working-class attendance at university in the US is considerably more widespread than it is in Britain where, for a variety of historical reasons, university education is more thoroughly mired in elitism, exclusivity and privilege. In Britain, Mike Fitzgerald, albeit without the qualification of a prison sentence, most closely approximates Irwin's role because of his work in the 1970s to promote prisoners' rights when few other people with academic credentials were interested in such work.

Fitzgerald was a student at Cambridge university in 1972 when Dick Pooley and several other ex-prisoners set up a small group to defend and promote prisoners' rights. Preservation of the Rights of Prisoners (PROP) brought together family and relatives of prisoners with community activists who shared a history of imprisonment and who had been prompted into action by their rising concern about the deteriorating state of prisoners' lives in British prisons, and the routine violence to which they were subjected. Fitzgerald became PROP's press officer and an organisational lynchpin for its activities. PROP was unusual in bringing to the foreground of campaigns the impact of imprisonment on prisoners' relatives, an issue which prison sociologists are only recently beginning to take seriously (see Condry et al, 2016).

The need for such an organisation can be gathered from the unremittingly bleak tone of Alan Clarke's 1979 film *Scum* which reflects the ingrained violence and racism that characterised much of the penal estate in Britain in the 1970s. Vivid personal testimony is provided in the autobiography of John McVicar (1974) but Fitzgerald's (1977) *Prisoners in Revolt* provides a compelling analytical and historical background that lists the riots and resistance that the appalling prison conditions generated.

PROP produced a Charter of Rights listing some 26 demands ranging from the right to adequate exercise to the right to vote. It decided there would be two classes of PROP membership, with prisoners and ex-prisoners taking precedence over those without records of imprisonment. Fitzgerald (1977, 140) explains why: 'The history of penal reform is filled with the largely futile efforts of middle-class liberals to improve the conditions inside prisons, without involving or even consulting with prisoners themselves.'

To avoid reproducing this historical pattern PROP offered full and free membership 'to any person who is or has been an inmate of any detention establishment in England, Wales, Scotland or Northern Ireland' (Fitzgerald, 1977, 140). Full members enjoyed constitutional rights of voting and could represent the organisation at external functions, and could stand for election to positions within PROP. In this way PROP modelled itself on a trade union structure, envisioning national, sub- and regional committees, and all the trappings of democratic hierarchy required of an internally accountable organisation. It established itself with the structure and ambition of a mass membership organisation, though in reality the number of active members struggled to exceed double figures.

Associate membership was available to anyone who had not been 'inside' but supported the aims and was willing to pay a yearly subscription. The £2[2] fee represented £1 for personal membership and £1 to cover the membership of a prisoner/ex-prisoner member. Associate Members were also required to 'establish and maintain contact with his or her Full Member associate and make reasonable efforts to assist in his or her rehabilitation'. Associate Members would not be entitled to sit on any PROP committees in anything other than an advisory capacity, and their potential impact on decision making was structurally constrained at every level of the organisation.

In 2015 it is sobering to read Fitzgerald's 1977 account of PROP. Even though they numbered little more than a handful of activists, within a few weeks of their first meeting the structure outlined above, and an ambition to recruit every prisoner in the country, had been made explicit. In Britain today barely a handful of convict criminologists struggle to meet on a regular basis, and in the last five years have barely begun to formulate an agenda to sustain ourselves. However, ambitious and far sighted as PROP was, it had different aims and objectives to convict criminology and may also have been slightly delusional, an affliction of many 1970s' radical organisations and one that British convict criminology has avoided. Despite professing to having 'around 500 members' in 'nine branches' around the country, Fitzgerald candidly admits that when it came to mobilising for a demonstration or prison picket, 'PROP never managed to find more than twenty-five or thirty people', and that while there were 'hundreds of people in general sympathy with the aims and strategies of the group...few actually made any sort of positive commitment to the movement'. It was a small group on the edges of the fringe of the political fringes. As parts of those fringes travelled toward the political centre-ground in the 1980s, and vice-versa, PROP was left isolated and collapsed.

As Fitzgerald's account goes on to describe, if the difficulties of mobilising mass support for its aims were substantial, sustaining a viable infrastructure and personal relations between its few members was no less daunting. In the end, despite its attempts to structurally constrain

---

[2] Equivalent to about £25 in 2015.

the dominant influence of resource- and time-rich, but prison-time poor, middle-class members, PROP was being run by 'a middle-class lecturer who provided office accommodation in Hull; a university lecturer in Sheffield, the only local group to get off the ground; and a student at Cambridge [Fitzgerald]' (Fitzgerald, 1977, 184).

Fitzgerald identifies the academic links built with the newly established National Deviancy Conference in 1968 as important, but insufficient. PROP struggled to develop alliances with academics, students, prisoners, ex-prisoners or prison reform groups and prison professionals. An organisation of women affected by imprisonment, the Prisoners' Wives Union, was briefly and productively associated with the group, but the tendency toward fragmentation and dissolution remained strong. In addition, other organisations and campaigning groups began to compete for the prisoner/ex-prisoner constituency that PROP had first identified. Relatively well-funded and firmly established groups such as the National Association for the Care and Rehabilitation of Offenders (NACRO), the National Council for Civil Liberties (NCCL), or the Howard League for Penal Reform began to encroach on PROP's agenda for supporting prisoners, but from a more mainstream perspective (see Van Swaanigen, 1997, 138–41). Within the counter-cultures of the 1970s PROP also suffered from being dismissed by the socialist and revolutionary Left for its singular focus on prisoners, rather than the wider destiny of the working-class movement.

Viva KROM: the unfinished in Norway

The same flourishing of radical struggles against capitalism that gave rise to GIP in France and PROP in Britain, brought forth in Scandinavia a novel and more durable alliance between prisoners, academics and penal reform groups. In 1966 a 'Parliament of Thieves' (Mathiesen, 2000) was convened by prisoners, ex-prisoners and radical activists in Sweden. Out of it came the prison pressure groups KRUM (Sweden), KRIM (Denmark) and KROM (Norway).

A key figure in the formation of KROM was Thomas Mathiesen whose 1965 research had revealed men in the Norwegian prison system to be isolated, dejected and vulnerable (Mathiesen, 1965). He found little sign of the self-sustaining solidarities identified by Sykes in the US prison system, and his work highlighted the intrinsic violence of prison and its consequences for prisoners. Mathiesen's response was to insist on prisoner involvement in prison research and prison reform strategies.

KROM organises an annual three-day long meeting that brings together serving prisoners, ex-prisoners, academics, researchers and prison policy activists. It has been almost unique in maintaining a radical, abolitionist stance while becoming progressively more influential in policy reform. Most groups established elsewhere in the heydays of the 1960s have either withered, atrophied, disappeared or become unrecognisably conformist in approach; not KROM. The reasons for this are complex, and analysed in some detail by Mathiesen (2000). They include the benefits of long, hard and evolving work on a strategy which is reconciled with being perpetually unfinished, incomplete and always in process. The consensus operates around two principles: (i) positive reforms that ameliorate the intrinsic harms of imprisonment, and (ii) negative reforms that promote abolitionist or size- and scope-reducing change in penal systems. Positive reforms are short term and conditioned by their alignment with the long-term strategy of negative reforms that prioritise abolition of penal systems per se.

Imprisonment in Scandinavian countries is less heavily invested in degradation and civic expulsion than in the UK and the USA. Prisoners remain citizens with entitlements rather than being reduced to virtual non-persons. Mathiesen (2000) indicates that the relative success of KROM compared to other radical penal pressure groups is partly down to its determination to maintain alliances with prisoners through grass-roots community building and the construction of an 'alternative public space'. The independence of this space, he says, is crucial. It must be free of mass-media driven agendas and bring together intellectuals, prisoners and ex-prisoners working 'towards re-vitalisation of research taking the interests of common people as a point of departure'. This, as he says, 'is not new' in itself, but it is distinct from the needs of the prison system, wider criminal justice procedures and the government, in whose interests most prison research is conducted.

Mathiesen is careful to qualify the history of KROM as being anchored in Norwegian contexts, and stresses that it cannot be assumed to be 'an ideal model to be replicated in other countries'. It is not convict criminology, but it creates an environment in which it may prosper. Of the three non-North American papers included in the special issue of the *Journal of Prisoners on Prisons*, two were written by ex-convict writers based in Finland (Hytonen, 2012; Ekunwe and Jones, 2012). These writers are drawn from prison populations that are among the smallest in Europe which makes their presence and contribution all the more remarkable. The third was from one of the co-founders of British convict criminology, Andy Aresti (2012).

The crimes and politics of criminology

Politics, social theory, sociology and criminology all overlap as academic disciplines, and forms of human practice, although perhaps not quite as much as they did for Peter Kroptkin in the nineteenth century. It is clear that prisons in Europe have propelled, detained or otherwise influenced academics from each and all of those academic disciplines, but Luke Hulsman draws an important distinction around the issue of criminal stigma. As Hulsman notes, though the political prisoner may suffer, he or she does not necessarily lose 'face' in the same way that someone convicted of a 'conventional' crime may do, with its accompanying potentials for shame, disgrace and rejection. Dejection and abjection can be avoided, or mitigated, by political prisoners who access a countervailing legitimating context or narrative for their actions that (dis)qualifies the judicial process to which they have been subject and the social opprobrium they might face. For Saul Alinskey (see Chapter 2), swindling a cafeteria out of the price of a meal was a simple economic necessity, and sharing the practice, a political imperative. It prompts no cause for shame even if it were exposed to judicial sanction. In a wider political context, he does not see himself as criminal, and thus won't become a convict, or for that matter a criminologist. Even where the crimes are harsher, or more violent, political prisoners may be ontologically insulated from some of prison's most elemental psychic debilitations.

As we have seen in this and the preceding chapters, convict criminologists in both the USA and Europe operate at a complex interface between crime and politics, academic discipline and personal experience, censure and stigma, complicated by our knowledge of two worlds, the prison and free society. Our capacity to negotiate and make sense of our transition between the two remains underdeveloped and its potentials under-appreciated. For those whose path into prison was hedged in politics, such as Tannenbaum and Alinskey, the paths out and into, or away from, academic life may be very different to those who, like Irwin, discovered the tangled relationship between politics, crime and social order after or during their incarceration. Both Jackson and Irwin's experiences were marked by the racial politics of the US prison system, and the blurred boundary between crime and politics (Cohen, 1996). However, as Hulsman notes, a key feature of the convict experience is stigma and a sense of being 'marked' for exclusion. The next chapter examines tendencies toward exploiting this stigma and administering exclusion on the basis of criminal records.

FIVE

Indelible stains: convict criminology and criminal records

POLICING THE CRISIS (1)

They park outside a municipal block of flats and we climb the stairs to a flat on the third floor, the two uniformed police officers in front. The door is open and they walk in announcing themselves to the elderly resident 'It's alright dear, we're here now. What can we do for you?' She explains about having heard noises around her door at night and one of them makes a series of comforting remarks, indicating gently that she isn't to worry, they are 'here now' and will take a look round. The tone is kind and reassuring. They offer to make the old woman a cup of tea. She seems to be known to them but I feel very out of place, and embarrassed. I feel the two officers are deliberately showing me their policing, demonstrating to me something they want me to know, and this is confirmed when we walk back down to the patrol car and one says, 'We shouldn't have really done that, taken you with us like that. But it's not all like you think.' It was a performance for my benefit, and I was affected by it. Their kindness to the old woman was genuine, her relief to be visited and attended to, equally so.

In 1980 the Campaign for Nuclear Disarmament (CND) began to publicise central government's contingency plans in the event of a Soviet nuclear strike. Norwich is situated in the middle of East Anglia not far from what were then the largest US airbases outside of the USA, at Mildenhall and Lakenheath. As part of a group researching these plans I drove my moped to a radio mast on the edge of town that was widely suspected to be situated on top of one of the Regional Seats of Government. These are camouflaged fortified bunkers where the local civic hierarchy would be housed while the radiation fallout from a nuclear explosion killed everyone else and made government a bit difficult. I drove down the lane to a small and apparently empty lodge where a notice informed me that I was on Ministry of Defence property that was private and didn't welcome trespassers. So, after peering further down the lane I turned around and drove home. The next morning a police officer knocked on the door and arrested me on suspicion of committing an offence on Ministry of Defence property. The two police officers seemed a bit bemused by the arrest, and I knew I'd done nothing but be a bit nosey. However, they insisted I had to be taken to the police station for enquiries to be made. I got in the back seat of the police car and off we went. The car's police radio intercom crackled into life and the officers discussed the request they'd just received to respond to a call nearby. 'On our way' they reported down the intercom, then turning to me one said, 'It's just a quick call we've got to make. It's on the way. You can come with us.'

POLICING THE CRISIS (2)

I'm in a central London police station in a large cell with about 12 other white men I've never met. They are fascists, members of the National Front and we have all been arrested at the annual Bloody Sunday demonstration commemorating the day British paratroopers opened fire on a civil rights demonstration in Derry in January 1971. I've spent the last half an hour keeping my head down. The small talk among the young men concerns their arrest, and how their organisation, 'Excalibur House', would take care of the costs. One of the group eventually turns to me, saying 'You're quiet. Where were you nicked?' 'Oh, at the beginning, at the Embankment,' I mumble unconvincingly, though it was true enough.

I went to London with a group of friends from Norwich. The demonstration usually attracts about a thousand supporters and sometimes half as much again in people who want to kick our heads in; fascist groups such as the National Front and its various splinter organisations. As we spilled out of the van toward the gathering crowd I spotted someone I knew and walked toward the end of the column of people, banners and placards. After a few minutes chat I walked toward the front of the demo where I had agreed to meet my Norwich friends. The police were gathering in strength at the front of the march before its departure, and seeing them start to close ranks I tried to nip between them and join the crowd. 'No you don't, mate' I heard a voice tell me. A policeman pushed me back to the pavement and said, 'Off you go, clear off.' I explained I was going to join friends on the march, pointing to them, waving at them. 'Not today, you're not,' he declared. I persisted, trying to keep calm and perplexed by his actions. 'I've come a long way today to do this,' I explained. 'I'm warning you' he said 'if you try and join that demonstration, I'm going to arrest you.' I can't believe he's serious and walk away from him further down the column, and then try in to slip through the thin blue line. As I do so I am grabbed from behind and swung onto the pavement. 'I warned you. You're under arrest!' Now my friends have seen me and rush to help, as I am pulled quickly and roughly to a waiting police van. An hour passes and eventually I am driven to the police station.

'You're a Red aren't you? He's a fucking Red! Fuck! He's been listening to every word!' A silence falls. 'How much trouble am I in?', I ask myself. They can't beat the shit out of me here in the cell. But if we all get booked out at the same time I am in serious 'out of the frying pan into the fire' kind of trouble.

Then my luck changes. An officer comes and calls me out. 'You first. Time to go.' As I step over the legs a boot swings but misses. I hear curses and talk rise as I'm escorted to the custody sergeant and I get released on bail. How long have I got to get away from the police station before the others are released and come looking for me? Thankfully I am met at the doors of the police station by my friends from Norwich with the van, and we disappear from London as quickly as we can.

Some weeks later I receive a notice to attend Bow Street magistrates' court to face a charge of 'Obstructing a police officer in the course of his duty'. It was all a big mistake I explain to the duty solicitor. The police officer must have thought that with my short haircut and army fatigue trousers I was part of the counter-demonstration organised by the National Front. They were only doing their job putting me in the cell with a large group of fascists. Was there malice aforethought? Probably. If I plead 'not guilty', and pursue the issue of an honest mistake, I'd probably have to make at least another two trips to London, and then it would be a police officer's word against mine. The duty solicitor at Bow Street advises me to get it dealt with quickly, with a conditional discharge highly likely. Another conviction I could do without.

Experiencing disqualification: how old convictions trump new qualifications

In 2012 the first elections were held in England and Wales for local Police and Crime Commissioners (PCCs). The policy of introducing Commissioners to replace local government-run police authorities was pushed through by the coalition government with the intention of raising the profile of the local management of crime and policing. The elections were widely ridiculed as an expensive fiasco with less than 15 per cent of the eligible population turning out to vote in most constituencies. However, the elections were effective in demonstrating the lasting and damaging consequences of even a minor criminal conviction. Two high-profile and potentially popular candidates were unexpectedly disqualified from standing for election as a Commissioner because of their criminal convictions.

The first was Simon Weston, a veteran of the Falklands/Malvinas war who survived horrific burns when HMS Galahad was sunk in the south Atlantic by an Argentinian Exocet missile. His recovery and rehabilitation from terrible facial scarring and his determination to overcome his disfigurement propelled him into public life and he was awarded the OBE. He withdrew his candidacy to stand for election as PCC when it emerged that his conviction, aged 14, for being found in a stolen car, would automatically disqualify him from standing for election.

The second was Bob Ashford who had many years of local public service behind him as manager of a Youth Offending Team before he moved into national policy development as a member of the Youth Justice Board, the body that co-ordinates youth justice services in England and Wales. Good qualifications, he felt, for a Police and Crime Commissioner. He reluctantly withdrew his candidacy following advice from the Home Office and the Electoral Commission that his convictions for trespass and possession of an offensive weapon at the age of 13 automatically disqualified him.

His account of the events that led to these convictions illuminates the literally overwhelming and transformative power of the criminal label that so concerned Frank Tannenbaum. His experience also demonstrates the inadequacy of attempts to diminish or qualify this power. The Electoral Commission guidelines specify that only 'imprisonable offences' would bar people from standing as Police and Crime Commissioners, a distinction that seems to suggest a degree of seriousness to the actions and behaviour. However, the vast majority of criminal offences are imprisonable.

'Trespass' and 'Possession of an offensive weapon' sound pretty serious. Here's what happened. As a boy Bob liked to play outside and one day he and his friends went down to the local railway sidings and crawled under a fence to the waste ground beyond. One of his friends produced an air pistol so they could line up tin cans and shoot them. They were spotted by the police who had been alerted by someone who saw the boys crawling under the fence. As the boys panicked and scattered the older boy thrust the air pistol into Bob's hands and made off. Bob was not so quick or so savvy, but wouldn't tell on his mates. His account is poignant in revealing his sense of panic and distress at the time. He was the only one not to run, the one who got left behind and caught by the police. Even though the pistol was not his and despite being only 13, criminal charges were pressed against him. On legal advice, he plead guilty having been assured that a conditional discharge was the most likely outcome and unlikely to have any further effect.

Fifty years later those criminal convictions arising from a bit of childish play were sufficient to cancel out Bob Ashford's years of public service and honourable achievements. Simon Weston's solitary conviction as a child for 'allowing himself to be carried' in a stolen car trumped all his active military service as an adult and his medal for an exceptional and sustained contribution to civil society. For both men, their long record of public service was completely subordinate to their minimal, nominal, criminal record. It was quite extraordinary to witness.

The two cases demonstrate just how thoroughly assumptions about 'criminality' have become embedded in the fabric of our lives and the institutions of the societies in which we live. It is understood as a durable, inherent condition that needs to be recorded. Conventional criminology is not a neutral bystander to this process: 'It has encouraged the view of crime whereby criminality in some way inheres in the personality of offenders, so that, come what may, they will seek out their opportunities for crime' (Hough et al, 1980, 3, cited in Hough, 2014).

For Thomas (2007) the burgeoning use of criminal records arises from their commodification, implying that they have entered a consumer's market and now circulate according to its principles. Convict criminologists are well placed to ask how this has happened because we often remain tangled in its consequences, forever negotiating the shadows and snares that criminal convictions set in our path. We are personally invested in establishing how the marking of someone as 'a criminal' has become so commonplace and so indelible with so little appreciation of the destructive consequences. For a convict criminologist these two episodes in the introduction of Police Commissioners have profound criminological and personal resonance, but they passed almost completely without comment in the criminological community in the UK. For conventional criminologists the principle issues were around the reconfiguration of police accountability and the influence of policy migration from the USA where Police Commissioners are an established part of the political landscape (Lister, 2013; Newburn, 2012). Fair enough, but not enough, criminologically speaking.

Spent convictions? The sad story of the Rehabilitation of Offenders Act 1974

The origins of the disclosure of criminal convictions arrangements in the UK are to be found in the Rehabilitation of Offenders Act 1974, and the wider efforts in the 1960s and 1970s to promote welfare and rehabilitation in criminal justice. The Act itself was the culmination of a sustained lobbying campaign from the three most prominent criminal justice pressure groups in England: the Howard League, Justice and NACRO. In 1972 they established a committee, led by a Conservative peer, Lord Gardiner, to consider the problems of a criminal record to 'rehabilitated persons'. Their report, 'Living It Down: The Problem of Old Convictions'(Gardiner 1972), catalogued the indignities endured by people having to reveal their criminal convictions to potential employers or others of social authority. It also pointed out that, at the time, of all the countries in the Council of Europe only the UK had no form of rehabilitation law that constrained disclosure of previous convictions. Parliament was urged to draft legislation that would ensure that after a certain period of time a person should be 'no longer liable to have his present pulled from under his feet by his past'. The committee report demonstrated how someone with a 'past' was frequently unable to shake off the label and faced considerable discrimination, stigma and prejudice, particularly in the field of employment, insurance and in the courts.

The Act that was eventually passed two years later in 1974 was a long way from the original proposals of the Gardiner committee, but it did establish in law the principle that criminal convictions need not, and should not, mark someone out for life. It introduced the idea of 'spent convictions' and gave formal effect to the concept of 'a rehabilitated person'. In its simplest form, this establishes that after a specified period of time without further offending a rehabilitated person is to be treated as never having committed the offence, full citizenship rights are restored and the slate is wiped clean, the offence is fully dismissed. The practical and symbolic significance of the Act was substantial in that it established both the legal principle of a 'spent conviction' and the general responsibility of the State to limit the damage incurred by social stigma, prejudice and stereotypical views that accompany a criminal conviction. The Act is particularly important for those interested in restorative justice in that it gave legal effect to the principle of restoring a person's full civil status, to lifting the civil disability imposed by a criminal conviction (Van Zyl Smit, 2003). The Act recognised that 'to wipe the slate clean' the person needed the help of the State, on whose slate their conviction was otherwise indelibly marked. It is this emphasis on the State taking responsibility for its actions in 'marking the criminal', so frequently at a young age, and hence it's corresponding responsibility for unmarking them in later life, that is so neglected in restorative justice theory and practice (Maruna, 2011).

Minting stigma and handing out certificates: the Criminal Records Bureau

The tragic difference between what the State is doing now and what it was doing with the 1974 Act, in terms of criminal records, is that rather than taking them out of circulation it has started to mint them as the official currency of stigma. The Criminal Records Bureau (CRB) and its disclosure certificates are to stigma what the Royal Mint is to money. Taking criminal records from the relative obscurity of a few recruitment procedures, it has established them in public and popular discourse. Criminal records now circulate as certificates of unworthiness and execration that almost completely cancel out the principles of the Rehabilitation Act. In the United Kingdom, a country of around 60 million people, between 2002 and 2009 over 19 million criminal record disclosures were issued by the CRB (Padfield, 2011). All this, with barely a murmur of concern or a ripple of protest. All this, in a period when crime policy was trumpeted as being evidence-based and delivered on the principles of 'what works', without a shred of evidence as to their efficacy.

Criminal record checks in England and Wales are carried out by the CRB, which was established under Part 5 of the Police Act 1997 and became operational on 1 April 2002. Its stated aim was: 'to help employers and voluntary organisations make more informed recruitment decisions through improved access to Government and police records' (CRB, 2002, 7). The Bureau acts as a 'one-stop-shop' for organisations, checking police records and, in some cases, information held by other government departments. The Act provided for two levels of CRB disclosure, called Standard and Enhanced Disclosures.

The two CRB checks were available in cases where an employer was entitled to ask 'exempted questions' under the Exceptions Order to the Rehabilitation of Offenders Act (ROA) 1974. Such exemptions from the Act's provisions are made in the interests of national security, the protection of particularly vulnerable people, maintaining confidence in the administration of the law and ensuring probity in areas of banking and financial services. Exempted professions include teachers, healthcare and childcare professionals.

Before the advent of the CRB in 2002, access to police checks for criminal convictions was mainly confined to organisations in the statutory sector for staff members who had 'substantial unsupervised access' to children. For other sectors, checking of police records was often carried out using the inappropriate and inefficient practice of 'enforced subject access' (ESA) in which individuals applying for jobs or roles where scrutiny of their police records was eligible under the ROA would be 'required' to obtain a copy of their police record under ESA provisions in the Data Protection Act 1998. In a review of these procedures the Better Regulation Task Force (1999) indicated that such practice was regarded by many, including the Data Protection Registrar, as a misuse of a right of access that was created for another purpose.

The launch of the CRB in 2002 established a massive expansion in the procurement of criminal records and a phenomenal rise in their public profile. Criminal record checks rapidly became a significant part of public life as they acquired vastly increased social visibility. The momentum behind their introduction, as imagined by the 1997 Police Act, was originally relatively low key. It was seen as a bureaucratic and procedural formality of marginal public interest. However, other events that coincided with emergence of the CRB in 2002 brought the issue of past offending and the scrutiny of criminal records into every home in the country, and gripped the heart of anyone who had one.

Overtaken by events: tragedy by television

In August 2002 two Cambridgeshire school children, Jessica Chapman and Holly Wells, were reported missing from their school in the village of Soham. As concern mounted for their welfare, the local community and the wider population were caught up in the increasingly desperate search to find them. When their bodies were discovered the murder enquiry eventually identified and arrested a key suspect – the school caretaker, Ian Huntley. Initially shielded by his girlfriend, a classroom assistant at the girl's school, Huntley had no previous convictions, but police in his home county of Northumbria had recorded a series of accusations against him for rape, underage sex and burglary. Huntley applied for his job using another name, and the CRB disclosure process failed to reveal the record of allegations against him.

The public and media focus on the case, and its exceptionally traumatic and tragic features, prompted enormous public concern. The revelation that various authorities were aware of allegations, from a number of sources, that Huntley had probably committed one act of indecent assault, four acts of underage sex and three rapes, although none of these had resulted in a conviction, caused widespread outrage.

Lord Bichard was commissioned by the Home Secretary to lead an Inquiry into the police investigation into the murders and the specific concerns about the management and handling of intelligence by the police and social services about Ian Huntley. The Bichard Inquiry and the traumatising events at Soham all combined to propel the issue of criminal vetting procedures firmly into the public domain. They combined with growing but largely unspecified anxiety about men's sexual behaviour and violence against women. These subterranean misgivings extended to other aspects of men's relationships, professional and caring, with children, that settled on particular individuals and cases. Despite the evident failure to protect schoolchildren as CRB checks were intended to do, most publicly and tragically in the case of Soham murders, CRB checks entered the vernacular of popular culture in much the same way as Anti-Social Behaviour Orders. They are commonly referred to by their acronyms, ASBO and CRB, as a knowingly sceptical shorthand for possessing a certificate of, respectively, unspecified menace or general virtue: 'yeah, he got an ASBO' or 'It's OK, I've been CRB-checked'.

In its first year of operation 1.4 million checks were issued by the CRB, and by 2005 this annual number had risen to 2.5 million. In 2007 it issued its 10 millionth check and by 2008–09 it was issuing 3.8 million checks per year. In 2010 it issued 4.3 million, and, by 2011 it had issued 19 million since its inception in 2002 (Padfield, 2011). When it was first established the CRB anticipated that of the two available disclosures, the majority would be for Standard disclosures regarded as suitable for most occupational categories allowed for under the exemptions of the ROA. The extent of the confused enthusiasm for criminal records and the defensive anxiety they foster is revealed by the fact that in 2004 89 per cent of disclosures were of the enhanced variety, and only 11 per cent were 'standard'. Ninety-five percent of all the disclosures issued were blank, that is, with no convictions recorded (Padfield, 2011).

The popular appeal of disclosure certificates and the reassurances they appear to offer rests on complex combinations of the circumstances surrounding their introduction and the anxieties they address and paradoxically foster. In my capacity as a college lecturer, social researcher, ex-convict and a school governor I have often felt these anxieties swirling around me. I have presented my various CRB forms to a number of institutions, and been asked to scrutinise other people's, sometimes in circumstances clearly in breach of the guidelines. Taking my son to the local Scout group I hear men nervously joking about them, and their implications. But I have been lucky only to be mildly discomforted.

Collateral damage, toxic contamination

The unintended consequences of the extraordinary proliferation in the use of criminal record disclosures in the UK have been relatively slow to attract critical academic scrutiny. In 2008 the experiences of Majid Ahmed attracted national media attention and came to exemplify rising concerns over the obscured negative impacts of CRB disclosures (Shepherd, 2008).

Seventeen-year-old Majid had secured an offer to study medicine at Imperial College, London. Growing up in an impoverished part of Bradford, northern England, where unemployment rarely dipped below 37 per cent, Majid had defied expectation by securing the best ever A-level results in his school. Growing up in a small house shared with his three brothers, three sisters and mother in an area where 49 per cent of the inhabitants have no formal qualification, Majid felt that he had earned his right to study medicine. He wanted to become a doctor. However his offer was withdrawn by Imperial College when he told them that he had failed to disclose on his application form that he had a criminal conviction. The college routinely run Criminal Record Bureau checks on all their applicants for medical courses but Majid had been misadvised by a friend that he need not make a disclosure.

Aged 16 Majid had plead guilty for his involvement in a local burglary, for which he received one of the new 'restorative justice' type sentences introduced by the New Labour Government – a referral order. In this type of order, the young person must attend a panel made up of local community volunteers, the victim or their representatives, and any other relevant individuals. The panel discuss the circumstances of the crime and agree a contract setting out a plan of action to remedy the situation. Majid accepts that for a short while he fell in 'with a bad crowd' but had put his life together, as his exam results suggested. He was utterly overwhelmed by the decision of Imperial College to bar him from the course.

Under the restorative justice provisions of the referral order, young people are told that their convictions will immediately be regarded as 'spent' (that is, dismissed) under the provisions of the Rehabilitation of Offenders Act 1974 if they satisfactorily complete their order. What Majid was not told, and what few people involved with referral orders, or restorative justice more broadly in the UK, appreciate is that this kind of dismissal of a criminal conviction has become largely meaningless. A criminal record is for life. It has become a negative credential certifying a person's eligibility for peremptory discrimination and exclusion.

Majid's case is far from being a rare exception and organisations, such as Nacro and UNLOCK, the National Association of Ex-Offenders, have become increasingly alarmed by the proliferation of checks that are both unlawful and unnecessary. Their damaging collateral consequences are also becoming increasingly obvious. Nacro's 'Change The Record' campaign, launched in 2010, (www.changetherecord. org/stories/) presents a series of case studies, many of which describe the lasting impact of minor convictions imposed on children. What they repeatedly reveal is the way complex life events are reduced to a single explanatory coda, a criminal conviction.

Take the case of 'Vicky' whose life spiralled out of control following her being raped at the age of 15. Unable to talk about the event, the trauma precipitated a sustained period of behaviour destructive to herself and others. However, subsequent convictions for criminal damage and assaulting the police continued to trump her self-rehabilitation as one of Europe's leading practitioners of Taekwondo. She says that after years of training others, with her instructor:

> "I set up my own franchise. However, as soon as I tried to go solo, I started facing problems. I would get asked for a CRB check and when it came back I would be told I wasn't suitable. Recently I have been told I am not suitable to volunteer either."

With the help of Nacro Vicky has managed to get such decisions overturned. She says it hasn't been easy but she wants to

> "overcome some of the difficulties in my past and move on with my life. I want to be able to give that chance to others and be able to teach other young people about my passion. I just need employers to see past the piece of paper that is stopping me from fulfilling my dream." (Change the Record, 2011, cited in Earle and Wakefield 2012).

Moving shadows subject to monitoring

The 2004 Bichard Inquiry produced extensive recommendations concerning police IT systems, data quality and sharing, and recording standards concerning allegations of sexual offences against children. It also proposed that all those working in schools should be subject to enhanced disclosures but the most far-reaching recommendation was for the establishment of a new registration scheme for those working or wanting to work with children or vulnerable adults.

These recommendations went on to form the basis of the Safeguarding Vulnerable Groups Act 2006 which attempted to revise and consolidate CRB procedures into a more comprehensive and co-ordinated national vetting procedure. It established a Vetting and Barring Scheme (VBS) to be overseen by a new Independent Safeguarding Authority (ISA) under which it was estimated that over 11 million people would be required to register to secure a 'passport' to work with children and vulnerable adults on the basis that their criminal records had been checked. They would then remain 'subject to monitoring' on a continuing basis. In 2008, these provisions moved toward implementation. As they did so they gathered increasingly critical publicity, particularly after a group of well-known novelists, among them the multi-award winning writers, Phillip Pullman and Michael Morpurgo, were informed that they would be required to present CRB disclosures and register with the ISA to continue their voluntary readings in schools. They indicated that they would boycott such procedures or suspend their visits to read to children in schools, protesting that it was absurd that their occasional visits to school classes should prompt such a bureaucratic intervention. They also pointed out that the implication of such certification procedures was to reverse the presumption of innocence, that they were guilty until proven innocent. They resented the shadow of suspicion being placed over them, and the responsibility of paying to have it lifted.

In June 2010, in the face of mounting concern over the both the cost and viability of the proposed Vetting and Barring Scheme the newly elected coalition government suspended the implementation of the scheme. In February 2011, it recommended the merger of the ISA with the CRB and promised to develop new procedures for vetting the criminal records of people seeking work with children or vulnerable adults. In 2012 the Disclosure and Barring Service (DBS) was established as a non-departmental body of the Home Office. It launched a complex new terminology of disclosure that includes new 'filtering' systems and eligibility time frames for spent convictions. New criteria for spent convictions were subsequently established in the 2013 parliamentary amendments to the Rehabilitation of Offenders Act. The new system promises to improve the portability and updating of disclosure certificates with on-line access.

The CRB operates independently of the sex offender register that was established after the 1997 Sex Offender Act was passed, though the legislation itself makes no provision for such a register. Anyone convicted or cautioned of sex offences has to notify the police with details of their address and inform them of any changes. The police also operate and manage another database, the Violent and Sex Offender Register, VISOR. Provisions for the consultation of these registers are now managed by the DBS (see Padfield, 2011).

Conviction and surveillance: Criminal record vetting internationally

In the early 1970s England and Wales, as a single jurisdiction, was regarded as out of step with the rest of Europe in not having rehabilitative legislation. Most countries now have procedures for the erasure and/or disclosure of criminal records. The review of the Rehabilitation of Offenders Act 1974 (Home Office, 2002) included an international summary of criminal record disclosure provision in other countries. It revealed a wide range of disparate practice that reflects the diversity of criminal procedures in the various jurisdictions examined. These vary according to principles and traditions of law that apply in the country, and, in turn, the cultural ambience around crime, accountability, social and personal security. It is not the intention of this chapter to assess whether there is an international trend toward more routine disclosure (for this see Pijoan, 2014) or provide a comprehensive summary of provisions elsewhere. However, even a brief review indicates a range of different approaches and some consistent themes. It indicates possibilities for a positive 'right to move on', and different ways in which people with criminal convictions can be protected from undue suspicion, unnecessary scrutiny and unwarranted discrimination.

In the Netherlands there are detailed provisions for both retaining and erasing penal convictions, and employers have no right to consult criminal records. However, employers can request an employee's Mayor, via the Ministry of Justice, to provide a 'declaration of good conduct', an official document indicating that the State has 'no objection' to this person's employment in the specified position. Furthermore, for certain public sector jobs, such as the civil service, the Mayor can scrutinise a complete criminal record including those otherwise 'erased' (spent convictions). This bears some resemblance to the procedures considered, but not taken up, by the UK Independent Safeguarding Authority (ISA). It circumvents the direct scrutiny of personal criminal records by employers, and thus reduces both the proximity of the decision maker, and the potential for improper discrimination or informal dissemination of disclosure information. Screening decisions are not devolved to individual people in each particular application, as they are under CRB/DBS procedures, but are retained within an accountable and identifiable external authority, the Mayor. The personal information about an applicant therefore remains less widely circulated and more private in a way that potentially safeguards their rights. Boone (2011) provides a detailed discussion of procedures in the Netherlands, and the specific cultural and legal contexts that apply.

In Spain the National Conviction Register records crimes but it is not a public register and access to it is severely restricted. As with the UK's ROA, sentences become 'spent' or 'sealed' after a specified period, and, as with the UK, a number of caveats apply. Larrauri (2011, 60) concludes that 'the somewhat negligible role convictions play in Spain is demonstrable by their public inaccessibility' but she cautions against false optimism because of the paucity of empirical research into the way they are used or the impact they may have.

In France criminal records are handled by the National Judicial Record (NJR) and French citizens have on-line access to their own records via a security system designed to ensure their own exclusive access. Every French citizen has a record, which is divided into three 'bulletins' each of which may be 'empty'. Employers may request presentation an 'empty' record, but France is unique in having court based procedures for expunging criminal records and for the explicit restoration of full citizenship rights (Herzog-Evans, 2011).

Two jurisdictions with strong historic links to the UK and its legal and cultural traditions have recently taken paths that attempt a more explicit balance between disclosure and the right to rehabilitation. In New Zealand legislation was passed in 2004 that, nominally at least, appears to prioritise rehabilitative sentiments rather than security-minded vetting priorities. The Criminal Records (Clean Slate) Act is relatively unique in this respect and addresses a long standing deficiency in New Zealand whereby there had been no such pre-existing legislation of this kind. The Act provides for criminal records to be erased, the slate to be cleaned, after a period of seven years with no convictions. Specified offences involving offences against children or sexual violence are exempt, as are all custodial sentences.

The Clean Slate Act, as it is commonly referred to in New Zealand, is a long way from prohibiting the disclosure of an individual's previous criminal career, as its name might imply, but it is notable for seeming to respond to a prevailing concern about rehabilitation rather than a generalised sense of threat and risk posed by certain people. In this respect it bears similarity to the Rehabilitation of Offenders Act 1974. The Clean Slate Act is significant in that it not only makes it a criminal offence to disclose someone's criminal record inappropriately, but also makes it an offence to ask someone to disclose their convictions if they are not eligible for such an inquiry to be made. The penalties are substantial and had a high profile in government sponsored public education programmes accompanying the passage of the Act. These combine to assert that those with criminal convictions have rights and that these rights require both recognition and protection if they are to be fully restored as citizens. Such emphasis, and provision, is sadly missing from the 1974 Act in the UK.

In Australia, legislation varies across its eight states and territories but most limit disclosure and one jurisdiction, the Northern Territory, provides positive protection against discrimination on the grounds of 'an irrelevant criminal record'. A national review of 'guidelines for the prevention of discrimination in employment on the basis of criminal records' conducted by the Australian Human Rights and Equality Commission (AHREC, 2005) affirmed an anti-discriminatory framework for disclosure. This framework cites the significance of the 1958 International Labour Organisation Convention, ratified by Australia in 1973, which requires signatories to actively pursue 'equality of opportunity and treatment' along the by now conventional grounds of race, ethnicity and gender but also leaves open further grounds for other inappropriate discrimination to be included.

In 1989 Australia added clauses to the ILO convention specifying that unfair discrimination in respect of a criminal record could occur if the 'inherent requirements' of a particular job were not in conflict with their criminal record. The significance of the 'inherent requirement' clause is that it helps to disaggregate the generic criminal record as applying to a general category of persons (criminals) who are prone to 'criminality', to something more behaviour- and incident-specific. Unless the crime(s) in question can be connected positively to the qualities of the employment a prima facie possibility of discrimination is established. This offers some clarity, and coherence, to those individuals concerned because it indicates that their earlier misdemeanours will not be so easily removed from their wider context. Those episodes will not be allowed to be seen, in perpetuity, as representative of their general character and personal qualities. These principles are consistent with those endorsed by Larrauri's (2014) review of the potential for legal protections to be developed that limit the intrusion of 'background checks'.

Simon Weston and Bob Ashford would both have been protected by such an approach because their childhood convictions would not demonstrate a conflict with the 'inherent requirements' of being a Police and Crime Commissioner. Presuming that it would amounts to inappropriate discrimination, and a profound malaise in political culture. The shift in emphasis from the assumption of intrinsic corruption and criminality in the body of the person to the 'inherent requirements' of the job is simple but noteworthy.

Naylor (2011, 81), however, reports that 'criminal history information is increasingly sought by employers in Australia' and notes the presence of commercial providers entering what they identify to be an emerging market in web-harvested crime data. CrimeNet is a private company offering Australians criminal history information based on 'any public records available' (Naylor, 2011, 83). By way of contrast, Australia's original inhabitants, the aboriginal people, continue to insist on the value and viability of their own long-established approaches to conflict resolution, as well as pointing out the limitations of 'settler justice'. Naylor (2011, 79) quotes the testimony of Jack Charles, an Aboriginal Elder and actor in his dispute with the Crown:

> "For the record I see Black and Whitefella law as both punitive. Eye for an eye, tooth for a tooth. Kill, and in either system it's get out of town if you can. But under Blackfella law, crimes down from the capital, a period of exile, spear in the leg...Exile ends. Wound heals. Better now Jack? Yes, I'm better now Uncle. Warm yourself at the fire old son...And I'd be accepted back in the fold. Whitefella way: the Convict Stain endures, lingers, and your past Shadows, Stalks your present, and Stymies, Jinks your future."

In the USA, ex-convicts face drastic, widespread and institutionally reinforced discrimination. Anyone with access to the internet can find information about the criminal convictions and arrest records of neighbours, friends, work colleagues or complete strangers. A criminal record bars entry to a wide range of jobs, including working as a barber, a real estate agent, a plumber, a septic tank cleaner and an embalmer (Pager, 2007).

The US government ensures that it retains an exceptionally harsh regime against ex-convicts. As with other aspects of its criminal justice system, it succeeds in doing it bigger and better. Love (2003, 112) reports that US Congress has endorsed 'a new level' of irrationality by extending the collateral consequences of a single conviction to 'automatic exclusion from a whole range of welfare benefits'. A conviction for a single drug-related offence can result in someone being denied housing assistance, food stamps, education loans and the right to vote). Unsurprisingly, the possibilities of lifting these collateral effects by redemption of the record, or restrictions on its effects, are confined to 'a hodge-podge of inaccessible and over-lapping provisions…riddled with qualifications and exceptions' (Love, 2003, 13). The power to punish in the US has been radically decentralised to include employers, insurers, housing agencies and anyone with a capacity to exert leverage over the life-chances of someone with a criminal conviction (Henley, 2014).

Such extended penalisation multiplies the damaging impact of conviction. Pinard (2010, 463) reminds us that these policies are 'extensions of historic and contemporary criminal justice policies that target racial minorities or that systematically ignore the disproportionate impact of these policies on racial minorities'. The 'malign neglect' of race in US criminal justice exposed by Michael Tonry (1996, 6) as far back as the mid-1990s has been sustained at an enormous human cost. As he declared then, so it is now: 'The text may be crime. The subtext is race.'

Not condemned to be free but free to be condemned

In the UK the restrictions on people with criminal convictions standing for election were first introduced after the election to Westminster of an IRA prisoner in Ireland, Bobby Sands. The Representation of the People Act 1981 was rushed through parliament to prevent other hunger-striking prisoners following him. It is an irony of politics that the attempt to exclude Irish republicans from the parliamentary process resulted in their radical re-engagement with it. A further irony is that these struggles over the enmeshment of crime and politics would resurface some 30 years later to exclude a British war hero and a civil servant from being allowed to 'represent the people'.

Henley (2014) refreshes the criminological imagination by revisiting Herman Mannheim's (1939) examination of the principle of 'non-superiority' that has lingered in the shadows behind the more well-known Benthamite principle of 'less-eligibility'. The recent extension to the availability of criminal records draws on the implicit principle that 'the condition of the criminal when he has paid the penalty for his crime should be at least not superior to that of the non-criminal population' (Mannheim, cited in Henley, 2014, 22). Convict criminologists can both expose and transcend this principle as they emerge into public view from the 'civic purgatory' created for them. In doing so they reveal the bankruptcy of the 'moral mortgage' that criminal records have become (Henley, 2014; see also Stacey, 2015a; 2015b).

In the 1980s and 1990s as rates of recorded crime began to soar one of the animating concerns of critical criminologists was that the number of crimes recorded bore little resemblance to the number of crimes committed. Crime and victimisation surveys, such as the British Crime Survey suggested huge numbers of crimes go undetected and unrecorded by criminal justice systems. According to Left Realist criminologists, such "Crime is the tip of the iceberg. It is a real problem in itself but it is also a symbol of a far greater problem" (Lea and Young 1993:55). To switch metaphors, the criminal justice system operates like a very inefficient traffic management system that only detects a small proportion of the problematic traffic. It then invests heavily in attaching clamps and tracking devices to particular vehicles while doing very little about, say, the congestion, pollution, accidents and injuries the wider transport system is generating.

Even though crime is far more widespread through the social structure than recorded crime suggests (Young and Lea, 1993), and even though all criminologists know that criminal justice sanctions are unevenly applied to focus on those at the lower end of the social structure, there is a growing momentum toward more permanent tagging of those who do get caught and processed by criminal justice agencies. Tannenbaum's early insights have become foresights. The commodification of criminal records brings with it a corresponding degree of fetishisation as people are persuaded that criminal records have a power far beyond their actual material potential. They enter the realm of fantasy and nightmare. Digital technologies that facilitate ever more widespread circulation of data achieve very little in the way of reassurance. What they can do very successfully is reinvent for a digital information society, the tattoos and branding discarded by a more optimistic and liberal generation. Criminal convictions have become theatrical props in the state-managed choreography of 'spoiled identities' (Goffman, 1959). People with criminal convictions are at risk of being condemned to a new dark age of digital suspicion and exclusion, the identified personal objects of an unidentified social malaise. The next chapter attempts to sketch the outline of this malaise by reference to its gender and racialised characteristics.

SIX

Race, class, gender: agitate, educate, organise

DIFFERENT CLASS, COMMON PEOPLE, ORDINARY MEN

Darren struggled at school. Then he started getting arrested for being in cars that didn't belong to their owners anymore. At times he was a danger to himself and to others. He was only 15 years old and no school would have him or he it. In 1992 he started to come to the project I worked at in south London. We provided him with a low-key education, a more tolerant timetable and a series of structured activities designed to capture his imagination, find his talents and thereby keep him out of more trouble. We succeeded in parts. He made some new friends. He reached 16 without going back to court (or to school). He left the cars alone.

Fifteen years later I am in one of the cell blocks at HMP Maidstone and I see him again. He sees me. A glimmer of recognition, but then I get called away to the interview I have arranged. I am profoundly unsettled and upset. I check the prison roll and find his name and identify which cell he is occupying. A few days later as I am doing some more observation and hanging around the cell block during the evening association period, I pop up the stairs to find his cell. I knock and enter. He is sitting on the bed and I say 'Darren? Isn't it? Remember me, Rod, from the Lambeth project?' 'Yeah,' he says 'I thought it was you when I see you the other day.' 'How you doing?' I blurt out before I can stop myself, before I realise what a stupid question it is. 'It's been a bumpy ride, yeah' he says flatly, answering my question.

At 15 he was a boy with his whole life ahead of him, and now, 15 years later, he is a wreck of a man who tells me that most of it is behind him. He looks forward to nothing. He is on medication for depression. He says has done terrible things, hurt people he loved, done 'crazy, crazy things, things you wouldn't believe'. He has no-one now, but God helps him he tells me and 'these people from the church that come to see me'. We talk some more but I am struggling to hold back tears and make my excuses to go. I say I'll be back for another chat in a few days.

Several times during the prison research project the drive home in the car has felt like the journey back from a deep dive, the car acting as a decompression chamber slowly easing me back into my world. Inside the car's metal shell, the routine activities and passive attentions of driving keep me from being overwhelmed by sadness and sorrow. Keeping the bends at bay, adjusting to normal atmospheric pressure. Meeting Darren is an unexpected shock. I was his keyworker at the project, responsible for his progression. What of that now? Can I still help him? Did I ever help him? Should I even try? What am I to do?

Our two trajectories to prison, out of prison, to this prison, are driven by motors deep in the social structure, engines of difference churning me along one route, him down another. The bumpy ride has left him broken. My ride is smoother, accelerating, I ride on. Darren is not going anywhere fast. His predicament reminds me of the feelings I had among the prisoners in HMP Norwich. I found that prison is not a hellhole full of terrible monsters and scary beasts but a sump where ordinary men, some sad and broken, like Darren, are left to waste their lives away. Some, like Jimmy, get by and pass through. Too many don't.

I couldn't face Darren again. I couldn't untangle myself from the research project's concerns about men's ethnic and masculine identities in prison, and my former keyworker role in helping to guide Darren through a difficult phase in his life.

Punishing differences, securing hierarchies

As is well known among criminologists, the USA generates nearly one quarter of the world's prison population from a mere 5 per cent of the global population. The rate of incarceration is up to ten times higher than rates in Western Europe and results in a society where nearly two million people are locked up. This means that in the second decade of the twenty-first century there are more people in prison in the USA than there were in the Soviet Gulags of the 1950s during Stalin's reign of terror. If you are a black person in the USA you are seven times more likely to be sent to prison than if you are a white person. There are more black men in prison, jail or on parole than were enslaved in 1850. More than half of all black men without a high-school diploma go to prison at some time in their lives, and in many US states ex-convicts cannot vote (Alexander, 2012).

In 2014 26 per cent of the adult prison population of England and Wales (21,769 people) was from an ethnic minority, that is, approximately one in four, in contrast to their proportion in the general population of one in ten (PRT, 2014). In England and Wales 40 per cent of the children in custody were from black and minority ethnic backgrounds (PRT, 2015). When the Home Office last published comparative rates of incarceration (in 2000), they revealed that for white people the rate was 188 per 100,000 people in the population, but for black Caribbeans it was 1,704 per 100,000. For black Africans the rate was 1,274 per 100,000, while for people of Pakistani or Bangladeshi heritage the rates were 329 and 183 respectively (Phillips and Webster, 2014). In the USA in 2009 the rate of incarceration for black men was a staggering 3,119 per 100,000 and 142 per 100,000 for black women (Fields and Fields, 2012).

Meanwhile, at the other end of the social structure, in institutions of higher education in the UK, the picture is rather different. For every African Caribbean male undergraduate at a Russell Group[1] university, there are three African Caribbean men aged 18–24 in prison. In this age group, 7 per cent of the prison population is made up of African Caribbean men, but they constitute only 0.1 per cent of the undergraduate population of Russell Group universities (Sviensson, 2012).

The uplift provided by a university degree in terms of future earnings and social status is widely recognised. The lockdown that a prison sentence provides in terms of social and spatial mobility is also acknowledged in the research literature, if somewhat less well appreciated. With a degree you emerge from university with a qualification to rise up the social hierarchy (or – more likely – secure your already elevated position in it); you get out of prison with a record that potentially disqualifies your right to belong, to work and to travel. You leave prison with negative credentials, an invisible digital diploma pre-loaded with stigma, fear and ignorance designed to hold you down and keep you back.

---

[1] The Russell Group is composed of 24 'elite' research-intensive universities, self selected from the 130 UK universities and university colleges. They award nearly 60% of UK doctorates.

Simple truths, complex unities: articulation of race and class

Loïc Wacquant (2007; 2009a; 2009b; 2010b) provides an extensive analysis of prisons' place in the transformations occurring in modern life. He characterises these transformations as neoliberal in character and 'epochal' in scale – that is, they are of world-historical proportions, equivalent to the shifts (in the West) from feudalism to capitalism. According to Wacquant, the penal state represents a newly ambidextrous state arising from the dynamic coupling of 'the maternal and nurturing social arm of the welfare state' with its more conventionally paternal 'virile and controlling arm'. These transitions from the feminised 'nanny state' of the Fordist–Keynesian era to the strict 'daddy state' of neoliberalism amount to 'the re-masculinization of the state' (Wacquant, 2009a, 290). In the process, the velvet that once gloved the iron fist of the state is discarded as it 'mans-up' and gets down to the increasingly urgent business of pacifying the marginal and dispossessed populations of a polarised neoliberal world order, by putting them in prison. Lots of prisons, bigger prisons and prisons that can be subcontracted to private enterprise. This new penal infrastructure, according to Wacquant, is central to the neoliberal project, an essential element of its statecraft. In this respect, he echoes Sykes's (1958, 8) cautionary remarks that: 'The prison is not an autonomous system of power, rather it is an instrument of the state, shaped by its social environment, and we must keep this simple truth in mind if we are to understand the prison.'

Wacquant (2010a, 79) also insists that the ethnic transformation of the US prison population is both more dramatic and more complex than most penal commentators allow for. Driving the transformation are class dynamics: '[C]lass, not race, is the first filter of selection for incarceration…inmates are first and foremost poor people', but whereas this has been a historical constant, the newly expanded dimensions of US penal enclosure are constituted by the additional force of racism. As a result a 'double selection' occurs that scoops those who are poor and black from the ghetto to the prison, and back again. And again. Waquant describes it at length and with forceful eloquence as a 'deadly symbiosis'.

In some respects, Wacquant's analysis of tectonic shifts in global politics are similar to those offered by Stuart Hall and the intellectuals gathered around British Communist Party's magazine, *Marxism Today*. Wacquant's contemporary outputs concentrate more on the toxic and continuing global aftershocks they each identify emerging from the mid-1970s. The focus of *New Times* (Hall and Jacques, 1989) was on the 1980s in the UK and its international relations, particularly Europe, and like Wacquant, Hall stresses the importance of race and class in this process. Hall however is more circumspect than Wacquant, indicating the changes are somewhat less than epochal and more consistent with previous transitions within the fluid dynamism of twentieth-century capitalism.

Hall emphasises the historical 'specificity of those social formations which exhibit distinctive or ethnic characteristics' (1980, 308). The Althusserian terminology of 'articulation' is central to Hall's depiction of the relative autonomy of race and class, and is helpful in distinguishing the significance of their interaction in specific historical conjunctures. This interaction is a perennial question of social theory, and Hall's formulation bears repeating, lest it is forgotten. Articulation is:

> 'a metaphor used to indicate relations of linkage and *affectivity* between different levels of all sorts of things... [These things need to be linked, because though connected they are not the same. The unity which they *form is thus not that of an identity*, where one structure perfectly recapitulates or reproduces or even 'expresses' another; or where each is reducible to the other;...The unity formed by this combination or articulation, is always, necessarily, a 'complex structure': a structure in which things are related, as much through their differences as through their similarities...It also means – since the combination is a structure (an articulated combination) and not a random association – that there will be structured relations between its parts, that is, relations of dominance and subordination. Hence, in Althusser's cryptic phrase, a 'complex unity, structured in dominance'. (Hall, 1980, 325, emphasis added)

The persistent and growing ethnic disproportionality in prisons in the US and the UK (see, respectively, Alexander, 2012; Phillips, 2012) as well as other jurisdictions, provides an abundance of 'brute facts' (Wacquant, 2002) but the articulation of race and class continues to frustrate theoretical explanation. It is a feature of 'complex unity, structured in dominance' that resists intelligibility. For criminologists the response is sometimes to bracket race and class apart and continue with business as usual. Bosworth and Hoyle (2012), for example, berate criminology and criminologists for their neglect of social theory and for inadequate engagement with political discourses of race, class, gender and nation. It is a big theoretical challenge. In popular culture and some academic discourse there is more talk about the demise of race, the insignificance of class and the irrelevance of gender than there is about their complex unity or their articulation (D'Souza, 1995; Hughey, 2014; Bhattacharyya, 2013; Rodriguez, 2014; Ikuenobe, 2013; Goldberg, 2012). It is a strange kind of post-racial, classless society that fills its bloated criminal justice system with working-class young men, and when to be black and male is to be more likely to end up in prison rather than university. It is a fantasy against which sociologists and criminologist must argue, and a reality against which we must mobilise (Belknap, 2015).

Hall's (1980) account of societies structured in dominance provides a series of advisory indicators that can continue to guide both argument and mobilisation. Hall is adamant that the 'rigorous application' of the 'premise of historical specificity' (Hall, 1980, 336) must be applied when addressing the racialised characteristics of social formations. As such, racism cannot be 'dealt with as a general feature of human societies' (Hall, 1980, 336) that recurs with similar functional characteristics, but rather must be understood in terms of 'historically specific racisms' (Hall, 1980, 336). This begins with an 'assumption of difference, of specificity rather than of a unitary, transhistorical or universal "structure"' (Hall, 1980, 336). It is vital, argues Hall, to 'distinguish those social features which fix the different positions of social groups and classes on the basis of racial ascription (biologically or socially defined) from other systems which have a similar social function' (Hall, 1980, 336). He reiterates his warning against 'extrapolating a common and universal structure to racism, which remains essentially the same, outside of its specific historical location. It is only as the different racisms are historically specified – in their difference – that they can be properly understood' (Hall, 1980, 336). The place and the time of race are as key to Hall's analysis as the permutations of class. As he memorably concluded '"race" is the modality through which class is lived, the medium through which class relations are experienced, the form in which it is appropriated and "fought through"' (Hall, 1980, 342), and this is as true for middle-class white people as it is for working-class black people. But very different.

Wacquant is widely congratulated and celebrated for bringing a wider sociological range to conventional criminological analysis that sometimes struggles to move beyond a narrow focus on penality (Squires and Lea, 2013). Nobody would accuse him of the neglect of social theory that Bosworth et al (2012) find in other branches of the criminological tree. However, many of his specific claims about the reach and novel character of neoliberal penality are deeply contested (Daems, 2008; Lacey, 2010; Cheliotis and Xenakis, 2010; Nelken, 2010; Newburn, 2010). Vivid, illuminating and eloquent as his work is in tracing historical and empirical connections from slavery, the Jim Crow system and the US urban ghettos, generalising his account across the Atlantic, Wacquant has struggled to accommodate the diversity of penal experience, the specificities of ethnicity and differences in the historical and local conditions of racism. I suspect that for most white people in Britain, the brute facts of racial apartheid in the post-war US southern states are as obscure as the term used to describe it, Jim Crow. As with the apartheid system in South Africa, it serves mainly as a convenient, finger-pointing generality of another nation's flaws that deflects from the specificities of domestic racisms.

For Stuart Hall (1989, 132) the imperative has always been to analyse specific reworkings of race that account for its contradictory forms, and accommodates the vagaries of resistance to it. As he noticed '[a]ny attempt to delineate the politics and ideologies of racism which omit these continuing features of struggle and contradictions win an apparent adequacy of explanation only by operating a disabling reductionism'. Hall was the first to identify that the alarming transition in Britain from the post-war Keynesian compact to neoliberalism rested on the specific cultural dynamics mobilised under the rubric of Thatcherism. He warned, though few paid attention, that one of 'its most powerful, enduring, effective – and least remarked – sources of strength' was cultural racism.

Convict criminologists can help avoid the pitfalls of 'disabling reductionism' by bringing their particular expertise on prison and prisoner interiors to bear on the analysis of race, class and gender. The emphasis on ethnographic and auto-ethnographic techniques among convict criminologists offers significant resources for developing analysis of carceral dynamics in the articulation of each of these categories. Convict criminologists are involved in nothing if not a reflexive project and as such we can attend to the specificities of our experience and presence within criminology and/or prison. Hendricksen and Mobley's paper, discussed in Chapter 3, is an exemplar of this approach and its potential. For my part, I have found it challenging to theorise the intersections of race, gender and class in the penal landscapes I have studied (Earle, 2011a; 2011c; 2012). Moving from the grain of ethnographic detail to the sweep of theory and building this knowledge is a slow, painstaking but collaborative enterprise and a work in progress for convict criminologists.

In what follows I explore some theoretical perspectives on new ethnicities and studies of whiteness, in the spirit outlined by Phillips and Webster (2014, 179): 'lest we become complacent that racialized thinking resides externally, only in the agents [and objects] of social control...we should be attuned to the imprint of slavery and colonialism on the psyche of criminologists'. It is my contention that this imprint is pressed hard by imprisonment, if differentially on either side of the Atlantic, and thus, as convict criminologists we can be particularly sensitive to its forms.

Post-race or new ethnicities

Hall's 'new ethnicities' paradigm is intended to disrupt the essentialising tendencies of cultural racism that sees cultures as stable entities with fixed boundaries. Noting the complex ambivalence of ethnicity he indicates its powerful affective register. There is no 'return to nature', no guarantees for humanity in biology other than mortality, and we all now live in the 'secondary universe' where 'culture' trumps 'nature'. The new focus on ethnicity, and its frequently reactionary form, is a result of 'the astonishing return...of all those points of attachment which give the individual some sense of "place" and position in the world' (Hall, 1989, 133).

For Hall the implications of embracing new ethnicities are profound in that they involve exchanging the bogus guarantees of biology and the toxic alibi of national culture for the uncertain contingencies of attachment 'to particular communities, localities, territories, languages, religions or cultures'. This involves exchanging racial hierarchy for a new and more horizontal planetary humanism (Gilroy, 2000). It is a transaction that has yet to be realised and is both resisted and neglected by those most heavily invested in race on both sides of the Atlantic. As Hall pointed out, the new ethnicities paradigm is no simple replacement discourse that just falls off an academic shelf and into place in cultural life, displacing and cancelling a history in which, until comparatively recently, race has been explicit as a central organising principle. It is a struggle 'for position' that demands 'others [that is, not just ethnic minorities] recognise that what they have to say comes out of particular histories and cultures'.

In England, the struggle over the meaning and futures of contemporary multicultural realities is played out in vivid form in prison (Crewe, 2009, 2011; Phillips, 2012; Earle and Phillips, 2015). Since the landmark 1999 Macpherson Inquiry, and Commission for Racial Equality reports that followed the murder of Zahid Mubarek

(CRE, 2003a; 2003b), the criminal justice system, and specifically Her Majesty's Prison Service (HMPS) has been at the forefront of a certain kind of multiculturalism (Earle, 2011c; Lentin and Titley, 2010). The struggles around multicultures require sustained critical scrutiny because of the symbolic importance of the institutions of criminal justice in the politics of race and their unprecedented power to have such a heavy impact on people's lives (Gilroy, 1987; Solomos, 1993).

Phillips (2012) describes in meticulous detail how multicultural realities generate complex and fluctuating patterns of racialisation.[2] Phillips' study, in which I was the co-investigator, reveals a complex and contradictory picture of social relations among imprisoned men in which ethnic differences were frequently seen as quite an ordinary and unremarkable aspect of their lives, both inside and outside the prison. Black and minority ethnic men tended to have stronger senses of ethnic identity, sometimes expressed in styles of hair care, idioms of speech, modes of greeting, social interaction and ways of wearing prison-issue clothes. Some white prisoners also felt comfortable with such stylings, but for others they seemed challengingly different and were resented. However, many white and ethnic minority prisoners told us that they preferred to ignore differences and focus on a sense of 'common humanity' in which differences of skin colour and culture was dismissed in favour of a kind of dissolute egalitarian humanism. Following Gilroy (2004) we have dubbed these relations as expressions of a tentative con-viviality (Earle, 2011c; Earle and Phillips, 2012), elements of which transcend conventional habits of racialisation.

In England's multicultural prison race had a mercurial presence; sliding in and out of view, it was everywhere and nowhere, something and nothing, active and inert. It could surface in any institutional interaction and also had a spectral presence in less formal relations where it was managed accordingly on personal terms. Many prisoners denied that race was an issue at all, and although there was no dominant consensus about race, a recurring feature of the way it was talked about reflected the now dominant position that 'race is a construct' that is, it doesn't really exist because it is a discredited invention. This reversal of the conventional sociological wisdom that 'if men define situations as real, they are real in their effects' (Thomas and Thomas, 1928, 572)

---

[1] Racialisation is a process in which differences between people are taken to represent essential, fixed differences derived from biology and/or culture, and positioned in a hierarchy of superiority and inferiority. It refers to the kind of contagious fiction of race, which is no longer recognised to have any basis in fact.

to 'if something is not real it can have no real effects' has profoundly perverse effects, and has become a primary constitutive element of white identities (Garner, 2007). The triumph of the sociological concept of 'race as a construct' now provides a cruelly ironic alibi for the reactionary notion that race is irrelevant to modern life, and is only animated by partisan agitators promoting an accusatory, self-serving 'political correctness'.

Nowadays, it seems, almost nobody 'believes' in 'race', or at least explicitly states that they do, but it is middle-class white people who tend to be more likely to think of 'race' in abstract terms as a kind of intellectual unicorn that has wandered off-stage into some kind of harmless neverland. In this wishful post-racial schema 'race' does not exist, so neither does its history or any material effects. Race has been reduced to a kind of pantomime villain dressed up in 'scare' quotes. It surfaces in a theatrical or rhetorical flourish where individuals can be exposed as 'racists' in a moral register of accusation and personal damnation. Individual acts and personal agency are the targets of policing and policy, race is recognised in exceptional incidents, violent disruption and, in a sublime irony, it 'works both ways'. It has a symmetry, so you get 'reverse racism' where white people are the victims of black people's prejudice. Racism is presented in zero-sum terms – you are one or you are not, you are a victim or a perpetrator. This polarised construct is so remote from everyday experience, the complexity of real life and the confusions sown by racism, it sets up enormous cognitive dissonance. Race is traduced – it is not about systems, history and structures, it is simply a personal defect to be identified, exposed, stigmatised, and more effectively criminalised.

The irrelevance of the social scientific truth that there are no races can be contrasted to the approach taken to gender in feminist theory. Feminist theory distinguishes the ahistorical biological fact of anatomical difference, sex, from the social historicity of gender. Feminist theory, however, does not insist that because gender is socially constructed it is meaningless but invests heavily in its experiential and ontological dimensions. Feminist critique has traced the way power differentials shape gender rather than cancel it. They have traced more of its intersections with class, race and ethnicity and theorised their implications for experience and practice (see McIntosh, 1988; 1989). Men's experience and masculinities are clearly integral to theorising gender, and suggestive of how white identities and perspectives are increasingly incorporated into critical race studies. In both, the dominant order is rendered invisible only to itself; that is, men are less aware of the privileges of masculinity and white people the privileges of whiteness. The oft-repeated statement that races do not exist is simply an invitation to see the privileges of whiteness vanish in a post-racial puff of smoke.

The alibi of biology that feminism contests so productively and effectively has no equivalence in phenotype when it comes to race, or any inherent referent when it comes to class. As the early biologism of race has been historicised and discredited it has been substituted with what Anthias (2013, 324) refers to as 'the culturalization of social relationships'. Nowhere is this more obvious, in prison and elsewhere, than in the way ideas about essentialist identities and radical, irreconcilable otherness appear to be settling on Muslim populations, rendering them at a collective and personal level, 'the new blacks' (Sayyid, 1997; Earle and Phillips, 2013; Kundnani, 2014).

Racialisation and the epistemology of ignorance

The persistence of racism as a determining feature of experience and the variable forms that it takes in society and people's lives has produced new analytical approaches. Among these is one that favours the term 'racialisation'. Racialisation refocuses attention more directly on a process, or series of processes, rather than the existence or non-existence of 'a thing', such as race. Using a vocabulary of racialisation it is easier to understand that there are varying degrees of experience of racism. It is a term which allows for different mixes of biological and cultural connotations of difference, and for the disparate valences of superiority and inferiority to be traced. Deploying the terminology of racialisation acknowledges that the labels 'racism/racist' obscure a complex spectrum of meanings and misunderstandings. It can accommodate the incoherence of race because rather than referring to a singular, doubtful entity, it emphasises a process in which a number of meanings are compiled according to specific circumstances. The ways in which Islam has come to dominate ideas about difference and belonging in Western Europe are a good example of racialisation. It involves the imposition by a dominant group of a narrow set of characteristics onto a diverse group and serves to cement their exclusion from a wider community.

Most people would agree that Muslims come in all shapes and sizes, all shades of skin colour, and a variety of national and ethnic cultures. Racialisation refers to the way they are presented as a homogenous threat and the extent to which this threat is located in a set of innate and essential qualities. In the USA racialisation accounts for the way that, for example, all Latin Americans in the city of Atlanta were construed by Atlanta's white communities as 'Mexicans' (Yarborough, 2010). It can also accommodate 'self-racialisation' where, for strategic purposes, a group may reflexively adopt a categorical identity.

The terminology of racialisation helps to understand the dynamics of racism because the power relationships involved in the hierarchies it establishes are made more prominent and are exposed as not being based exclusively on colour but culture. It weakens the association of race with biology, or phenotypical differences. Thus, 'white' groups can be subject to racialisation, and in the British context this includes people categorised as Jews (see Kushner, 2005), Irish Catholics (see Garner, 2003) Gypsies/Travellers (see Taylor, 2008) and East European migrants (see Dawney, 2008). In each case, the dominant group constitutes itself against what it purports itself not to be – that is, by characterising the negative features of the other culture, it establishes its own positive ones by implication and inference. This can reveal a great deal about dominant groups, the racialising groups, at least as much as it does the subordinate group. For example, the current obsession with Islam in the West has exposed aspects of its Christian, liberal and secular traditions to renewed scrutiny. Muslim cultures are frequently (mis)characterised in the terms of the European Reformation that established formal relations between two interpretations of Christian faith, imposing a contested Eurocentric historical experience of religious schism onto the distinctive histories of Islam (Kundnani, 2014).

Most of the theoretical literature associated with work on racialisation in the UK, and specifically the racialisation of white identities has been largely independent of the theoretical structure provided in the United States by 'critical race theory' and 'critical whiteness studies' (Mills, 1997; Roedigger, 2007; Garner, 2007). This theoretical literature highlights the concept of white privilege and the ways in which it is sustained by 'epistemological ignorance' (Mills, 1997). This is a kind of constructed ignorance rather than a simple lack of knowledge, an ignorance that is produced and maintained by a specific form of social practice that makes the existence of discrimination towards people of colour, and white people's agency in it, almost completely invisible to the latter. This 'ignorance' is not a personal defect but a structural social problem (Alcoff, 2007). It is not a passive deficit, but an active practice – (white) people choose ignorance to protect the position it gives them, and to avoid the work involved in changing the way those positions are made available.

Tuana (2004; 2006) develops a taxonomy of ignorance that is helpful for understanding how the diverse social practice of white people accumulates to sustain and perpetuate their relative privilege. According to Tuana there are four principal modes of ignorance: (1) knowing that we know, yet not caring to know, (2) not even knowing that we do not know, (3) not knowing because (privileged) others do not want us to know, and (4) wilful ignorance.

The first type might apply to ignorance of widespread and long-standing evidence of disproportionality in prison populations that Tonry (1996), in the US context, long ago accurately diagnosed as 'malign neglect'. The second type of ignorance occurs when we utterly fail to recognise that we do not know certain things because 'our current interests, beliefs and theories obscure them' (Tuana, 2006, 6) as possible objects of knowledge. This might apply in the UK where fleeting and passing reference is made to the ethnic disproportionality of prison populations, but there is widespread ignorance of the fact that the probability of being imprisoned if you are black is slightly higher in England than it is in the USA (Langan and Farrington, 1998; Phillips, 2012). Indeed in England, the extraordinary scale of US imprisonment is allowed to act as a shield against such knowledge of domestic penal dynamics. The link with simply not caring in the first type is the logical corollary of this type of ignorance.

The third type is less identifiable in the relatively open democracies of the West, but would apply at different times in more totalitarian regimes. The fourth type, wilful ignorance, is perhaps the most toxic and the most widespread. This is an ignorance of the persistence of white privilege and the pervasive evidence of racism that is actively cultivated and maintained. As Tuana (2006, 11) puts it: 'Wilful ignorance is a systematic process of self-deception, a wilful embrace of ignorance that infects those who are in positions of privilege, an active ignoring of the oppression of others and one's role in that exploitation.' It is a self-serving ignorance because it appears to be in one's interests to be ignorant. However, this form of ignorance operates at the same level as Sartre and de Beauvoir's notion of 'bad faith', a duplicitousness that is not entirely a matter of conscious volition (see Judaken, 2008).

'Whiteness' operates through the unconscious in complex ways as a signifier 'that generates a combinatory with its own set of inclusions and exclusions that determine the subject' (Seshadri-Crooks, 2000, 24). It means that to be racialised is to be put in a position relative to the master signifier of 'whiteness'. Being white means living in an accumulation of ignorance, disavowal and denial, a combination of partial omissions and incomplete commissions of knowledge. The resulting subjectivity is deep rooted and characterised by a kind of strategic, self-serving, self-perpetuating ambivalence in the face of the realities of racism. In the absence of effective and militant anti-racist pedagogy the 'white unconscious' persists. It is sustained by the inertial benefits of white privilege, a passive reflexivity that recognises the difficulty, disturbance and discomfort associated with doing something about the condition, but fails to assemble the necessary motivations and resources to act on the knowledge. The classic ambivalent symptoms of post-colonial melancholia take shape in a kind of destructive 'learned helplessness' (Seligman, 1975).

Theorising ignorance and the manufacture of both uncertainty and ambivalence are now gathered together under the banner of 'agnotology' (Proctor and Schiebinger, 2008). Agnotology has much to offer the ways in which convict criminology can understand the penal status quo, the way things change but also remain the same. It does this by developing tools that can expose the historicity of how some knowledge assumes power and leverage, while other forms of knowledge acquire a more passive weight akin to forms of ignorance. It involves a form of 'symptomatic reading' (Althusser and Balibar, 1997) which analyses texts for their 'silences' as much as for their explicit statements with a view to revealing the possibility of underlying problematics or stretching their analytical reach. Mills's (1997, 18) analogy with the familiar tropes of the social contract is a good example of a symptomatic reading' in relation to race: 'the Racial Contract prescribes for its signatories an inverted epistemology, an epistemology of ignorance, a particular pattern of localised and global cognitive dysfunctions (which are psychologically and socially functional), producing the ironic outcome that whites will in general be unable to understand the world they themselves have made'.

Developing anti-racism in convict criminology

Criminologists have tended to neglect the over-representation of racialised people in criminal justice systems, and relegated the issue of race to one of 'special interest' marginality within criminology. Convict criminology can align itself with efforts to consider more explicitly and extensively how 'notions of race have simply been written into the entire notion of punishment itself' (Bosworth, 2004b, 237). This means attending to the seminal works of Du Bois, and the contemporary work of scholars such Gabbidon (2007; 2014) in the US and Phillips (2012) and Phillips and Webster (2014) in the UK.

Toni Morrison's proposal (1993) for the examination of the 'impact of notions of racial hierarchy, racial exclusion and racial vulnerability... on nonblacks who held, resisted, explored or altered these notions' has begun to gather support and momentum. She noted how race had already become metaphorical – 'a way of referring to and disguising forces, events, classes and expressions of social decay and economic division far more threatening to the body politic than biological "race" ever was' (Morrison, 1993, 63) – but also that race was subject to a 'willed scholarly indifference' (Morrison, 1993, 14) that reflects the whiteness of the scholarly community. White liberal colour-blindness has become the hegemonic form of whiteness, with white being the only colour it is blind to.

Polarisation is the stock-in-trade of racism, and sometimes, anti-racism. Anti-racism frequently falls into the trap of setting up simplistic binary dualisms and straw 'bogey-men' that are 'inattentive to the dramatic ways racial identity is rapidly transforming', and fails to accommodate 'the contradictions, inconsistencies and ambivalences in white and non-white identities' (Hartigan, 2005, 231–41). Anti-racism has frequently taken on a moral register at the expense of a political one. Racists are regarded simply as 'bad' people to be identified and condemned. This is a profoundly ill-informed approach for criminologists to take, and a painfully ironic one for convict criminologists. As a by-product of this simplistic binary approach, victims of racism are also reduced to an equally two-dimensional existence as necessarily hapless and virtuous innocents. This kind of reductive over-simplification is a comforting short cut that leads nowhere. No one is intrinsically more evil or more good than anyone else. The critical issue is that not everyone has the same power to activate racism, or align themselves with its historical force, social institutions and political resources.

Racism privileges all white people but only some people activate racism more explicitly than others, have greater access to its resources, benefit more from its accumulated influence in the institutions of power and can mobilise its cultural force more easily. It is important to stress that a focus on white racism and aspects of whiteness is not a moralistic project, but a political one. White people are not bad people, as is sometimes suggested in caricatures of anti-racism, but the power and social privileges of whiteness cannot be ignored. This is a political critique not a moral one, it involves recognising the complexity of racism, and its affective dimensions in personal life.

One of the most toxic political features of racism is the intrinsic fragility of the racist construct. Because of its instability and contradictions it is uniquely prone toward paranoia. Racists tend to be paranoid not because they are scared of the people they are racialising but because they are scared of themselves (Hage, 1998; 2003). A self-declared white racist is someone who is trying to live up to an ideal created in their own mind that has an explicit racial collectivity: 'we whites are the best, and best together'. These openly racist identities are relatively rare, and even more rarely articulated, but even the more common features whiteness draw on a similar sense of collectivity and unconscious affinity. The experiential reality of difference, and the impossibility of purity, always belies this sense of affinity. The stronger the investment in this sense of affinity, the deeper the insecurity it breeds at a personal level around the failure to live up to the image and expectation of white superiority. Thus, a self-referential cycle is set in train where people who are most insecure about the privileges of whiteness deploy more racism to defend against the anxiety it generates, which then reinforces their beleaguered sense of entitlement and fuels increasingly bitter resentment at the predicament in which they find themselves. Rage, resentment and an erupting suppressed anger are the emotional markers of white privilege, expressed with such lethal effect in the USA through the persona of Dylan Roof. Roof's slaughter in 2015 of the congregation of a black church in Charleston appeared not out of nowhere but out of whiteness, likewise the Black Lives Matter campaign.

In the UK, such rage and resentment usually take less violent form but shape dangerous tendencies toward both disabling sentimentality and melancholia (Gilroy, 2004). In Norway Anders Breivik's obsessive militarism emerged in the attacks he launched on a children's holiday camp in 2011. Breivik's actions were unusual in drawing such explicit ideological justification from whiteness. This he persists with in prison in Norway where he indicates a desire to pursue a course of study in political science. That he continues to receive and respond to large amounts of fan mail from admirers around the world indicates the extent and variable form of whiteness.

The implications of this perspective on race for convict criminologists is that we know as well as anyone, and probably better, prison is a place where the hardest person to avoid is yourself. It is a place where arbitrary authority and institutionalised disempowerment catalyse the usual ingredients of paranoia. Add drugs, whether to dull the pains or to escape, and the resulting cocktail may account for the particular segregational virulence of US prison racism, and the convoluted permutations of con-viviality in English prisons. Convict criminologists can build on direct experience of these dynamics to build a stronger anti-racist pedagogy in the struggles over the future of prison.

Can I get a whiteniss?

Thinking about prison and looking for answers to the questions posed by Stuart Hall involves working beyond the boundaries of conventional anglophone criminology. Being so closely involved in Phillips' (2012) study of race and ethnicity in men's prisons brought home to me the ways in which whiteness has profound epistemological implications. As convict criminology attempts to expand the criminological imagination and develop new pedagogical potentials it needs to explicitly address the blindspot of racism and its own whiteness.

Henry Giroux (2008) insists that the meanings and definitions of racism alter for each generation, and so the challenge for scholars is to develop a new language for understanding how racism redefines social relations between people. Convict criminologists need to understand more about the different forms racism takes in prisons and criminal justice procedures, and how it has structured criminology. We need to appreciate and articulate its different intensities, and how it circulates in society. How are prisons implicated in the way racism captures people, hurts and destroys them? How is it that racism makes you feel the way you feel in its presence? Claustrophobic? Anxious and miserable? Disoriented in a world in which you need to find your place, but in a way you can't put your finger on? How is it so strongly bound to criminal justice that it makes a mockery of the second term? What does racialisation, a process that articulates exclusion, inferiorisation, subordination and exploitation (Anthias and Yuval-Davis, 1993), share with criminalisation – a process that so effectively and consistently renders similar groups of people subject to the state's power to punish?

Stuart Hall's *New Ethnicities* (1992) provides a starting point and I've tried to identify other neglected resources in this chapter. Perhaps it might help just to listen to Timmy Thomas's *Why Can't We Live Together?* (Thomas, 1972). Does Rahsaan Roland Kirk's 'Blacknuss' (Kirk, 1972) get across something of an affective space that constitute, with apologies to Kirk, a more helpful sense of 'whiteniss'. perhaps 'whiteniss', by inferring a process of witness and acknowledgement to the powers of racialisation, can disrupt some of the more prescriptive terms currently available to account for how we can live together with our differences and without indifference.

Was there a bit of 'whiteniss' in Rowan Atkinson's one-finger synthesiser performance during Danny Boyle's Opening ceremony to the 2012 London Olympics?[3] His comical rendition of the repetitive signature in the *Chariots of Fire* tune hinted at a parody of precious masculine and imperial themes, the whiteniss smuggled through his hapless Mr Bean 'everyman' persona deflating the familiar code of imperial pomp. And then there is the young, white Londoner, Ben Drew. As Plan B he presents an ambitiously apocalyptic urban parallel vision of Olympic London in which white and black youth of the riot-torn city seethe with inchoate frustration and anger. Echoes of the Specials 1983 hit 'Ghost Town' are unavoidable as his lyrics grope awkwardly toward the insurrectionary politics of class war; *ill Manors* is an album, a film and a vision with inventive attitude – another lens through which particular aspects of social relationships can be apprehended (Garner, 2007). Is it whiteniss?

The next two chapters do not answer this question but explore ways in which it might contribute positively to convict criminology by opening up its reflexive potentials. Questions of masculine identity, social class and ethnicity are explored alongside the way men make sense of incarceration, both as a system of punishment and a personal experience. It extends the foundational hypothesis of convict criminology that having been imprisoned can provide particular criminological insights into these and other questions.

[2] www.youtube.com/watch?v=h17gIW9paO0

SEVEN

Methodologies, epistemologies, ontologies

OLD TIMERS AND HARD TIMERS

On the first day of my prison sentence I was joined in the reception cell of HMP Norwich by an older man, probably in his late forties, also starting his sentence. We exchanged a few cagey formalities: 'How long are you doing?' he asked, 'Three months' I said. 'F*** me!' he scoffed 'I done more than that in a Panda car.'[1] I believe he had and he faced a long haul on his latest sentence. He was the saddest, most broken man I met in the prison. The first days of a long sentence in prison can be like that, I'm told – no road ahead, no road back. I thought of him as I read *Doing Harder Time*, a book by Natalie Mann (2012), which recounts the experiences of men in a growing and ageing UK prison population. It makes grim reading, but it is also a compelling account of an issue few people will find compelling. It tells the story of men in prison who will, most likely, die there of old age, their lives progressively degraded by growing infirmity and permanent incarceration.

Reading *Doing Harder Time* I was reminded of how short my time inside was, and how long prison sentences have become since.[2] Not for the first time, I feel lucky. I had the same feeling listening to a radio programme that interviewed the governor of a vast American prison. He indicated the extent of his prison by saying 'Pretty much all you can see between here and the horizon, that's us.' Then, according to the reporter, he gestured to a workshop building, 'That's the busiest place here, that's where they make the coffins.' In addition to providing the local community with coffins, long-term inmates prided themselves on the kind of coffin they could make for themselves. They knew it was how they would leave the prison and they wanted to do it in style.

---

[1]   Police vehicle, so called because of its black and white marking.
[2]   Crewe (2014) notes that the average life tariff in England and Wales increased from 12.5 years in 2003 to 21.1 years in 2012. For an early account of the dynamics involved in sentence inflation see Hough, Jacobson and Millie (2003).

Mann declares that her book is an attempt 'to give a voice to all those individuals who have been systematically ignored by governments, by prison service policy, and until very recently, by criminologists'. She is concerned not only by the limited quantity of literature on the topic, but also by its tone. What there is, she says, tends to characterise the men as 'powerless and accepting of their fate'. Albeit that it is a picture at least partially drawn out of sympathy with their predicament, it is one that Mann says unhelpfully compounds the denial of their agency.

Why should we care? Does it matter what happens to old men in prison? Surely there are better candidates for our concern, people who haven't done terrible things. When it comes to compassion fatigue it certainly doesn't help that one of the reasons the prison population in the UK is ageing is that it increasingly includes not the wrinkled and grey anti-heroes of a criminal underworld, such as Reggie Kray or Ronnie Biggs, or the mature men in suits who bankrupted the country, but men serving long sentences imposed relatively late in their life for historic sex abuse convictions.

Some convict criminologists align themselves with prison abolitionists who want to get rid of criminal justice systems altogether because they recognise them as false short cuts in complex struggles. I count myself among them. Abolitionists point to the way criminal justice systems have a consistent historical tendency to lock up large numbers of people from working-class, minority ethnic and indigenous populations. Men convicted of sexual offences, historic and otherwise, are not the usual suspects. Their demographics are somewhat older, whiter and more middle class. They do not, however, provide the basis for abandoning such abolitionist struggles.

In UK prison systems men who commit sexual offences are usually categorised as 'vulnerable' and special provisions are made for them to keep them apart from other prisoners through segregation on special wings, or VPUs (vulnerable prisoner units). Mann was told by some of the older prisoners whom she interviewed who were not convicted of sexual offences, that being compelled by their age and infirmity to join these pariahs among pariahs was one of the worst indignities imposed upon them, the final insult to what was left of their manhood; being forced to do their time 'with the nonces' – the sex offenders.

By exposing the irony in which the traditional markers of power in open society, such as being white, being middle class, being older men, are turned over to become signs of risk, stigma and vulnerability can, I think, tell us a lot about how our society works, and the currents flowing through it, bearing it through history. It is as if in prison, the crude simplicities of the regime, the stripping down of life to a minimum set of requirements, reveals important and illuminating truths about who we are and how we can live. How men die, so obviously and exclusively in the arms of society, even if they are prison arms, reveals much of society's capacities and capabilities for care, for life, for accommodating vulnerability.

Mann's book closes with a useful summary discussion of the ways in which the pains of imprisonment for older men in prison can be both recognised and mitigated. Ironically for me as a reader, HMP Norwich in the east of England, where I served my sentence is held up by Mann not so much as a beacon of good practice, but an exemplar of the problems of the new policy of providing specialised age-segregated housing for the 'greying prison population': 'Many of the prisoners in the sample referred to such units as "God's waiting room", and many were frightened about ending up in such a facility.'

Giving and getting: the inside story

When a young man I was interviewing in a prison in England remarked that what I really needed was someone who had been in prison themselves to do the research, I didn't know what to say. I hadn't come across convict criminology, and certainly didn't think of myself as one. I didn't know what to say because although I had been in prison at a similar age to him, I didn't feel I was like him. He was barely 20 years old, bi-lingual, called himself 'white Asian' and was immersed in London's youthful and convivial multicultures (Phillips and Earle, 2010). I was nearly 50 years old, mono-lingual, with three children and living in an ethnically mono-cultural white village. My three months in HMP Norwich seemed a long way back, and yet I knew he had made a good point and I had a decent card to play on it. I didn't, but I felt I had missed an opportunity, withheld something I needn't have.

Convict criminology is founded on the idea that people who have been through a prison sentence can themselves fashion distinctive contributions to criminology. This idea is taken from the ethnographic traditions of anthropology: 'In order to explain a cultural product it is necessary to know it. And to know it, in matters of thought and emotion, is to have experienced it' (Malinowski, 1962, 291). For most people, becoming a criminologist involves a lot of reading and perhaps conducting some research. Convict criminologists have another, more direct source of knowledge: themselves. They can bring their own insider's view from prison to establish a richer dialogue with broader criminological scholarship (Warr, 2015). In this chapter I discuss how this has been accomplished and try to demonstrate some of its potential.

The convict criminology established in the US stresses the importance of ethnographic and auto-ethnographic methods because of their capacity to provide a counterweight against the burgeoning production of quantitative data about people in prison. This growing mountain of studies about prison, prisoners and prison policy can obscure the people most directly involved and reduce them to a collection of variables and policy outcomes. Jewkes (2015), for example, refers to the 'dazzling' effect of this data and how the result is to disguise the harshest aspects of imprisonment and render its interiors even more impenetrable.

Qualitative and ethnographic studies of prison life set out to overcome such barriers but as prison populations in the USA expanded Loïc Wacquant (2002) warned that there was a simultaneous 'eclipse' of qualitative studies of prison interiors. Thus, he declared there was a danger that at the very moment in history when they were most needed, inside and insider views of prison life would disappear from view. This bleak prognosis is qualified by Drake et al (2015) who present an impressively diverse range of ethnographic studies of prison life. Nonetheless, the promise of convict criminology to provide richer and more challenging accounts of prison life through the eyes and experience of prisoners cannot be taken for granted. The epistemological privileges of ethnographic research cannot be assumed, they can only be earned and demonstrated (Hammersely, 2015).

C Wright Mills' (1959, 196) advice to sociologists resonates particularly strongly with convict criminologists: 'You must learn to use your life experience in your intellectual work: continually to examine and interpret it. In this sense craftsmanship is the centre of yourself and you are personally involved in every intellectual product upon which you work.'

For a criminologist with a past in prison, it is not just C Wright Mills who is setting the intellectual agenda. Long before convict criminology was formally established in the USA, Jim Jacobs (1974, 232) highlighted the challenge we confront. He reports the perspective of a prisoner, who, with commendable economy and precision, identifies the issues: 'Instead of doing your bull-shit research from an armchair, why don't you come in as an inmate so you could find out what it's all about, you phoney cock-sucker.' If most prison researchers have not been confronted with such a directly phrased challenge, few will have avoided sensing something similar: how can a non-prisoner know what it is like to be a prisoner?

Bill Davies (2015) provides a lucid account of finding a positive resolution to the dilemmas of disclosing his criminal convictions and ex-prisoner status. Davies is confronted with time-limited access to young men in an English prison to conduct a series of semi-structured qualitative interviews. He opts to use his ex-prisoner status as an icebreaker, an opportunity to establish some sense of common ground and a platform for easier and more open communication. He describes how the conventional 'prison research bargain' of providing the prisoner with additional time out of their cell and someone new to talk to is redrawn by presenting an unexpected opportunity for rapport and identification. Davies suggests that his interviews could more quickly become 'a two-way street' by offering up his prison history at the outset – 'the offence I had committed, the sentence that I had received, the time I had served'. He further unsettles the conventional procedure by inviting his respondents to question him and his story, if they want to, quickly establishing grounds for genuine dialogue around an experience in common. His disclosures elicit and enable theirs in a more egalitarian, horizontal exchange. As Davies phrases it, 'The fee I paid to my respondents was not one of money or goods, but information, personal information' (Davies, 2015, 469). He dubs this approach, borrowing from Bulmer (1982, 232) 'retrospective participant observation'. His creativity and candour immediately enlarge the methodological repertoire for prison research, though he is careful to acknowledge both its limitations and its antecedents in Finch's (1984) feminist approach to interviewing women and Quraishi's (2008) deployment of his Muslim identity in interviewing Muslim prisoners. Davies stresses that 'simply having one connection is not necessarily enough to build trust', but being a convict criminologist offers him one more point of possible connection to the men in prison.

Other academic disciplines have been more open to these potentials and quicker to recognise the significance of personal biography. One example can be found in Chinua Achebe's (1977) account of the hitherto unremarked racism of Joseph Conrad's novella, *Heart of Darkness*. Achebe's analysis is justifiably famous, but gathers additional force when he introduces his personal experience into the account as a kind of inside knowledge of the pernicious qualities of racism. Situating Conrad's fiction in his own reality provides Achebe with a revealing juxtaposition. Conrad, he says, was born in 1857, 'the very year when Anglican Missionaries were arriving among my own people in Nigeria' (Achebe, 2001, 1790). Conrad's journey down the river Congo that provided him with the dubious source material for *Heart of Darkness*, occurred in 1890 when Achebe's father in Nigeria 'was a babe in arms' says Achebe (Achebe, 2001, 1791). Achebe's trenchant diagnosis of the racism running through Conrad's (non)account of the African people encountered by the novella's protagonist, Marlow, is leant extra force by the contrasting intimacy and immediacy of Achebe's perspective. The assault Conrad performs on Africans in the Congo through his writing by portraying them as simpletons without language, is trumped by Achebe's brief biographical asides. It places in the reader's mind starkly contrasting images of the father of the Nobel laureate and Conrad's depictions of Africans as animalistic brutes. At least some of the power of the critique comes from Achebe's distinct African voice, refuting with biographical presence the ugliness in Conrad's text.

Getting inside perspectives as an ethnographic researcher involves complex questions about the recognition of similarity and difference, of being an insider *and* an outsider (Hammersely, 2015; Hodkinson, 2005). Because these are not *either/or* questions but the predicaments of *both/and* the most important issue is that of reflexivity: a self-awareness of your personal characteristics, of your emotional and biographical hinterlands and, summatively, the significance of your positionality in respect of those whom you are researching. Reflexivity allows for this to be more explicit in the accounts we give of our research (Phillips and Earle, 2010; Jewkes, 2012; Drake and Harvey, 2014).

Reflexivity and convict criminology

Reflexivity is a widespread and controversial term in social science, qualifying its claim to objective knowledge because of the way the personal qualities of the researcher filter and shape the data collected and thus the knowledge that emerges from it. Unfortunately, reflexivity has also developed a reputation for making academics even more socially awkward and self-absorbed than usual. Reflexivity, so it is argued, indulges academic egos and fosters narcissistic navel gazing. As such, it is a diverting hall of mirrors, best passed through quickly. Does anyone really want to know about the agonising doubts of a heroic ethnographer who negotiated his or her path into the social margins and back again? Who cares if they were 'nearly arrested, almost beaten up and didn't quite go crazy' (Hobbs, 1993, 62) as they found themselves in worlds that are simply an everyday reality for many people? Reflexivity, poorly practised, or uncritically indulged, simply turns the voyeurism of the researcher back on themselves, degenerating into a narcissistic self-absorption (Skeggs, 2004).

In the study of ethnicity and social relations in two English men's prisons, Coretta Phillips and I struggled with the complexity of our subject matter and our respective identities. It became obvious that my being a white, middle-class man contrasted with Coretta being a working-class, black and mixed-race woman and that this would be a significant feature of our fieldwork, shaping the data we collected and our encounters with respondents. This was forcefully brought home to us on our first full day 'in the field' when we decided to go onto the prison wings and explain a bit about our research and approach. Returning to our office in another part of the prison to compare notes it was clear Coretta's experiences, and thus her account, had been very different from mine. While I had struggled to get any attention or generate much interest in our research from the young men, Coretta had to contend with an avalanche of attention and brought back numerous stories about prison officers and their racism, largely, but not exclusively, from black prisoners.

Perhaps the novelty of the appearance on the wing of a black, mixed-race woman had something to do with it. Nearly all prison officers are white and most are male (in men's prisons). As Coretta pointed out, they all looked a bit like me, but none looked like her. Some months later Coretta asked if I'd noticed how the prison officers always seemed to address me first when we encountered them on our walks around the prison. I hadn't but she said that it wasn't unusual, and that much the same, and worse, happened at the university in which she worked. As we progressed through the research we came to appreciate the complexities of our identities and their various impacts on the data we collected. Our different experiences of social class entwined with visual markers of ethnicity and gender, revealing variable points of connection with, and distance from, men in the prison, their experiences and backgrounds.[3]

Coretta and I were able to side-step some of the self-indulgent traps of solipsism largely because there were two of us engaged in a process of structured reflection. We could counterpose any over-investment in scrutinising our 'selves' because we were also scrutinising each other through specific lenses of class, ethnicity and gender where we were

[3] For further such reflections on this topic, such as the time she was mistaken by a white academic, at a conference on ethnicity, for a hotel cleaner, or the occasion she was mistakenly treated as a clerical assistant and asked to photocopy someone's documents at a journal editorial board meeting composed, other than herself, entirely of white academics, see Phillips and Webster (2013). 3

each positioned so 'differently' (Phillips and Earle, 2010). Working together, we could understand more clearly how the everyday omissions and opportunities of fieldwork were shaped by our respective positions. We developed ways of using these differences, and situating them in the emerging ethnographic narrative.

Other ethnographers, such as Mitch Duneier (2004) have come across similar issues and enriched ethnography by writing reflexively about the process. For convict criminologists negotiating the ethnographic points of connection and disconnection around a convict/ex-convict identity are likely to be similarly enriching but complex and challenging to develop. In the UK context, convict criminologists such as Bill Davies (2015) have opened some methodological doors and David Honeywell's PhD research will generate novel empirical data about academics and aspiring academics with criminal and prison pasts. Andy Aresti (2012; 2014; Aresti and Darke, 2015) is establishing a new synthesis of personal experience, supporting prisoner activism and writing collaborations.

The benefits of reflexivity are not always straightforward or easily accomplished. The pitfalls are many and easy to fall into (Lynch, 2000; but see also Pels, 2000). There is, for example, a trans-Atlantic tendency for irritating neologisms, such as 'mystory' (as opposed to history, etc) and 'Me-search' (research!), or 'I-witnessing' (eye witnessing!) that can be off-putting to read and that offer little more than epistemological cul-de-sacs (Back, 2012). Geertz's (1988, 97) warnings about 'unbearably earnest' confessional writing can help convict criminologists avoid adding to this literature. It is a difficult balance to strike between recognising that there is no 'view from nowhere' (Bourdieu, 2000, 2) and that you are not the story, you are the storyteller.

The forms of triangulation and co-working across identities, as described above with Coretta Phillips, can be a helpful strategy for convict criminologists to establish if, when and how experiences as a prisoner provide additional elements to be included in the reflexive mix. Because very few ex-prisoners become academics and of those that do only some become criminologists, it will inevitably mean we are a small minority among prison ethnographers and criminologists. Convict criminology in the USA has demonstrated how entry into the discipline can be developed, supported and encouraged. What ex-prisoners can bring to prison research are not just the usual characteristics of their ethnicity, class and gender, but some 'practical wisdom' of prison life and the additional opportunities it might provide for ethnographic connection (see Davies, 2015). They can also create opportunities, as Achebe demonstrates, for cancelling the ugliness of caricature, prejudice and ignorance with simple biographical detail. They can help change public perceptions of prisoners and criminals as a lesser breed, doomed and destined for social marginality by taking up positions in universities and making their presence felt.

There is a tension within some currents of convict criminology around the extent to which 'insider/ex-con' auto-ethnographic perspectives may be assumed to provide privileged insights, intrinsically superior, more authentic, and thus more valid, than conventional prison research accounts (see Bosworth, 2004a; Newbold et al, 2014). Convict criminology is inevitably and necessarily diverse in approach. It enriches large and growing critical currents within criminology to which I am keen to contribute, but I am also wary of over-claiming from my relatively limited experience of being imprisoned (three months). Although some convict criminologists draw from much longer experience, any automatic association of convict criminology with intrinsic epistemological privilege derived from authentic experience must be made with caution and caveats.

Authenticity, masculinity and prison life

For most of my working life since my final conviction in 1982 I have resisted any direct reference to my prison experiences, for a variety of reasons, not least a degree of confusion, embarrassment and indecision about their significance. I think very few people who have been sent to prison want to be defined by the experience or remembered for it. Most of us are acutely aware of its defining power and our lack of control over how we will be regarded under its lingering shadows.

I have also been conscious of not wanting to 'cash-in' on experiences that were, to me, exceptional but that to others less fortunate (that is, less middle-class, less white) are, if not a matter of destiny, a kind of routine hazard, more of a 'commonplace'. For the most part prison is an experience that blights lives and leaves scars (or worse) that I am thankful to have avoided. In short, a prison sentence did me no harm, but I have been reluctant to allow it to do me good, not least because this could mean implicitly colluding in its most pernicious myth ('it works') and affirming liberal faith in the benefits of prison's rehabilitative role (see Carlen, 2008).

I have also wanted to avoid granting any kind of currency to the macho myths of prison and the capital it trades in, that is, of being tough and being tough enough to shrug it off or smart enough to trade in its reputations and perverse allure. This kind of masculine capital buys into the fantasies of power, invulnerability and omnipotence that men need to challenge rather than invest in. This choice for me although not always easy or straightforward, is as loaded with class privilege as it is with gender virtue.

Most convict criminologists are men, and heterosexual men are often over-invested in the 'authenticity' of their masculinity, not least because their position within the gender order is less readily acknowledged as a construct (Connell, 1983; 1995; 2003). Masculinities are socially contingent rather than naturally occurring. They vary through history and according to place, albeit that for most men masculinity is popularly regarded as innate. Authenticity in experience, biography and self-presentation are thus highly prized aspects of hegemonic masculinity. Its opposite, camp, is almost invariably associated with homosexual men, the subordinated masculinity. The status attached to the effortless accomplishment of being a man in a man's world, of taking 'naturally' to its social rhythms and expectations, or moving easily through its territory, are features of most men's experience. They are all brought into the foreground, or closer to the surface, in prison and become more explicitly negotiated. Direct but involuntary experience of these exclusively masculine and heavily masculinised environments provides convict criminologist with potentially valuable resources with which to engage with gender theory.

Being inside, being alone, being possessed – and other worries

Erwin James served a long prison sentence before developing a successful career as a writer. Few others can write on or about the complexities, peculiarities and pains of prison with such power, care and insight. In a Foreword to a collection of prisoners' writings he points out '[W]hoever you are and however long your sentence, in prison you live inside your head' (James, 2013, 7). Convict criminologists are well placed to address this aspect of men's experience more closely and sensitively than most. Men's interior, subjective worlds are thrown back at them by force of circumstance in prison, exposing them to both new and familiar challenges of making life liveable.

In prison the question of looking after your basic needs for food, shelter and hygiene is radically repositioned by the fact that the prison has assumed the basics of that role. These broadly domestic, frequently maternal, roles are radically reconfigured in a paternal register subordinated to the primary penal function of delivering pain. Unsurprisingly, the experience is only rarely regarded positively. Even the most widely accepted forms of male domesticity, gardening and

DIY, are usually denied to prisoners. All the treasured fundamentals of the Victorian domestic revolution which anchored men's identities between the twin poles of work and home life, are disrupted by imprisonment (Tosh, 1999). The structured engagement, within a household, of women's domestic regimes and power, with children and comfort, are replaced with austere, homosocial masculine regulation.

If you are imprisoned, you are taken away from those whom you care about and who care for you. Even when these domestic or intimate relations are strained, fragile or fraught, or worse, the pains imposed on those involved, family members close or distant, have only recently come to be included within penal scholarship (Comfort, 2008; Condry et al, 2016). Convict criminologist's direct experience of negotiating these pains, and working through their implications can contribute to this new scholarship. To what extent, for example, are our academic interests and appetites conditioned or supported by these personal networks? How are the ruptures to them repaired, remade or abandoned through the transition from prison to university? How, if at all, are these experiences analogous to other transitions? By bringing family networks firmly back into the picture, not simply as instruments of rehabilitation but as participants subjected to the pains of punishment, Condry et al (2016) widen the field of opportunity for convict criminology's epistemological contributions.

From being a part of family and social networks, however strained or supportive, malign or benign, as a prisoner you belong unequivocally to the state. It assimilates you. You are fed, clothed and provided with shelter, but excluded from society and deprived of liberty and property. Once you become a prisoner, you become the property of the state. You are brought down close to a feudal form of bondage, being chattel, that is, owned by someone. This possessive relationship is complex and involves basic care and concern as a condition of ownership. For prisoners the relationship is experientially relatively obscure in the modern prison environments with which I am familiar, but is no less real for all that. One of the first things a prison officer said to me in HMP Norwich was, "Basically, you've got no rights in here. It's not quite that simple, but that's pretty much how it is." Imprisonment is an ironic form of self-dispossession which rhetorically promotes the liberal contract of autonomy, rights and personal responsibility – by removing them! The prisoner's rights to himself/herself are suspended for the duration of their incarceration, and their return made conditional on demonstrable good behaviour. The obscure political abstraction of the social contract becomes a practical reality for the prisoner, a lesson in politics for which no grades or academic credit are available.

The right to yourself, and its removal, was something that confronted Bernard Stiegler in prison (see Chapter Four). For Stiegler (2009) it was such an intensely disorienting and profoundly disturbing experience that it propelled him into the arms of philosophy and politics, for survival and comfort. The stage-managed withdrawal of his personal agency by the prison left the robber feeling robbed, violated and undone. Being in prison, Stiegler discovered, takes away the usual human capacity to inhabit a place and to inform its shape with your own. In phenomenological terms this active relationship between place and self is the fundamental source of life (Merleau-Ponty, 1962) and although its removal in prison is not total, it is powerful. It is a kind of induced lifelessness that is referred to in the sociological literature as the 'weight' and 'tightness' of a prison sentence (Crewe, 2011). It is a state of suspended animation in which life goes on because it is still, just, a bit better than the alternative.

For prisoners the lack of creative transaction and possibility between themselves and the immediate environment throws them into themselves, into their heads, as Erwin puts it. The result, according to Stiegler (2008), is a profoundly alienating individuation. The ideal man individuated by prison is discrete from his environment, closed off, ontologically still and stable, like the prison. At one level this is akin to the stoicism described by Toch (1998) as a form of adaptation, but at another it is a form of half-death, a sacrificing of the vital life, the kind of life lived in a social world which involves perpetual amendment around the flux of social and environmental interaction. It exchanges a multiple world one occupies *with oneself* for a world simply *of oneself*.

The life that requires openness and engagement, that is a vulnerable life and a sociable life, is not for the prison or the prisoner. In stark contrast to the kinetic and liquid properties of modern life, the western prison persists in stasis and immobility. The emergent social relations of modernity that Marx and Engels (1848) identified are turned around to haunt the prisoner – all that is melted into air becomes solid, fluid relations are fast-frozen and 'man is at last compelled to face with sober senses his real conditions of life and his relations with his kind'. Prison is thus a kind of communist nightmare in which society has withered away leaving only the state and the individual. You don't have to be a communist to find the horror of it palpable, but if you are, as Serge was, it hurts all the more so.

If these theoretical formulations of prison life seem remote from daily experience as lived by prisoners, it is because they are concerned with the ideological function of prison life as a form of experience. When you are in prison, the implications of the daily practice of life in prison pass you by and it is only afterwards that it is possible to make sense of it at a higher level of comprehension. The subtle habituations and stasis of prison life ambushed me on release from my short sentence. Even after just three months inside I found myself thrown off balance, literally physically, by the scale and speed of objects in motion, particularly cars, buses all the more so, but even people. Everything seemed to move so fast. Roads were a hazard, if only for a day or so. It was an unexpectedly physical reaction to the kinetic dimensions of social life that the prison had stilled. The release into chosen rather than frozen relations was sublime.

Prisons are a form of involuntary, immobile human commune where you are forced to live in the kind of close proximity with others that fascinates philosophers and political scientists. Sykes (1958) observed that for prisoners one of the hardest things to bear was being around other prisoners. Prisons, with their potential for solitary confinement ever-present, confront the prisoner with the classic polarities of existential ambivalence: hell is other people and hell is no people at all. In prison, aged 24, I wasn't much given to existential reflection, I'm sorry to say, though Samuel Beckett's *Waiting for Godot*, studied at school and memorised for performance, began to make considerably better sense than it did at the time. More recently, as a criminologist returning to prison as an ethnographic researcher concerned to integrate social theory into my work, I increasingly found myself recognising, post hoc, in my prison experience innumerable features of modern social life and the classic existential dilemmas with which Beckett played. There are no bars on Beckett's stage, only a tree, but Vladimir and Estragon are famously inert, prisoners toyed with by an unseen power, and toying with their predicament.

Jean-Paul Sartre (2004) turned Marx's investigation of class consciousness into a one of personal ontology that prison life is rather good at exposing. The individualised passivity and immobility of prison life is an exemplary existential condition, the 'serie', the individual-in-itself in a 'plurality of isolations'. Sartre, and others, have used the symbolism of the queue to evoke this condition. The queue represents an ideal form of order, moving ever closer towards a goal, each person in their place, it is an idealised form of governmentality. To this familiar form of queueing the prison adds its own distinctive variety, the circular string of the exercise yard, not so much a queue quietly infused with the hope of arrival, as a fatalistic rehearsing of the prison sentence itself. Going round and round in circles.

UNIVERSITY OF WINCHESTER
LIBRARY

Men of state and the state of men

Because (western, white) men often tend to see themselves as ungendered, as the index of all humanity at large, it is particularly tempting for such men to see men's prisons as a microcosm of a whole society, despite the persistent and glaring gender dimensions of their constitution. Several eminent male social theorists suggest ominous and portentous analogies from relatively limited contact with the institution. Foucault (1979, 14), notwithstanding his close work with prisoners in GIP (see Chapter 4), presents an analysis of prison's panoptic features that declares them part of 'a machine in which everyone is caught, those who exercise power as well as those subject to it'. For Deleuze (1992) prisons serve as the ultimate analogical model of a particular kind of 'society of control'. Bauman (1993, 122) advises that prisons are fertile ground for sociological research because 'penal practice may serve as a laboratory where the tendencies attenuated and adulterated elsewhere can be observed in their pure form; after all, control and order are the outspoken objectives of the prison system'. Wacquant (2002, 386) suggests that we recognise the prison as a 'template or vector of broader social forces, political nexi, and cultural processes that traverse its walls'. Jerome Miller (2000, cited in Shalev, 2009, 28) tells us that 'Prisons and jails are an early warning system for society. They constitute the canary in the coalmine, providing an omen of mortal danger that often lies beyond our capacity to perceive.' These perspectives suggest that prisons provide evidence of social processes otherwise obscured, possibilities impending. The living death of a prison sentence manifests as bare life, life excluded and reduced to a minimum by the power of the state (Agamben, 1998). Who better, then, than convict criminologists who have been 'inside the monster' to consider and present that evidence?

Convict criminologists are well placed to conduct the kind of anthropology of prisons that Lorna Rhodes (2001; 2015) advocates. This involves bending the criminological toward the anthropological and putting ourselves into the question (Levi-Strauss, 2011). Anthropology began as an investigation of human culture beyond the immediate dynamics of capitalist modernity, but an anthropological interest in prison rests on its position at the heart of capitalist modernity. Criminology invites us into customs and practice that can shock, astonish and repulse but usually with policy and correction in mind. Anthropology has no such agenda. An anthropological approach within convict criminology might reveal prison's 'minor realities' as the primitivist anthropologists once did of 'old world' cultures, but it can also engage critically in the prison's radical alterities. It can steer inquiry elsewhere than correction and system improvement to difficult spaces, awkward silences, uncertain outcomes and radical politics (Hage, 2012).

There is often something intrinsically sad, or at least bleak and compulsive, about institutions that exclude women and build themselves exclusively around men, whether that is the priesthood, schools, armies or prisons. That other criminologists (Crewe, 2014; Sabo et al, 2001; Maycock and Hunt, 2017) also note the neglect of these gender dimensions in men's social lives in prison means that you don't have to be a convict criminologist to do so, but if you are, your resources are enhanced by your personal experience of the transition between the carceral and the academic institution, between the practice and the theory.

During my research in a young men's prison in England I was struck by the young men's descriptions of, and investments in, a type of heavily muscled upper body strength that they referred to as 'hench'. This masculine physicality and muscular enhancement presents the male body as a kind of fortress that seems uncannily analogous with the 'crustacean' features of the state that Karl Polanyi (1957) describes. Polanyi shows that in the Middle Ages the pre-Westphalian states of Europe invested heavily in boundary fortification, armour and shows of martial strength as a way of asserting their presence in the shifting economic landscape of Europe. The 'crustacean state' is how he describes the resulting formation, states relatively hollow on the inside in terms of infrastructure, but brittle and well defended on their margins. Both for individual men, and their collective interests as men gathered into state formation (Connell, 1990), this structuring reflects a certain kind of orientation to the social and personal management of ontological vulnerability (Gilson, 2014).

'Crustacean' is a term that evokes comic-book images of heavily armoured super-heroes as much as it does crabs, lobsters or nation-states. The hard-looking sculpted body so highly prized by many young men in prison (and elsewhere) is one that is apparently impervious to harm, full of extravagantly showy body strength. Generating this semblance of invulnerability provides men with a sense of control and potency which the experience of incarceration is designed to diminish. It is a defiant gesture of ontological assertion. In the process, body shape and appearance become the primary locus of affect and experience, the principal means of representing the self to the world (Bordo, 2003; Russon, 2003).

The popularity of the new cinematic action-hero genre of techno-brutalism, especially Marvel-comic movies, such as *The X-Men, The*

Avengers or *Iron Man*, rests on a spectacular valorisation of a bizarre fantasy of omnipotence, invulnerability and 'raw', brute, power. Now beyond its third iteration, the *Iron Man* movie franchise, for example, is successful for explicitly combining the tension between an omnipotent exterior ready for action and the vulnerable interior poorly equipped for reflection. It takes cinematic form in the famously troubled, once drug-addled, Robert Downey Jr as Iron Man/Tony Stark, a character who simultaneously celebrates the capacity of the super-rich to flout society's laws and conventions.

Body shape and appearance then tends to take precedence and slides toward an objectification that desensitises other capabilities and capacities. This investment, especially by heterosexual men, in surfaces and appearance is often at the expense of interiors and metaphysical resources. It can foster a mind/body dualism which exacerbates the inner self/outer appearance dichotomy by stressing the image of physical control and other characteristics of hegemonic masculinity such as strength and physical competency. The sense of control and self is reduced to mastery of the body, a masculine essence of subjective authenticity (Heyes, 2007) in perpetual dissonance with the prison's project of control. Even though prisoners might 'live in their head', they often let their bodies do the talking because no one listening, only watching.

Being inside: prison with Levinas and Buber

> Humanity, to which proximity properly so called refers, must...not be first understood as consciousness...Why does the other concern me?...Am I my brother's keeper? These questions have meaning only if one has already supposed that the ego is concerned only with itself, is only a concern for itself. In this hypothesis it indeed remains incomprehensible that the absolute outside-of-me, the other, would concern me. (Levinas, 1981, 88, 117)

Victor Serge's description of 'the throngs of men thrown together' in prison captures one of the abiding features of prison life. It is an experience that is at once banal and laden with layers of moral, ethical and philosophical resonance. Almost in an instant, on being thrown into prison as the cliché has it, the apparently abstract existential questions posed by Levinas (above and below) surface as urgent dilemmas. Does (prison) society depend:

on the limitation of the principle that men are predators of one another, or if to the contrary it results from the limitation of the principle that men are for one another[?]. Does the social...result from limiting the consequences of the war between men, or from limiting the infinity which opens in the ethical relationship of man to man? (Levinas, 1981, 88, 117)

Am I among strangers or friends? Neighbours or aliens? The reality – confusingly, horrifyingly and comfortingly – is both. Fellow prisoners can be alien neighbours, stranger friends, predators and protectors but they are always physically close. Proximity has powerful moral effects, and is unavoidably affecting. Living in this way, I discovered at HMP Norwich, requires the cultivation of special skills not learned since childhood. They are soft skills of interactions and meetings, the micro-politics of egalitarian practice, ways of being together for common good and harmonious living. They are the 'countless tokens' and 'the thousand nothings' (Bourdieu, 1981, 7–8) that make life matter but have become increasingly marginal (see Overing and Passes, 2000).

One consequence of this predicament is the mismeeting, Martin Buber's term for the management of unchosen proximity. The mismeeting is one without genuine dialogue, a degradation of what Buber defines as the ethical interactions of 'I–Thou' relations (Buber, 1958). In other areas of life where proximity presses people together for extended periods, such as academic conferences, these encounters might be recognised benignly as 'face time'. This is a condition of being face-to-face, and dealing with close human presence, both fleeting and more fulsome. Often they are the most valuable and enriching of encounters. Even so, conferences can induce in academics a degree of 'face fatigue'. The work is tiring. It can sap your energy and vitality. It is a small and more dilute measure of the ethical work a prisoner contends with and must accomplish on a daily basis.

Goffman (1971) refers to the habits of 'disattention', another skill the prisoner must learn quickly, and one I recognise as being also present in the academic conference hall. The mismeeting and habits of disattention are necessary to relegate proximate others, the Other, into the background, into an irrelevant presence. A prisoner must find ways of living in a perpetual but lonely crowd, of avoiding unwanted contact; ordinary and familiar skills perhaps, but ones loaded with ethical significance. A moral void beckons; Levinas's nightmare of instrumental sympathy and strategic hostility must be managed, loss of face avoided. One solution is to disappear, to not have a face. Prison environments can easily become dangerously de-ethicalised, purged of I–Thou interaction (Leibling, 2015).

Simmel (1969, 52) recognised these dangers in the modern city's tendencies toward civil indifference. His description of the preponderance of 'an evenly flat and grey tone' where 'no one object deserves preference over any other' is a reasonable approximation of the effect prison interiors strive for, except for the ostentatious presence of security measures. Richard Sennet's (1974) diagnosis of the potential ills of city life are also a good guide to the difficulties of life inside a prison; they are 'place[s] to pass through, not to use', 'place[s] to move through, not to be in'. If the coping options of moving or passing through are available for city dwellers, they are ones much less available to prisoners, with predictably harsh existential consequences. Prisons can be alarming analogues of dystopian city-states. They give operational form to the ideals of governing an inert society.

Convict criminologists are more aware than most that someone is sent to prison to 'teach them a lesson'. Unfortunately, the lesson is that 'the Other does not have to become an enemy, if [he] can simply be stripped of his ethically commanding humanity' (Bauman, 1990, 29). The lesson offers social endorsement of the human condition imagined as inherently depraved and permanently requiring 'societally administered coercion' (Bauman, 1990). Bauman closes a bleak assessment of the ethical consequences of modernity without reference to prison life, though his earlier work on the Holocaust (Bauman, 1989) provides him with plentiful dystopian reference points. He warns that any 'social scientific doctrine which endorses the separation of politics from morality by lending its authority to the assumption of the moral depravity of man and thereby replacing the issue of moral substance with that of legal form does not exactly help [the development of a new ethics]'. This, to my mind, is the risk criminology poses. In the next and final chapter I consider whether convict criminology can mitigate this risk and help steer a different path.

EIGHT

Concluding with convictions!

GUNS OF BRIXTON, BABYLON'S BURNING!

The gun pointing at me is held by a teenager. It is almost as big as he is. The whole thing is faintly ridiculous and terrifying. Although he is younger than me, still distinctly boy-ish, the gun is very real and loaded. I can see his finger, his hand steady, his eyes not. He is scared and so am I. A small group of us have marched up to the gates of a large British army fort squatting on Andersonstown Road in West Belfast. We are carrying our banners and shouting 'troops out!'. The local Irish guys with us cannot believe we have got so close to the fort without being warned off. As we push our luck and advance on the small group of soldiers, including the teenager, they are ordered back into the fort. We carry on shouting, beating on the corrugated iron walls for added effect.

The next day I get my second close-up view of a gun. It is a pistol, held up in the air in the middle of a crowd of cheering men, women and children. The speeches have just finished, the rally commemorating the introduction in 1971 of internment without trial is almost over. Just behind me there is a commotion and then there he is – balaclava pulled slightly awry over one eye, a plastic gloved hand waving the gun aloft. The clinical glove surprises me almost as much as the gun. No prints, no forensics. The crowd begin to chant 'I–I–IRA! I–I–IRA!' and next to me a man lifts his young son up over his shoulders for a better view. The mood is ecstatic. Nervously, I take a couple of hasty pictures, but no one minds. It's a show of force, it's for the cameras as much as the crowd.

Later, in the customary riots that gather around the street bonfires, plastic bullets are fired as the Royal Ulster Constabulary and the British Army try to reclaim streets that are clearly not theirs. It's scary but exciting.

Back in England a few weeks later, punk fanzines fizzle and pop with protest against the Thatcher government and everything it represents. Calls to all kinds of action are in the air. A new Irish band, U2, are on tour promoting their first album, *Boy*. In January 1981 they play Norwich University where I get backstage with the 'editor' of a local fanzine that I print. Dubliner Paul

Hewson, or Bono as he has decided to let himself be called, is becoming a star, a spokesman for a generation that doesn't want one.

My editor friend tells me that Bono and The Edge – the guitarist David Evans – have agreed to a short interview. I want to know what Bono/Hewson thinks, and will say, about the recent hunger strike in Long Kesh prison. About the war in Ireland. When we meet he mutters evasively and defensively that he can see we are both people who care deeply about our world, and then my friend leads Bono away before I lose him his chance of an interview.

The fanzine is called *Final Straw*, aptly enough as it turns out. Disgusted with Bono's interview platitudes, his rock pretensions and appetite for stardom, I determine a response, asking the 'editor' if I can put a page of graphics in the fanzine. Using a crude collage of lurid text alongside images I have found of the Pentagon grafted onto the head of a boiler-suited worker, I craft my riposte to Bono and everything he represents.

I include an anarchist symbol, mention something about death culture, banks that are like vampires. Then that petrol emotion kicks in, and I provide the recipe for a Molotov cocktail, suggesting suitable targets – banks, the unemployment office, McDonald's. Burn and run, like in Belfast. It's about six lines of crudely typed, roughly pasted lines of text, over a slightly obscure but striking image of the military–industrial complex's colonisation of our souls. It probably takes me less than an hour, but will shape my future.

In March Bobby Sands begins the second hunger strike in Long Kesh prison to demand the restoration of prisoner's political status and derail the British government's criminalisation strategy.

In April, the fanzine pages printed, I hand them over to the 'editor' to staple together and distribute. I hitch down to London to visit my sisters, one in Brixton, the other in Finsbury Park. It's an uneventful weekend, or so I think until I turn on the telly. I'm in Finsbury Park, just back from Brixton and Brixton is on the evening news. There's burning. And looting. Four years after the Sex Pistols mere anarchy is loosed upon the UK. The centre cannot hold. No-one appears to know why.

The next day I hitch back to Norwich and drop into the radical bookshop I've helped to set up over the last couple of years. My friends there are agitated. They've been raided and tell me that the police are looking for me. The local paper got hold of a copy of the fanzine and called the police about my collage. It didn't go down well with the news on TV. The police have seized all the copies of *Final Straw* from the local shops, and want to interview me.

The next morning at dawn they arrive at my home and arrest me. About nine months later I am charged with Incitement to Commit Criminal Damage by Fire – it's arson by another name. And slowly the wheels of justice turn until I am convicted and sentenced to three months in prison.

I should probably be grateful, the maximum sentence is 'life' and until then I thought that mortification was what happened when you said that 'Take Me to the River' was Talking Head's best song, and then someone told you it was Al Green's. And you didn't even know who Al Green was.

In Ireland Bobby Sands and nine other young men die slow, unimaginably horrible deaths in prison as Margaret Thatcher consolidates her hold over the political imagination in Britain.

England's dreaming: class, convictions, criminology

The possibilities of insider perspectives, of ex-prisoner scholars contributing to criminological knowledge, and knowledge of prison in particular, are rich and exciting but 'insiders' are never positioned in a single or fixed place. George Orwell (1937), for example, talks candidly of his position as a kind of class insider in examining both the upper and lower reaches of the English class system. According to Raymond Williams (1971), Orwell possessed a special advantage because he could look at England with an insider's first-hand knowledge of the British Empire. Taken from his time working as a colonial police officer, this simultaneously equipped him with an outsider's perspective on domestic English life. Like Chinua Achebe speaking from a West African perspective on racism in English literature, Orwell can speak from inside the metropole, and from outside. It gives his writing about England and Empire a visceral force:

> I was in the Indian Police Force five years, and by the end of that time I hated the imperialism I was serving with a bitterness which I can probably not make clear. In the free air of England that kind of thing is not fully intelligible. In order to hate imperialism you have got to be part of it. (Orwell, 1937, 145)

Orwell knew that having been a part of the imperial machine provided him with special insights into its mechanisms and sentiments. The prevailing myths of its civilising mission were transparently false to him because of his intimate knowledge of the brutality he encountered and then rejected. He knew from experience that the elevated material position of England was the product of exploited labourers who spanned a large part of the world. He had been among them himself. As he put it in his 1939 essay 'Not counting niggers', 'What we forget is that the overwhelming bulk of the British proletariat does not live in Britain but in Asia and Africa…This is the system which we all live on' (Orwell, in Orwell and Angus, 1968, 397).

There is equivalent potential in convict criminology to furnish criminology with richer insider perspectives on prison and criminal justice that draw on direct personal experience of being imprisoned. Many former prison officers, prison governors, police and probation officers have taken to criminology like ducks to water but not many ex-prisoners. Academics passing through prison on research excursions can provide insightful accounts of prison life, but there are missing voices and perspectives from inside prisons. The realities of prison life, like life in 'the colonies' according to Orwell, are not 'fully intelligible' to those living or working exclusively in the academic equivalent of England –the university.

Few criminologists will admit to hating prison because to do so would be regarded as unprofessional, revealing unscientific bias and prejudice. I cannot escape the fact that my feelings about prison will always be based on both direct experience of imprisonment and academic study of its social effects. Its academic fascinations and peculiar charisma are tempered with experience. A convict criminology critique of prison may or may not bear traces of hatred, but such sentiments derive from having been personally subject to the distance between the rhetoric and the reality of prison life, the sentimentality of its civilising mission and the sometimes casual, sometimes calculating brutality of the institution.

Writing in the 1930s, Orwell is unequivocal about the role of class society in fostering the kinds of contempt for humanity he discovered in Britain's colonies. Educated at Eton, he recognised the way misanthropy is so easily dressed up as philanthropy, and he rejected the ruling-class ideas of his peers. However, he could not fully jettison the disdain for working-class people which remains such a pervasive, but usually undisclosed, feature of the English middle and upper classes: 'At a distance I could agonise over their suffering, but I still hated them and despised them when I came anywhere near them…To the shock-absorbers of the bourgeoisie, such as myself, 'common people still appeared brutal and repulsive' (Orwell, 1937, 142–3).

Williams (1971, 18,) makes an observation that the Eton-educated British Prime Minister, David Cameron, and his chums would do well to learn. Williams says it is almost impossible to convince middle- and upper-class people who have had 'a separated education that they are not, in the most central ways, English'. This is because the treasured myths of England which they have created, their idea of England and its history, have been almost exclusively in the hands of a small minority. But that is changing. Because people such as David Cameron and George Osborne belong to a class that, as Williams (1971, 18) points out, 'has done most of the writing, directed most of the institutions, and is most readily recognised abroad' does not mean that they are typical, simply more powerful. This class minority's images and imagination may have defined Englishness in the past, but they are struggling to find a future for it.

Parts of today's ascendant class, the property-owning 'middle' class, are still seeking the England that eluded Orwell, a replacement for a waning imperial England, even though a vibrant alternative frequently stares it in the face in the multicultural conviviality of the expanding urban polis (Gilroy, 2004). Liberal democracy has provided well for them. The once insurgent class who challenged the despotic aristocracy and landed gentry of the eighteenth and nineteenth century with a contradictory claim for universality and equality have ensured that as democracy spread it became increasingly identified with its shallowest aspects. The Men of Property, the bourgeoisie, put women, non-propertied labourers, the colonised and the natural world in a framework of domination and exploitation known as either 'modernity' or white-supremacist capitalist patriarchy, according your point of view (Plumwood, 1995). The state has been rolled out and rolled back according to the fluctuating balance of power between conservative reaction and radical progression.

It is no accident that for Europe and the US, the social relations of the twenty-first century are starting to resemble an amalgam of those of the sixteenth and nineteenth – the feudal and the modern (Retort, 2004). They are conditions that should remind us that the creation of modern criminal justice institutions, such as the police, was often opposed as much by the aristocracy and the gentry as they were the working class. Then, as now, the super-rich simply wanted to look after themselves and secure their assets. There was no such thing as society.

England's cocooned and conservative bourgeoisie cannot tear itself away from the rear-view mirror even though it finds no consolation in its rapidly receding images. Theirs is an England that no longer has a colonial frontier to drive it forward and enrich the metropolitan core. The various men and masculinities once mobilised for Queen, Country and Empire have few homes to go to and less territory to conquer. For everyone but the globetrotting cosmopolitan elite, 'England' is a dismal kind of politics in which to be stuck: no road ahead and no road back. In this post-colonial limbo, the criminal justice system has expanded to gather up the men of the marginalised precariat, the men of no property, who find themselves increasingly dumped into prisons or prison-like places (Wacquant, 2007; Standing, 2014). Prisons become simply the fullest expression of all those forces that exclude them from society, holding them apart, disqualified, down and out of sight.

The business of criminology as usual: fail better

'Ever tried. Ever failed. No matter. Try again. Fail again. Fail better' is the forlorn prescription that Samuel Beckett (1983) offers as a bulwark against the existential ennui his plays and prose explore with such confounding effect. Beckett's penchant for barren minimalism, delicate paranoia, insecurity and self-conscious marginality resonate powerfully with penal effects. Or perhaps, as Terry Eagleton (2006) observes, they may just indulge Irish vistas of passive colonial victimhood, implying 'you can do no more than sit and wait for deliverance'. 'Fail better' is what Foucault (1979) had in mind when he analysed the functional dimensions of the constant efforts to reform and reinvent prisons, efforts that Kropotkin had experienced, analysed and dismissed as futile in 1887.

Criminologists and criminology have largely failed to dislodge the popular modern myth that police control the level of crime in society. We have had very little impact on the widely held belief that the best way to control crime is to arrest offenders and put them behind bars somewhere. We have operated most successfully as Orwell's 'shock-absorbers', evening out the bumpy ride of modernity's juggernaut (Young, 2007) with reassuring scientific formulations rather than building resistance to its progress or plotting another horizon for it. To extend Orwell's analogies, if criminologists are to become something other than the 'the shock-absorbers of the bourgeoisie', fine-tuning their management of criminal justice systems that help secure the neoliberal order, we could do with something more than 'criminology as usual', perhaps something unheard of.

One of the ambitions behind the establishment of convict criminology both in the USA and, more recently in the UK, is to develop new partnerships and conversations with prisoners and ex-prisoners with a view to expanding the resources from which criminologists draw. Encouraging ex-prisoner academics in to criminology can significantly enlarge the criminological imagination (Young, 2011). Being involved with convict criminology means challenging the study of criminals as objects and crime as a 'thing' rather than a set of social relations. Prisons are not sociological zoos populated by exotic specimens of humanity. Neither are they politically neutral instruments gathering law breakers into containment and protecting citizens from harm. If criminology is to become something more than sociology stripped of an emancipatory agenda (Bauman, 2014) it must find a more effective way of challenging the relentless growth of prisons.

During the 1960s and 1970s in Italy, France, Ireland and other European countries prison populations were supplemented by the influx of thousands of radical socialist, republican and anarchist activists. Sociology and criminology were transformed by the dialogue that emerged from the critical convergence with Marxism, feminism and anarchism and the realities of penal life. In the incidental tumult of the times, prisoners and professors sometimes found themselves co-located and with coincident interests.

In the USA the failure to effectively challenge racism, the policing of the civil rights movements, and the degradations prompted by 'the war on drugs' shovelled growing numbers of black people into prison. The convergence in prison of black nationalism with Islam generated networks of solace, support and resistance. In the 1970s and 1980s these networks and forms of identification were simply anomalous to white America's sense of itself. Today, they reflect a different challenge as the modernity of 'the West' is confronted by insurgent Islamism (Hamm, 2013; Dearey, 2014; Silke, 2013; Sayyid, 1997). One of the triumphs of the neoliberal project is the installation of the belief that there is no alternative (TINA) to its relentless progression – known as the TINA doctrine. Islamism, by default or by design, has effectively positioned itself as an alternative, and as such it has become the primary threat to neoliberal hegemony.

In the second decade of the twenty-first century the two principal domestic institutions where the state identifies radicalisation as a threat are prisons and universities (Brown and Saeed, 2015). In each, the radicals it targets are not Marxists but Muslims. In the UK, Alison Leibling et al's (2015) work in high security prisons has established a unique dialogue with these prisoners, drawing explicit parallels with Laurie Taylor and Stan Cohen's pathbreaking studies of the 1970s. Though the new times are different times, Leibling et al (2015, 77) find in their prison 'the same processes of social control in polarising, labelling and confirming its own stereotypes'. Fashioning the conditions of possibility for dialogue proves hard work, but it opens minds if not doors. They find political consciousness rising in the face of lengthening sentences and harsher treatments, in recognition of connections they find between prison life, structural inequalities and their faith. Their dialogue group thrives as '[e]thical and political themes emerged with power and energy' prompting Liebling et al (2015, 78) to speculate whether '[l]ong term prisoners were the budding "new criminologists"' of the twenty-first century.

In the twentieth century the communist horizon (Dean, 2012) defined the prospects of radical thought and provided a narrative for why the world was the way it was and how it could become otherwise. It helped to dispel the myth that violence was something perpetrated only by 'thugs' or terrorists, by arguing that violence could be structural and systemic. Those earlier myths are returning. Today it is not Thomas Paine, the *Rights of Man*, Rosa Luxemburg and the *Communist Manifesto* that are the spectres stalking Europe, it is a fear of fundamentalism (Sayyid, 1997; see also Gordon, 2008). The religious vocabularies of Islam are securing social traction on increasingly complex political problems. Religious idioms redefine political protests, and discontent is increasingly articulated in the language of Islamic ethics. Western corruption, affluence and venal excess become sufficient explanations for underemployment, ethnic marginality and poor health or housing facilities. Religious metaphysics starts to replace political economy in the lexicons of street activists and international solidarity.

The resurgence of Islam is posing questions that Europe and America are struggling to answer and two very different institutions, prisons and universities, are in the front line of efforts to advance that struggle. Whether they are looking at the same questions, or are on the same side of the struggle should be an issue for criminologists. How, for example, are they connected to the questions Fanon (2001) posed when he diagnosed that the 'European game' was 'finally over' and urged a search for a new Europe and a post-colonial humanism that could fulfil its promises?

Predicaments of auto-ethnography

My research and direct personal experience of prisons is restricted to just three months' incarceration, three English prisons, two of them separated from the first by over 100 miles and more than 30 years. For as long as I have worked around the criminal justice system and criminology, having personal experience of imprisonment has troubled me, albeit in a low-key kind of way. I didn't realise how much I would appreciate working through these private troubles by connecting them to the public issues that I have found so compelling in criminology: issues of social justice, ideas about freedom, the problem of men, the role of law, the possibilities of social order and the significance of history.

Auto-ethnography is becoming more widely recognised as a viable method for deploying personal narratives to explore social or cultural issues, but within criminology it remains peripheral (see Jewkes, 2012). It is an approach sometimes dismissed as indulgent or merely experimental, and as such it exposes the author to an unusual degree of scrutiny (Dashper, 2015). I am still troubled that I risk claiming too much for my very brief experiences of imprisonment and the glancing blow they delivered to my prospects. I've now spent more hours in prison as a researcher or a guest than I have as a prisoner which somewhat undermines the primacy afforded to my notional convict perspective. But there are two kinds of time inside and they do, I think, in the end, make a difference to anyone approaching the prison again as a scholar, and particularly as a criminologist.

Something of this difference resides in a remark I recall, but cannot properly cite, from an eminent former Chief Inspector of Prisons in the UK. Reflecting, in a newspaper article, on his work revealing and reforming the way prisons operate, he noted that for all the good reform does, it was ever the case that prison 'sits on a road that leads ultimately to the concentration camp'. Society, he said, neglects this awkward fact at its peril. It is something, an immanent truth perhaps, that prisoners can sense more intuitively than most. Convict criminologists, ex-prisoners writing sociologically about the experience, the institution of prison and the way society thinks about crime and punishment, may have something valuable to offer criminology. They can be helpfully guided by what the poet Adrienne Rich writes about the way silenced experience gives way to language as people once muted begin to express themselves. She says that this involves 'not simply learning the jargon of the elite, fitting unexceptionably into the status quo, but learning that language can be used as a means of changing reality' (Rich, 1980, cited by Miles, 2005, xii).

Without wanting to sound too melodramatic I don't think anyone touched by prison, either as a worker or as a prisoner, is ever quite the same or will ever entirely forget the experience. It accounts, at least in part, for the determination and dogged persistence of the penal reform movement and the passion of the abolitionist. For a prisoner, it can leave a mark on your soul as much as a stain on your character, even if it doesn't totally re-shape it, as intended.

Prison's gruesome totalitarian implications, however far distant, are registered in personal experience and various levels of consciousness. This is not as fanciful or rhetorical as it may seem. Goffman (1961, 56, emphasis in original), for example, compares the 'secondary adjustments' men make in the asylum as 'lodgement[s] for the self, *a churinga* in which the soul is felt to reside'. Not so very different from Erwin James' (2013) remark about the way 'you live in your head when you are in prison'. Life behind bars means retreating behind your eyes. Not so very different, perhaps, from Voldemort's 'horcrux' in JK Rowling's saga, and the resulting scar that marks Harry Potter's encounter with the 'Dark Lord'!

The pacifist philosopher Simone Weil (1977) writes about the mutually corrupting effect of the use of force on those who wield it and those subject to it. Her remarkable re-reading of Homer's *Illiad* turns it into an extended allegory of the effects of force on a person. It illuminates so much out of which prisons are made:

> Might is that which makes a thing of anybody who comes under its sway. When exercised to the full, it makes a thing of a man in the most literal sense, for it makes him a corpse…The might which kills outright is an elementary and coarse form of might. How much more varied in its devices, how much more astonishing in its effects is that other which does not kill, or which delays killing. It must surely kill, or it will perhaps kill, or else it is only suspended above him whom it may at any moment destroy. This of all procedures turns a man to stone. From the power to transform him into a thing by killing him there proceeds another power, and much more prodigious, that which makes a thing of him while he still lives.[1]

In another essay Weil describes how the use of force transforms a person into 'a compromise between a man and a corpse' (Weil, 2009, 94), which is an excellent approximation of what a long-term prison

---

[1] This quote is taken from a brilliant discussion of Weil's work in a US prison workshop convened by Drewe Leder (2000). His collection of prison workshop discussions of philosophy, politics, ethics and religion is an exceptionally rewarding book to read.

sentence sets out to achieve. Working in socialist movements in the 1930s and 1940s, Weil is propelled to write by the rising prominence of fascism in Europe and her concerns about the threat it represents in terms of the generalisation of force in social relations. Her nightmare visions are uniquely effective in evoking what happens in prison, and to those that keep them there. Force corrupts those who wield it as much as it destroys those subject to it, according to Weil.

Stepping up for, or coming out with, convict criminology?

Chapter 1 discussed some of the troublesome images and terminology associated with the idea of convict criminology. This extends to and includes the issue of how to disclose the existence of criminal convictions and the academic identity of convict criminologists. In the USA where convict criminology is most firmly established and members, potential and otherwise, more numerous the issue is phrased in terms of 'coming out'. Stephen C Richards (2010, 173), for instance, tells of John Irwin's role in helping new members at conferences 'prepare for their "coming out"', where they introduce themselves to their audience by relating their criminal activity, convictions and prison time, to their research'. He concludes that '[O]nce they step out of the closet they are members of the Convict Criminology Group.'

Disclosure of criminal convictions is more complex than it might appear because of the implication of confession, and by extension the issue of reanimating shame, guilt and stigma. Even though it is central to the epistemological leverage that is claimed for convict criminology, the issue remains a sensitive and delicate one. In theoretical terms, Michel Foucault has muddied the waters with his analysis of the way the compulsions of confession have returned from distant ecclesiastical traditions to become one of the main rituals we rely on for the production of truth. 'Western man' says Foucault (1978, 59) 'has become a confessing animal.' Society has become obsessed with 'extracting from the depths of oneself, in between the words, a truth which the very form of confession holds out like a shimmering mirage'. Foucault challenges the idea that subjectivity in general and sexual identity in particular are authentic inner truths that are simply validated by being surfaced by, for example, 'coming out' as gay.

Some 'queer' theorists have argued against Foucault's problematisation and for the extension of 'coming out' narratives beyond gay and lesbian cultures to more general 'legal, cultural and political discourses' (Burgess, 2005, 128). Declared identities expose the structures of all identities and thereby challenge the essentialism of dominant race and gender identities that rarely tell their own story or position themselves in struggles. In critical race studies, for example, the 'coming out white' narrative has taken this approach, though not without controversy (Ryden and Marshall, 2012). In the 1980s, strategic essentialism encouraged building united struggles against racism through the endorsement of a strategic black identity that attempted to include the diverse peoples of the African diaspora and others subject to colonialism (Brah, 1996). In this version of strategic essentialism it was even possible to argue, persuasively, that the Irish (in Britain) were black (see Rolston, 1999; 2003; Garner, 2003, 2007).

Eve Sedgwick (1990, 71) notes how the terminology of 'the closet' and 'coming out' are 'now verging on all-purpose phrases' deployed whenever there appears to be a question of crossing politically charged lines of representation. In these terms, 'coming out' with a self-declaration of a specific identity is a way of claiming belonging to an otherwise devalued group of people, an assertion of pride against shame, presence against erasure, endurance against oppression. As Chirrey (2003) indicates 'coming out is typically viewed as the action of individuals on the margin of society whose lives, lifestyles, or personal characteristics are subject to social approbation'. It is a strategy of minoritised and stigmatised groups negotiating access and acceptance and the right to disrupt the hitherto conventional boundaries of belonging.

It is reasonably obvious that 'coming out' in the terms established by minority sexual communities is not really analogous with the 'coming out' of convict criminologists. There is no vital but suppressed history, no vibrant underground network or subjugated community of knowledge and experience that disclosing a conviction or imprisonment liberates. The cadence of defiance is necessarily absent, not least in deference to the feelings of victims and their families. The aspirant community of belonging is a small branch of social science, not an emancipatory political vision. There is no essentialism to unpack and no strategic need to construct one. I hesitate to recognise the utility of the rhetoric for convict criminologists and am reluctant to use it. A prison sentence is not a closet. Convictions are not identities. The 'self' of the convict criminologist is not remade by disclosure, and the suggestion even if only by implication, association or linguistic convenience, that the process is analogous or equivalent to gay and lesbian liberation struggles seems disingenuous.

Adding to the treachery of criminology

In the 1980s, as criminology expanded, one of the critiques levelled against it was that it was a discipline based on a single unitary category, crime, which could not withstand the empirical evidence and theoretical analysis of its diversity (Smart, 1990; Sumner, 1994). By virtue of nominative determinism, criminology was doomed to focus on crime, and as the critics insist, 'crime has no ontological reality': it doesn't exist and has to be invented. Criminology, the critics argue, simply colludes in this self-serving invention. What the critics did not anticipate was that rather than conceding to the infinite diversity of human behaviour by disappearing, criminology has itself diversified into a series of corresponding and overlapping specialisms. Victimology established a series of perspectives that focused less exclusively on perpetrators while more criminological genres have emerged on everything from hate crime to green crime. There are criminologies of sport, border criminologies focusing on migration, green criminologies examining environmental issues, developmental criminologies aiming at the life course, competing realist and hyper-realist criminologies, cultural criminologies, feminist criminologies, and, still, anti-criminology criminologists who call themselves zemologists, who prefer the vocabulary of social harms, and perhaps there's no harm in that.

Millie (2016) discusses the proliferations of contemporary criminology with reference to the ways in which the surrealists, such as Marcel Duchamp, disrupted the boundaries of what art was considered to be. For Duchamp, art was what artists did. Simple as. The surrealist painter, Rene Magritte elaborates on the theme of what art is or is not, with his famous picture, 'The Treachery of Images', which shows a picture of a smoker's pipe with the cryptic caption: 'Ceci n'est pas une pipe' (This is not a pipe). Perhaps they were both criminologists simply posing provocatively as artists because there is a recurring tendency among criminologist for this kind of disavowal. The multitudes of criminology discussed by Millie can certainly resemble what Alfred Jarry, another contemporary of Duchamp, refers to as the science of imaginary solutions (see Hugill, 2014).

Convict criminologists labour more heavily than most under the unifying category of crime at its most basic and legal. We are part of the illusions it invents, the 'criminals' that are not like other people. We are the type of people of whom Foucault warns, people sorted into neat categories to identify social boundaries, but our diverse biographies immediately give the lie to this typology. In the UK the number of convicted convict criminologists operating within the established definition can be numbered on the fingers of one hand. Or possibly two. My three-month conviction in 1982 for Incitement to Commit Criminal Damage by Fire (Arson) bears little in common with the convictions of Bill Davies from the University of Leeds, Dave Honeywell from University of York and Andreas Aresti from the University of Westminster. We're all relatively open about having been to prison and now teach criminology at various universities. We conduct research about prison and with prisoners, and prison personnel, but apart from that, we are as different to each other as we are from anyone else in criminology, with contrasting perspectives and priorities. What we have in common with each other, and with those from the US, Australia and New Zealand is time behind bars, and that we are nearly all white men. Dave, Bill and Andy are not particularly unusual ex-prisoners but are exceptionally unusual criminologists because their working-class backgrounds combine with a route to higher education that includes the diverting force of a prison sentence. This provides the basis for developing some further distinctive contributions to criminological knowledge, but it is work that remains to be done. It confronts us with a challenge of including women's perspectives, who form approximately 5 per cent of the prison population in the UK, and whose trajectories into and out of prison are distinctively different to men's.

The disproportionally large population of men from black and minority ethnic groups are absent from the publishing activity of the British Convict Criminology group, though there is some indication of their presence and potential in some of our other activities. These include supporting prison learners, and those ex-prisoners with an appetite to develop academic careers in criminology but who have yet to complete postgraduate qualifications. As discussed in Chapter Three, this sort of work was pioneered and developed by John Irwin and convict criminology in the USA. The result is a vibrant and expanding community of ex-prisoner scholars, aided and abetted by the Canadian *Journal of Prisoners on Prison* (*JPP*). The existence of the US group, and the *JPP*, is a beacon and inspiration. It may not be a model suitable for all, not least because US penal conditions are so specific to the US and a global scandal no-one would want to emulate, but in the US convict criminology has demonstrated the viability and vitality of the concept.

Convict criminology, or variations around the theme of making academic use of prison experience, can now be found in Europe. Chapter Four traced the diverse currents of European experience, and their various political contexts, retro-fitting Peter Kropotkin and Victor Serge into a capacious mould of convict criminology. The recent formation of British convict criminology has attracted widespread support from the membership of various criminology groups, such as the British Society of Criminology and the European Group for the Study of Deviance and Social Control. With the support of the US group it has established a webpage and contacts with KROM in Norway, and prison activist scholars in other European countries.

One of the features to emerge in the account presented in this book is the longer historical roots of convict perspectives in criminology, and the role of imprisonment in containing political dissent and protest. The term 'convict criminology' is not to all tastes for the way it tends to efface this political function of imprisonment. For Irish criminologists, for example, the terminology may be regarded as particularly toxic owing to the British tradition of suppressing Irish political activity through the development of criminal law and criminal justice institutions. It is no coincidence that the precursors of the British police, the Peace Preservation Force, were established in Ireland by Sir Robert Peel when he was Chief Secretary for Ireland between 1812 and 1816. For Peel, there was no contradiction between the first term and the third: peace meant pacification. Out of this experience the London Metropolitan police was established in 1829, with the aim of suppressing growing support in London for the Irish Republican Brotherhood, the Fenians. A longer and wider history of convict criminology thus illuminates some of the complex relationships between crime and politics that are as vital today as they were in the nineteenth century.

In the US, Frank Tannenbaum and Saul Alinskey each found their political imagination confronted by the force of criminal justice and unfolding global events. The fate of George Jackson and the neglected insights of WEB Du Bois reveal how closely prison and criminal justice go hand in hand with the politics of race, challenging convict criminology to raise its intellectual game and meet the theoretical task of explaining how it is that the US locks up black people at a higher rate than did the apartheid regime of South Africa while presenting itself as leader of 'the free world'.

The practices of 'tagging' that Tannenbaum identified have now taken new digital forms in the circulation and monitoring of criminal records, discussed in Chapter Five. Criminology has neglected these recent features of 'labelling' and their viral impacts. It has failed to appreciate the impact of being regarded primarily as a problem, whether it is at the border, at the threshold of work or in the possibilities of intimacy. No doubt some of this neglect arises from the masculinist blindspots of criminology that has funnelled research activity into the narrow concerns of risk management, public spaces and private property. Convict criminologists can usually shake themselves free of the stigma of a criminal record, but the metrics of risk provide an indelible digital trail that can seriously snag their careers and their mobility. Convict criminologists can theorise this relationship and build empirical resources to illuminate further the impact of criminal records, enriching criminology and engaging its emancipatory possibilities.

The steep upward gradient of the roads that lead to university and into academic careers is the opposite of that which tilts downward toward prison. It's a long hard climb back up. This presents ex-prisoner scholars with specific challenges and the roads into academic life are increasingly littered with administrative obstacles and financial hurdles. The simple facts of possessing a criminal record and the mandatory screening of students and academic applicants for criminal convictions aren't exactly helpful. Marshalling recognition of these difficulties and support in overcoming them is one objective of convict criminology groups. By encouraging prisoners and ex-prisoners with social science ambitions convict criminology can be well placed to provide theoretical, empirical and reflexive development of the emerging new potentials of criminology

Convict criminology: for a gendered criminology

Prison is a heavily gendered institution where men's behaviour and identities are the focus, but rarely analysed in critical gender specific terms (see Sabo et al, 2001; Maycock and Hunt, 2017). Convict criminology, which will inevitably be composed predominantly of men because of the enormous differential in rates of offending and incarceration, needs to ensure gender specific analysis becomes more commonplace and theoretically robust. Failure to do so not only projects men's experiences onto women as if it were the generality of prison life, thereby occluding women's experience of penality, it also denies analytical purchase on one of its most distinctive features. Men's prisons are very masculine places, places created almost exclusively by, and for, men. Reading much of the prison literature you might be forgiven for thinking this was simply an accident of fate, or just so obvious as to be unworthy of comment. It is my hope that by listening closely to how men who have been in prison as prisoners connect their experiences of prisons to their interest in criminology, convict criminology can provide new and telling insights into the relationships between men and society, between men and crime, prison and criminology.

Prison masculinities are becoming a distinctive theme in penal scholarship (Sabo et al, 2001; Maycock and Hunt, 2017). The characteristics and history of the institution suggest that just as military experience presents certain paradigmatic forms of masculinity, so the prison offers a variety of masculine archetypes collected around power, strength, protection and invulnerability (Young 2005) . Using Aristotle's original conception of human life as 'animal being with politics', Easton (2017) considers the potential of the prison to develop the political consciousness of the prisoner as a zōon politikon. Here, in the power play of prison and prisoner, is every kind of politics, suggests Easton, the pragmatics of ruling and being ruled, the management of needs and the negotiation of affection and intimacy.

The prison plays an important role in the culture of danger and risk that are central to the ascendancy of neoliberalism that casts everyone's vulnerabilities into a narrow, instrumental subtext of risk-management. Vulnerability has become increasingly misrecognised as an exclusively undesireable weakness, a liability to harm that generates, in turn, an obsessive risk-awareness. These risks become the personal responsibility of the individual (Gilson, 2014).

An alternative, less dichotomous, feminist ethics of vulnerability would recognise its potentials as a source of strength and creativity as well as alertness to dangers to be avoided (Cixous, 1986; Butler, 2009; Gilson, 2014). As Cixous (1986) suggests, these variable forms of vulnerability are not always easy or comfortable alternatives, and they can be wearing and wearying. They involve refusing to presume the threat of others, a stance which Bauman (1993) indicates is the pre-requisite of an emancipatory post-modern ethics. Vulnerabilities sustain important fragilities and receptivities, and foster a radical and more positive form of self-dispossession. This self-dispossession contrasts dramatically with the robbery practiced by the prison. In the radical version, self-dispossession becomes a refusal to accommodate the rationality prescribed by a prison vision of the individual: the requirement to master oneself, and possibly others; to capitalise the will and the conscience only in the service of the self; to establish the boundaries of the self and police oneself accordingly – to be tough not tender. The quest for privatisation, control and invulnerability draws from neoliberal dynamics in which personal danger and risk are regarded as omnipresent and forever proliferating. It calls forth an entrepreneurial subjectivity focused on controlling and managing socially generated uncertainties primarily through self-management and self-enhancement, the values so heavily promoted by the neoliberal prison's rehabilitative rhetoric.

The modern prison for men is now concerned to produce not a docile body submitting to the brute authority of law, but someone geared up to become an entrepreneur of himself. Although convict criminologists can ironically exemplify this fate, it can be avoided by living our vulnerabilities differently, more appreciably, more empathically, re-conceptualising the relationships between vulnerability, harms and criminology, and our own lives as criminologists and ex-prisoners. To challenge the cultivation of entrepreneurial subjectivities and the pursuit of invulnerability, convict criminology can take strength from the fragility, variety and ambiguity of the prison experiences on which it is based. In these terms, a critical ontology is particularly important to the development of convict criminology perspectives because our experiences of imprisonment provide us with particularly direct experience of the ways in which we are in society and society is in us.

References

Achebe, C, 1977, An image of Africa: Racism in Conrad's *Heart of Darkness*, *Norton Anthology of Theory and Criticism*, pp 1781–94, New York: Norton, 2001

AFSC (American Friends Service Committee), 1971, *Struggle for justice: A report on crime and punishment*, Philadelphia, PA: AFSC

Agamben, G, 1998, *Homo sacer: Sovereign power and bare life*, Standford, CA: Stanford University Press

Agonizo, B, 2007, Preface, in SL Gabbidon (ed) *WEB Du Bois on crime and justice: Laying the foundations of sociological criminology*, Farnham: Ashgate

AHREC (Australian Human Rights and Equality Commissions), 2005, *Human rights: On the record – Guidelines for the prevention of discrimination in employment on the basis of criminal record*, Sydney: AHRC

Alcoff, L, 2007, Epistemologies of ignorance: Three types, in S Sullivan, N Tuana (eds) *Race and epistemologies of ignorance*, pp 39–57, Albany, NY: SUNY Press

Alexander, M, 2012, *The new Jim Crow: Mass incarceration in the age of colorblindness*, New York: The New Press

Alinsky, SD, 1946, *Reveille for radicals*, New York: Random House, 1969

Alinsky, SD, 1971, *Rules for radicals: A pragmatic primer for realistic radicals*, New York: Vintage, 1972

Alinsky, SD, 1972, Interview, *Playboy*, www.bahaistudies.net/neurelitism/library/alinsky_interview_1967.pdf

Althusser, L, Balibar, E, 1997, Reading capital, London: Verso Anthias, F. (2013) 'Moving beyond the Janus face of integration and diversity discourses: Towards an intersectional framing,' *The Sociological Review*, vol, 61, pp. 323-343

Anthias, F and Yuval-Davis, N. (1993) racialized boundaries: race, nation, gender, colour and class and the anti-racist struggle, London. Routledge

Aresti, A, 2012, Developing a convict criminology group in the UK, *Journal of Prisoners on Prison* 21, 1 and 2,148-165

Aresti, A, 2014, Contraction in an age of expansion: A convict perspective, *Prison Service Journal* 211, 19–24

Aresti, A, Darke, S, 2015, Open prisons: An ex-prisoner perspective, *Prison Service Journal* 217, 14–16

Austin, J, 2003, The use of science to justify the imprisonment binge, in IR Ross, SC Richards (eds) *Convict criminology*, Belmont, CA: Wadsworth

Back, L, 2012, Take your reader there: Some notes on writing qualitative research, in *Writing on writing*, Durham: Durham University, www.dur.ac.uk/writingacrossboundaries/writingonwriting/lesback/

Bauman, Z, 1989, *Modernity and the holocaust*, Cambridge: Polity Press

Bauman, Z, 1990, Effacing the face: On the social management of moral proximity, *Theory, Culture and Society* 7, 5–38

Bauman, Z, 1993, *Postmodern ethics*, Cambridge: Polity Press

Bauman, Z, 2014, *What's the use of Sociology? Conversations with Michael Hviid Jacobsen and Keith Tester*, Cambridge: Polity Press

Becker, H, 1963, *Outsiders*, New York: Free Press

Beckett, S, 1983, *Worstward ho*, in Nohow On, New York. Grove Press

Belknap J, 2015, Activist criminology: Criminologists' responsibility to advocate for social and legal justice, *Criminology* 53, 1, 1–22

Benhabib, S, 1987, The generalized and the concrete other, in E Kittay, D Meyers (eds) *Women and moral theory*, New York: Rowman and Littlefield

Bennett, J, 1981, *Oral history and delinquency: The rhetoric of criminology*, Chicago, IL: University of Chicago Press

Beresford, D, 1987, *Ten men dead: The story of the 1981 Irish hunger strike*, London: Grafton Books

Berger, J, 1977, Cover endorsement, *Men in prison*, London: Writers and Readers Publishing Cooperative

Better Regulation Task Force, 1999, *Review of fit persons criteria*, London: The Stationery Office

Bhattacharyya, G, 2013, Regional narratives and post-racial fantasies in the English riots, *Journal for Cultural Research* 17, 2, 183–97

Blumstein, A, Wallman, J, 2006, *The crime drop in America*, Cambridge: Cambridge University Press

Bonilla-Silva, E, Dietrich, D, 2011, The sweet enchantment of color-blind racism in Obamerica, *The Annals of the American Academy of Political and Social Science* 634, 1, 190–206

Boone, M, 2011, Judicial Rehabilitation in the Netherlands: Balancing between safety and privacy, *European Journal of Probation* 3, 1 63–78

Bordo, S, 2003, *Unbearable weight: Feminism, western culture and the body*, Berkeley, CA: University of California Press

Boudin, C, 2011, Children of incarcerated parents: The child's constitutional right to the family relationship, *Journal of Criminal Law and Criminology* 101, 77–118

Boudin, K, 1998, Lessons from a mother's programme in prison: A psychosocial approach supports women and their children, *Women and Therapy* 21, 103

Bourdieu, P, 1981, Preface, in P Lazarsfeld, M Jahoda, H Zeisel (eds) *Les Chomeurs de Marienthal*, Paris: Les Editions de Minuit

Bourdieu, P, 2000, *Pascalian meditations*, Cambridge: Polity Press

Bosworth, M, 2004a, Review of J Ross, S Richards (eds) *Convict criminology*, *British Journal of Criminology* 44, 6, 988

Bosworth, M, 2004b, Theorising race and imprisonment: Towards a new penality, *Critical Criminology* 12, 2, 221–42

Bosworth, M, Hoyle, C (eds), 2012, *What is criminology?*, Oxford: Oxford University Press

Brah, A, 1996, *Cartographies of diaspora*, London: Routledge

Breiner, P, 1996, *Max Weber and democratic politics*, Ithaca, NY: Cornell University Press

Brown, KE, Saeed, T, 2015, Radicalisation and counter-radicalisation at British Universities: Muslim encounters and alternatives, *Ethnic and Racial Studies* 38, 11, 1952–68

Buber, M, 1958, *I and thou*, New York: Charles Scribner

Buhle, P, Schulman, N, 2005, *Wobblies: A graphic history of the industrial workers of the world*, London: Verso

Bull, M, 2010, *Punishment and sentencing: Risk, rehabilitation and restitution*, Victoria: Oxford University Press

Bulmer, M, 1982, The merits and demerits of covert participant observation, in M Bulmer (ed) *Social research ethics*, London: Macmillan

Burgess, S, 2005, Did the Supreme Court come out in Bush v Gore? Queer theory and the performance of the politics of shame, *Differences: A Journal of Feminist Cultural Studies* 16, 1, 126–46

Buroway, M, 2005, For public sociology, *American Sociological Review* 70, 1, 14–28

Butler, J, 2009, *Frames of war: When is life grievable?*, New York: Verso

Carlen, P (ed), 2008, *Imaginary penalities*, Cullompton: Willan

Change the Record, 2011, *Vicky's story*, www.changetherecord.org/stories/vickys-story,676,NAP.html

Cheliotis, LK, Xenakis, S, 2010, What's neoliberalism got to do with it? Towards a political economy of punishment in Greece, *Criminology and Criminal Justice* 10, 4, 353–73

Chirrey, D, 2003, 'I hereby Come Out': What sort of speech act is Coming Out?, *Journal of Sociolinguistics* 7,1, 24–37

Christie, N, 1977, Conflicts as property, *British Journal of Criminology* 17, 1–15

Cixous, H (1986) The Newly Born Woman, Minneapolis. University of Minnesota Press

Cohen, S, 1980, *Folk devils and moral panics*, London: Martin Robertson

Cohen, S, 1985, *Visions of social control: Crime, punishment, classification*, Cambridge: Polity Press

Cohen, S, 1996, Crime and politics: Spot the difference, *British Journal of Sociology* 47, 1, 1–21

Comfort, M, 2008, 'The best seven year I could'a done': The reconstruction of imprisonment as rehabilitation, in P Carlen (ed) *Imaginary penalties*, pp 252–74, Cullompton: Willan

Condry, R, Kotova, A, Minson, S, 2016, Social injustice and collateral damage: The families and children of prisoners, in B Crewe, Y, Jewkes, Y (eds) *The handbook of prisons*, Abingdon: Routledge

Connell, RW, 1983, *Which way is up: Essays on sex, class and culture*, Sydney: Allen and Unwin

Connell, RW, 1990, The state, gender, and sexual politics: Theory and appraisal, *Theory and Society* 19, 507–44

Connell, R, 1995, *Masculinities*, Cambridge: Polity Press

Connell, R, 2003, *Gender*, Cambridge: Polity Press

Connell, R, 2012, The poet of Autonomy: Antonio Negri as a social theorist, *Sociologica* 6, 1, 1–23

Cowburn, M, 2007, Men researching men in prison: The challenges for profeminist research, *Howard Journal of Criminal Justice* 46, 3, 276–88

Cowburn, M, 2013, Men researching violent men: Epistemologies, ethics and emotions in qualitative research, in B Pini, B Pease (eds) *Men, masculinities and methodologies*, pp 183–96, Basingstoke: Palgrave Macmillan

Cowburn, M, Featherstone, B, 2010, Editorial, *Fathers and fatherhood*, special issue, *Critical Social Policy* 30, 2, 163–4

CRB (Criminal Records Bureau), 2002, *Annual report and accounts 2001–2002*, London: The Stationery Office

CRE (Commission for Racial Equality), 2003a, *A formal investigation by the commission for racial equality into HM prison service of England and Wales. Part 1: The murder of Zahid Mubarek*, London: Commission for Racial Equality

CRE (Commission for Racial Equality), 2003b, *A formal investigation by the commission for racial equality into HM prison service of England and Wales. Part 2: Racial equality in prisons*, London: Commission for Racial Equality

Crewe, B, 2009, *The prisoner society: Power, adaption and social life in an English Prison*, Oxford: Oxford University Press

Crewe, B, 2011, Depth, weight, tightness: Revisiting the pains of imprisonment, B Crewe, Y Jewkes (eds) *Revisiting the pains of imprisonment*, special issue, *Punishment and Society* 13, 5, 509–29

Crewe, B, 2014, Not looking hard enough: Masculinity, emotion and prison research, *Qualitative Inquiry* 20, 4, 392–404

Crewe, B, Ievens, A, 2015, Closeness, distance and honesty in prison ethnography, in D Drake, R Earle, J Sloan (eds) *The Palgrave handbook of prison ethnography*, Palgrave Studies in Prisons and Penology, Basingstoke: Palgrave

Cuneen, C, Baldry, E, Brown, D, Schwartz M, Steel, A, 2013, *Penal culture and hyperincarceration: The revival of the prison*, Farnham: Ashgate

Daems, T, 2008, *Making sense of penal change*, Oxford: Oxford University Press

Dashper, K, 2015, Revise, resubmit and reveal? An auto-ethnographer's story of facing the challenges of revealing the self through publication, *Current Sociology* 63, 4, 511–27

Davies, W. (2015) Unique Position: Dual Identities as Prison Researcher and Ex-prisoner, in D Drake, R Earle, J Sloan (eds) *The Palgrave handbook of prison ethnography*, Palgrave Studies in Prisons and Penology, Basingstoke: Palgrave

Davis, A, 1971, *If they come in the morning: Voices of resistance*, New York: Third Press

Davis, A, 1983, *Women, race, and class*, New York: Vintage

Davis, A, 2003, *Are prisons obsolete?*, New York: Seven Stories Press

Davis, A, 2005, *Abolition democracy: Beyond prisons, torture, and empire*, New York: Seven Stories Press

Dawney, L, 2008, Racialization of central and east European migrants in Herefordshire, *Working Paper* 53, Brighton: Sussex Centre for Migration Research, University of Sussex

Dean, J (2012) The Communist Horizon, London. Verso.

Dearey, M, 2010, *Radicalisation: The life writings of political prisoners*, London: Routledge

Deleuze, G, 1992, Postscript on the societies of control, *October* 59, Winter, 3–7

Drake, D, Harvey, J, 2014, Performing the role of ethnographer: Processing and managing the emotional dimensions of prison research, *International Journal of Social Research Methodology* 17, 5, 489–501

Drake, DH, Earle, R, Sloan, J (eds), 2015, *The Palgrave handbook of prison ethnography*, Palgrave Studies in Prisons and Penology, Basingstoke: Palgrave

D'Souza, D, 1995, *The end of racism*, New York, NY: Free Press

Du Bois, WEB, 1903, *The souls of black folk*, New York: Dover Publications, 1994

Du Bois, WEB, 1923, Letter, http://oubliette.library.umass.edu/view/full/mums312-b023-i361

Du Bois, WEB, 1924, Letter, http://oubliette.library.umass.edu/view/full/mums312-b026-i396

Du Bois, WEB, 1935, *Black reconstruction in America 1860–1880*, New York: Free Press, 1970

Duneier, M, 2004, Three rules I go by in my ethnographic research on race and racism, in M Bulmer, J Solomos (eds) *Researching race and racism*, Basingstoke: Palgrave

Eagleton, T. (2006) 'Champion of Ambiguity', The Guardian http://www.theguardian.com/commentisfree/2006/mar/20/arts.theatre [accessed 17/03/2013]

Earle, R, 2009, Living in a box: Young men's prison identities, in W Taylor, R Earle, R Hester (eds) *Youth justice handbook: Theory, policy and practice*, Cullompton: Willan

Earle, R, 2011a, Boys' zone stories: Perspectives from a young men's prison, *Criminology and Criminal Justice* 11, 2, 129–43

Earle, R, 2011b, Prison and university: A tale of two institutions?, *Papers from the British Criminology Conference*, British Society of Criminology 11, 20–37, http://www.britsoccrim.org/volume11/pbcc_2011_Earle.pdf

Earle, R, 2011c, Ethnicity, multiculture and racism in a young offenders' institution, *Prison Service Journal* 197, September, 32

Earle, R, 2012, 'Who's the Daddy?' Ideas about fathers from a young men's prison, *The Howard Journal of Criminal Justice* 51, 4, 387–99

Earle, R, 2013, Inside white: Racism, ethnicity and social relations in English prisons, in C Phillips, C Webster (eds) *New directions in race, ethnicity and crime*, pp 160–77, Abingdon: Routledge

Earle, R, 2014, Insider and out: Reflections on a prison experience and research experience, *Qualitative Inquiry* 20, 5, 429–38

Earle, R, Phillips, C, 2012, Digesting men? Ethnicity, gender and food: Perspectives from a 'prison ethnography', *Theoretical Criminology* 16, 2, 141–56

Earle, R, Phillips, C, 2013, 'Muslim is the new black': New ethnicities and new essentialisms in the prison, *Race and Justice* 3, 2, 114–29

Earle, R, Phillips, C, 2015, Prison ethnography at the threshold of race, reflexivity and difference, in DH Drake, R Earle, J Sloan (eds) *The Palgrave handbook of prison ethnography*, Palgrave Studies in Prisons and Penology, Basingstoke: Palgrave

Earle, R. and Wakefield, A. (2012) Restorative justice and the right to move on: toward deinsti-tutionalising the stigma of a criminal conviction. In: Gavrielides, Theo ed. *Rights and Restoration within Youth Justice*. Canada: de Sitter

Easton, S, 2017, *The politics of the prison and the prisoner: Zoon politikon?*, London: Routledge

Ekunwe, I, Jones, R, 2012, Finnish criminal policy: From hard time to gentle justice, *Journal of Prisoners on Prison* 21, 1 and 2, 173–89

Empey, LT, 1970, Introduction: The players and the setting, in A Mannochio, J Dunn (eds) *'The time game': Two views of prison*, Beverley Hills, CA: Sage

Fanon, F, 1967, *Black skin: White masks*, London: Pluto

Fanon, F, 2001, *The wretched of the earth*, Harmondsworth: Penguin

Ferrell, J, 2010, Kropotkin, in K Hayward, S Maruna, J Mooney (eds) *Fifty key thinkers in criminology*, London: Routledge

Fields, K, Fields, B, 2012, *Racecraft: The soul of inequality in American life*, London: Verso

Finch, J. (1984) 'Its great to have someone to talk to: ethics and politics of interviewing women' in C. Bell and H. Roberts (eds) Social Researching: Politics, Problems Practice. London. Routledge.

Fisher, M, 2012, *Capitalist realism: Is there no alternative?*, Winchester: Zero Books

Fitzgerald, M, 1977, *Prisoners in revolt*, Harmondsworth: Penguin

Foucault, M, 1978, *The history of sexuality, Vol 1: An introduction*, New York: Random

Foucault, M, 1979, *Discipline and punish: The birth of the prison*, Harmondsworth: Penguin

Foucault, M, 1980, *Power/knowledge: Selected interviews and other writings 1972–1977*, New York: Pantheon Books

Frankenberg, R, 1993, *White women, race matters: The social construction of whiteness*, Minneapolis, MN: University of Minnesota Press

Freire, P, 1970, *Cultural action for freedom*, Harmondsworth: Penguin

Freire, P, 1985, *The politics of education: Culture, power and liberation*, Westport, CT: Bergin and Garvey

Gabbidon, S, 2007, *WEB Du Bois on crime and justice: Laying the foundations of sociological criminology*, Farnham: Ashgate

Gabbidon, S, 2014, *Race and Crime*, 4th edn, London: Sage

Gadd, D, Jefferson, T, 2007, *Psychosocial criminology: An introduction*, London: Sage

Gardiner. (1972) *Living it down - the problem of old convictions. A report of the Gardiner Committee*, London, Stevens & Sons, 1972

Garner, S, 2003, *Racism in the Irish experience*, London: Pluto

Garner, S, 2007, *Whiteness: An introduction*, London: Routledge Geertz, C, 1988, *Works and lives: The anthropologist as author*, Cambridge: Polity Press

Gilroy, P, 1987, *There ain't no black in the Union Jack*, London: Routledge

Gilroy, P, 1993, *The black Atlantic: Modernity and double consciousness*, London: Verso

Gilroy, P, 2000, *Between camps: Nations, culture and the allure of race*, London: Allen Lane

Gilroy, P, 2004, *After empire: Melancholia or convivial culture*, Abingdon: Routledge

Gilson, E, 2014, *The ethics of vulnerability: A feminist analysis of social life and practice*, Abingdon: Routledge

Giroux, H. A. (2008). *Against the Terror of Neoliberalism: Politics Beyond the Age of Greed*. Boulder CO.: Paradigm Publishers, University of British Columbia Press.

Goffman, E, 1959, *The presentation of self in everyday life*, New York: Anchor

Goffman, E, 1961, *Asylums: Essays on the social situation of mental patients and other inmates*, London: Penguin

Goffman, E, 1971, *Relations in public: Microstudies of the public order*, London: Allen Lane

Goldberg, D, 2012, 'When race disappears', *Comparative American Studies*10, 2–3,116–27

Goldman, E, 1931, *Living my life*, The Anarchist Library, http://theanarchistlibrary.org/library/emma-goldman-living-my-life

Gopink, A, 2012, The caging of America, *The New Yorker*, 30 January, www.newyorker.com/magazine/2012/01/30/the-caging-of-america

Gordon, A, 2008, *Ghostly matters: Haunting and the sociological imagination*, Minneapolis, MN: University of Minnesota Press

Gordon, P, 2013, *Vagabond witness: Victor Serge and the politics of hope*, Winchester: Zero Books

Gouldner, A, 1973, Foreword, in I Taylor, P Walton, J Young (eds) *The new criminology: For a social theory of deviance*, London: Routledge and Kegan Paul

Gramscii, A, 1971, *A Gramsci reader: Selected writings 1916–1935*, David Forgacs (ed), London: Lawrence and Wishart

Hage, G, 1998, *White nation: Fantasies of white supremacy in a multicultural society*, Annandale, NSW Australia: Pluto Press

Hage, G, 2003, *Paranoid nationalism: Searching for hope in a shrinking society*, London: Merlin

Hage, G, 2012, Critical anthropological thought and the radical political imaginary today, *Critique of Anthropology* 32, 3, 285–308

Hall, C, 1996, Histories, empires and the post-colonial moment, in E Chambers, L Curtis (eds) *The post-colonial question: Common skies, divided horizons*, London: Routledge

Hall, S, 1980, Race, articulation, and societies structured in dominance, *Sociological theories: Race and colonialism*, pp 305–45, Paris: UNESCO

Hall, S, 1989, The meaning of new times, in S Hall, M Jacques (eds) *New times: The changing face of politics in the 1990s*, London: Lawrence and Wishart

Hall, S, Jacques, M (eds), 1989, *New times: The changing face of politics in the 1990s*, London: Lawrence and Wishart

Hall, S. (1992). 'New Ethnicities' in J. Donald & A. Rattansi (Eds.), *'Race', Culture and Difference* London: Sage.

Hamm, MS, 2013, *The spectacular few: Prisoner radicalisation and the evolving terrorist threat*, New York: NYU Press

Hammerseley, M, 2015, Research 'inside' viewed from 'outside': Reflections on prison ethnography, in DH Drake, R Earle, J Sloan (eds) *The Palgrave handbook of prison ethnography*, Palgrave Studies in Prisons and Penology, Basingstoke: Palgrave

Hammerseley, M, Atkinson, P, 2007, *Ethnography: Principles in practice*, 3rd edn, London: Routledge

Hartigan, J, 2005, *Odd tribes: Toward a cultural analysis of white people*, London: Duke University Press

Hardt, M, Negri, A, 2001, *Empire*, Boston, MA: Harvard University Press

Hardt, M, Negri, A, 2011, *Commonwealth*, Boston, MA: Harvard University Press

Harcourt, B, 2001, Reducing mass incarceration: Lessons from the deinstitutionalisation of mental hospitals in the 1960s, *Ohio State Journal of Criminal Law* 9, 1, 53–88

Hendricksen, R, Mobley, A, 2012, A tale of two convicts: A reentry story about the impacts ethnicity and social class, *Journal of Prisoners on Prisons* 21, 1 and 2, 105–18

Henley, A, 2014, Abolishing the stigma of punishments served, *Criminal Justice Matters* 97, 22–3

Herzog-Evans, M, 2011, Judicial rehabilitation in France: Helping with the desisting process and acknowledging achieved desistance, *European Journal of Probation* 3, 1, 4–19

Hesse, D, 2003, The place of creative nonfiction, *College English* 65, 3, 237–41

Heyes, C, 2007, *Self-transformation: Foucault, ethics and normalised bodies*, New York: Oxford University Press

Hobbs, D, 1993, Peers, careers and academic fears: Writing as academic fieldwork, in D Hobbs, T May (eds) *Interpreting the field: Accounts of ethnography*, Oxford: Clarendon Press

Hobsbawn, E, 1993, The new threat to history, *New York Review*, 15 December

Hodkinson, P, 2005, 'Insider research' in the study of youth cultures, *Journal of Youth Studies* 8, 2131–49

Holdaway, S, Rock, P (eds), 1998, *Thinking about criminology*, London: University College Press

Home Office (2002) *Breaking The Circle – A Report of The review of The Rehabilitation of Offenders Act,* London. Home Office Sentencing and Offences Unit,

Home Office, 2007, *The Corston report: A report of a review of women with particular vulnerabilities in the criminal justice system*, Norwich: HMSO

Hough, M, 2014, Confessions of a recovering administrative criminologist: Jock Young, quantitative research and policy research, *Crime Media and Culture* 10, 3, 215–26

Hough, M, Jacobson, I, Millie, A, 2003, *The decision to imprison: Sentencing and the prison population*, London: Prison Reform Trust

Hughes, R, 2003, *The fatal shore*, London: Vintage

Hughes, K, 2010, Proportionality not presumption, *Cambridge Law Journal* 69, 4–6

Hughey, MW, 2014, White backlash in the 'post-racial' United States, *Ethnic and Racial Studies* 37, 5, 721–30

Hugill A, 2014, *Pataphysics: A useless guide*, Harvard, MA: MIT Press

Hytonen, M, 2012, An ugly fairy tale with an ending in hope: The founding of KRIS in Finland, *Journal of Prisoners on Prison* 21, 1 and 2, 166–72

Ignatieff, M, 1978, *A just measure of pain: The penitentiary in the industrial revolution 1750–1850*, New York: Random House

Ikuenobe, PA, 2013, Conceptualizing and theorizing about the idea of a 'post-racial' era, *Journal for the Theory of Social Behaviour* 43, 4, 446–68

Illouz, E, 2007, *Cold intimacies: The making of emotional capitalism*, Cambridge: Polity Press

Irwin, J, 1970, *The felon*, Englewood Cliffs, NJ: Prentice Hall

Irwin, J, 1980, *Prisons in turmoil*, Boston, MA: Little, Brown

Irwin, J, 2003, Preface, J Ross, S Richards (eds) *Convict criminology*, Belmont, CA: Wadsworth

Irwin, J, 2005, *The warehouse prison: Disposal of the new dangerous class*, Los Angeles, CA: Roxbury

Irwin, J, Cressey, DR, 1962, Thieves, convicts and the inmate culture, *Social Problems* 10, 2, 142–55

Jacobs, J, 1974, Participant observation in prison, *Urban Life and Culture* 3, 2, 221–40

Jackson, G, 1971, *Soledad brother: The prison letters of George Jackson*, Melbourne: Penguin

Jackson, G, 1972, *Blood in my eye*, Baltimore, MD: Black Classic Press, 1990

James, E, 2013, *Free to write: Prison voices past and present*, West Kirby: Headland Press

Jewkes, Y, 2012, Autoethnography and emotion as intellectual resources: Doing prison research differently, *Qualitative Inquiry* **18**, 1, 63–75

Jewkes, Y, 2015, Foreword, in DH Drake, R Earle, J Sloan (eds) *The Palgrave handbook of prison ethnography*, Palgrave Studies in Prisons and Penology, Basingstoke: Palgrave

Judaken, J (ed), 2008, *Race after Sartre: Antiracism, Africana existentialism, postcolonialism*, Albany, NY: State University of New York Press

Kirk, R. R. (1972) *Blacknuss*, Atlantic Records, Warner Music. USA.

Kropotkin, P, 1887, *In Russian and French prisons*, London: Ward and Downey, e-book, Les editions de Londres

Kropotkin, P, 1902, *Mutual aid: A factor of evolution*, CreateSpace Independent Publishing Platform, 2015

Kropotkin, P, 1975, Prisons and their moral influence on prisoners, in E Capouya, K Tomkins (eds) *The essential Kropotkin*, New York: Liveright

Kundnani, A, 2014, *The Muslims are coming! Islamophobia, extremism and the domestic war on terror*, London: Verso

Kunkel, B, 2014, *Utopia or bust: A guide to the present crisis*, London: Verso

Kurki, L, Morris, N, 2001, The purposes, practices and problems of supermax prisons, in M Tonry (ed) *Crime and justice: A review of research*, 28, 385–424, Chicago, IL: University of Chicago Press

Kushner, T, 2005, Racialization and 'White European' immigration to Britain, in K Murji, J Solomos (eds) *Racialization: Studies in theory and practice*, pp 207–25, Oxford: Oxford University Press

Lacey, N, 2010, Differentiating among penal states, *British Journal of Sociology* 61, 4, 778–94

Lander, I, Signe, R, Jon, N (eds), 2014, *Masculinities in the criminological field: Control, vulnerability and risk taking*, Farnham: Ashgate

Langan, P, Farrington, D, 1998, Crime and justice in the United States and in England and Wales 1981–96, *Bureau of Justice Statistics*, Washington, DC: US Deptartment of Justice

Larsen, M, Piche, J, 2012, Convict criminology and the journal of prisoners on prisons, *Journal of Prisoners on Prisons* 21, 1 and 2, 1–3

Latour, B, 2014, On some of the effects of capitalism, Lecture given at the Royal Academy, Copenhagen, 26 Feb 2014, www.bruno-latour.fr/sites/default/files/136-AFFECTS-OF-K-COPENHAGUE.pdf

Larrauri, E, 2011, Conviction records in Spain: Obstacles to reintegration of offenders?, *European Journal of Probation* 3, 1, 50–62

Larrauri E, 2014, Legal protections against background checks in Europe, *Punishment and Society* 16, 1, 50–73

Lea, J. and Young J. (1993) *What Is To Be Done About Law and Order.* London. Pluto Press

Leder, D, 2000, *The soul knows no bars: Inmates reflect on life, death and hope*, Lanham, MD: Rowman and Littlefield

Leibling, A, 2015, Descriptions at the edge? I–it/I–thou relations and action in prisons research, *International Journal of Crime, Justice and Social Democracy* 4, 1, 18–32

Leibling, A, Arnold, H, Straub, C, 2015, Prison research beyond the conventional: Dialogue, 'creating miracles' and staying sane in a maximum security prison, in DH Drake, R Earle, J Sloan (eds) *The Palgrave handbook of prison ethnography,* Palgrave Studies in Prisons and Penology, Basingstoke: Palgrave

Lemert, EM, 1967, *Human deviance, social problems and social control*, Englewood Cliffs, NJ: Prentice-Hall

Lentin, A, Titley, G, 2010, *The crises of multiculturalism: Racism in a neo-liberal age*, London: Zed Press

Levinas, E, 1981, *Otherwise than being or beyond essence*, Alphonso Linges (translator), The Hague: Martinus Nijhoff

Levi-Strauss, C, 2011, *L'anthropologie face aux problemes du monde modern*, Paris: Seuil

Lister, S, 2013, The new politics of the police: Police and crime commissioners and the 'operational independence' of the police, *Policing* 7, 3, 239–47

Loader, I, Sparks, R, 2010, *Public criminology?*, London: Routledge

Loader, I, Sparks, R, 2012, Situating criminology: On the production and consumption of knowledge about crime and justice, in M Maguire, R Morgan, R Reiner (eds) *The Oxford handbook of criminology*, 5th edn, Oxford: Oxford University Press

Love, MC, 2003, Starting over with a clean slate: In praise of a forgotten section of the model penal code, *Fordham Urban Law Journal* 30, 101–36

Lynch, M, 2000, Against reflexivity as an academic virtue and source of privileged knowledge, *Theory, Culture and Society* 17, 3, 26–54

Macey, D, 1995, *The lives of Michel Foucault*, London: Vintage

Macey, D, Rée, J, 2008, Perhaps there aren't any secrets: Jonathan Ree and David Macey in conversation on Michel Foucault, the impossible prison programme, in *Histories of the Present, Nottingham*, Nottingham: Nottingham Contemporary

McIntosh, P, 1988, White privilege and male privilege: A personal account of coming to see correspondences through work, *Women's Studies' Working Paper* 189, Wellesley College, www.iub.edu/~tchsotl/part2/McIntosh%20White%20Privilege.pdf

McIntosh, P, 1989, White privilege: Unpacking the invisible backpack, www.isr.umich.edu/home/diversity/resources/white-privilege.pdf

McLuhan, M, 1964, *The medium is the massage: An inventory of effects*, Harmondsworth: Penguin

McVicar, J, 1974, *John McVicar by himself*, London: Artnik, 2002

Malinowski, B, 1962, *Sex, culture, and myth*, New York: Harcourt, Brace and World

Mann, N, 2012, *Doing harder time: The experience of an ageing male prison population in England and Wales*, Farnham: Ashgate

Mannheim, H, 1939, *The dilemma of penal reform*, London: George Allen and Unwin

Maruna, S, 1997, Going straight: Desistance from crime and life narratives of reform, in A Lieblich, R Josselson (eds) *The narrative study of lives* 5, Thousand Oaks, CA: Sage

Maruna, S, 2001, *Making good: How ex-offenders reform and reclaim their lives*, Washington, DC: Transaction

Maruna, S, 2011, Judicial rehabilitation and the 'clean bill of health' in criminal justice, *European Journal of Probation* 3, 1, 97–117

Marx, K, Engels, F, 1848, *The Communist manifesto*, London: Verso, 2014

Mathiesen, T, 1965, *Defences of the weak: A sociological study of a Norwegian correctional institution*, London: Tavistock

Mathiesen, T, 2000, About KROM: Past–present–future, http://krom.no/hva-er-krom/

Matza, D, 1964, *Delinquency and drift*, New York: Wiley

Matza, D, 1969, *Becoming deviant*, Englewood Cliffs, NJ: Prentice Hall

Maycock, M, Hunt, K (eds), 2017, *New perspectives on prison masculinities*, Basingstoke: Palgrave

Merleau-Ponty, M, 1962, *Phenomenology of perception*, Colin Smith (translator), London: Routledge, Kegan Paul

Merton, R, 1972, Insiders and outsiders: A chapter in the sociology of knowledge, *American Journal of Sociology* 78, 9–47

Merton, R, 1988, Some thoughts on the concept of sociological autobiography, in M White Riley (ed) *Sociological lives*, London: George Allen and Unwin

Miles, S, 2005, Foreword to *Simone Weil: An anthology*, London: Penguin

Millie, A, 2016, *Philosophical criminology*, Bristol: Policy Press

Mills, C, 1997, *The racial contract*, Ithaca, NY: Cornell University Press

Mills, CW, 1959, *The sociological imagination*, Harmondsworth: Penguin

Moolman, B, 2015, Ethnography: Exploring methodological nuances in feminist research with men incarcerated for sexual offences, in DH Drake, R Earle, J Sloan (eds) *The Palgrave handbook of prison ethnography*, Palgrave Studies in Prisons and Penology, Basingstoke: Palgrave

Moore, J, 2014, Is the empire coming home? Liberalism, exclusion and the punitiveness of the British State, *Papers from the British Criminology Conference*, British Society of Criminology 14, 31–48, http://britsoccrim.org/new/volume14/pbcc_2014_moore.pdf

Morris, N, 1965, Prison in evolution, *Federal Probation* 29, 12

Morrison, T, 1993, *Playing in the dark: Whiteness and the literary imagination*, London: Vintage

Murakawa, N, 2014, *The first Civil Right: How Liberals built Prison America*, Oxford: Oxford University Press

NACRO, 2006, Getting disclosures right: A review of the use and misuse criminal record disclosures, with a guide to best practice and assessing risk, Clapham: NACRO

Nayak, A, 2005, White lives, in K Murji, J Solomos (eds) *Racialization: Studies in theory and practice*, pp 141–62, Oxford: Oxford University Press

Nayak, A, 2006, After race: Ethnography, race and post-race theory, *Ethnic and Racial Studies* 29, 3

Naylor, B, 2011, Criminal records and rehabilitation in Australia, *European Journal of Probation* 3, 1, 79–96

Negri, A, 1999, *The savage anomaly: The power of Spinoza's metaphysics and politics*, Minneapolis, MN: University of Minnesota Press

Negri, A, 2013, *Time for revolution*, London: Bloomsbury

Negri, A, 2015, *Pipeline: Letters from prison*, Cambridge: Polity Press

Nelken, D, 2010, Denouncing the penal state, *Criminology and Criminal Justice* 10, 4, 331–40

Newbold, G, Ross, J, Jones, R, Richards, S, Lenza, M, 2014, Prison research from the inside: The role of convict autoethnography, *Qualitative Inquiry* 20, 454–63

Newburn, T, 2010, Diffusion, differentiation and resistance in comparative penality, *Criminology and Criminal Justice* 10, 4, 341–52

Newburn, T, 2012, Police and crime commissioners: The Americanization of policing or a very British reform?, *International Journal of Law, Crime and Justice* 40, 1, 31–46

NRC (National Research Council), 2014, *The growth of incarceration in the United States: Exploring causes and consequences*, Washington, DC: National Academies Press

O'Donnell, I, 2004, Prison rape in context, *British Journal of Criminology* 44, 2, 241–55

ONS (Office of National Statistics), 2014, How have mortality rates by age changed over the last 50 years, London: ONS, www.ons.gov.uk/ons/rel/vsob1/death-reg-sum-tables/2013/sty-mortality-rates-by-age.html

Orwell, G, 1937, *The road to Wigan pier*, London: Penguin

Orwell, S, Angus, I (eds), 1968, *Collected essays, journalism and letters of George Orwell*, London: Penguin

Osterweil, W, 2015, How white Liberals used civil rights to create more prisons, *The Nation* 6 January, www.thenation.com/article/193977/how-white-liberals-used-civil-rights-create-more-prisons

Overing, J, Passes, A (eds), 2000, *The anthropology of love and anger: The aesthetics of conviviality in Native Amazonia*, London: Routledge

Padfield, N, 2011, Judicial rehabilitation? A view from England, *European Journal of Probation* 3, 1, 36–49

Pager, D, 2007, *Marked: Race, crime and finding work in an era of mass incarceration*, Chicago, IL: University of Chicago Press

Paseta, S, 2013, *Irish nationalist women 1900–1918*, Cambridge: Cambridge University Press

Pearson, G, 1975, Misfit sociology and politics of socialisation, in I Taylor, P Walton, J Young (eds) *Critical criminology*, London: Routledge and Kegan Paul

Pels, D, 2000, Reflexivity: One step up, *Theory Culture and Society* 17, 3, 1–25

Pfiel, F, 1995, *White guys: Studies in postmodern domination and difference*, London: Verso

Phillips, C, 2012, *The multicultural prison: Ethnicity, masculinity and social relations among prisoners*, Oxford: Oxford University Press

Phillips, C, Earle, R, 2010, Reading difference differently? Identity, epistemology and prison ethnography, *British Journal of Criminology* 50, 2, 360–78

Phillips, C, Earle, R, 2011, Cultural diversity, ethnicity and race relations in prison, in B Crewe, J Bennett, Jamie (eds) *The prisoner*, pp 117–30, Abingdon: Routledge

Phillips, C, Webster, C, 2013, *New directions in race, ethnicity and crime*, Abingdon: Routledge

Phillips, C, Webster, C, 2014, *New directions in race and criminal justice*, Abingdon: Routledge

Pijoan, L, 2014, Legal protections against criminal background checks in Europe, *Punishment and Society* 16, 1, 50–73

Pinard, M, 2010, Collateral consequences of criminal convictions: Confronting issues of race and dignity, *New York University Law Review* 85, 2, 457–534

Platt, T, 1980, John Irwin: Prisons in turmoil, Review, *Crime and Social Justice*, Winter, 70–5

Plumwood, V, 1995, Feminism, privacy and radical democracy, *Anarchist Studies* 3, 2, 97–120

Polanyi, K, 1957, *The great transformation*, Boston, MA: Beacon Press

Proctor, R, Schiebinger, L, 2008, *Agnotology: The making and unmaking of ignorance*, Standford, CA: Stanford University Press

PRT (Prison Reform Trust), 2014, Bromley Briefings prison factfile autumn 2014 http://www.prisonreformtrust.org.uk/Portals/0/Documents/Bromley%20Briefings/Factfile%20Autumn%202014.pdf)

PRT (2015) Bromley Briefings prison factfile summer 2015 http://www.prisonreformtrust.org.uk/Portals/0/Documents/Prison%20the%20facts%20May%202015.pdf

Quraishi, M, 2008, Researching Muslim prisoners, *International Journal of Social Research Methodology* 11, 5, 453–67

Ree, J, 2010, 'Perhaps there aren't any secrets' Jonathan Ree and David Macey in Conversation, *The impossible prison*, Nottingham. Nottingham Contemporary

Retort, 2004, Afflicted powers: The state, the spectacle and September 11, *New Left Review* 27, May–June

Rhodes, L, 2001, Toward an anthropology of prisons, *Annual Review of Anthropology* 30, 65–83

Rhodes, L, 2015, Ethnographic imagination in the field of prison in DH Drake, R Earle, J Sloan (eds) *The Palgrave handbook of prison ethnography*, Palgrave Studies in Prisons and Penology, Basingstoke: Palgrave

Richards, SC, 2010, John Irwin, in K Hayward, S Maruna, J Mooney (eds) *Fifty key thinkers in criminology*, London: Routledge

Richards, SC, 2015a, Personal email communication with author

Richards, SC, 2015b, *The Marion experiment: Long-term solitary confinement and the Supermax movement*, Carbondale, IL: Southern Illinois University Press

Rock, P, 2014, The public faces of public criminology, *Criminology and Criminal Justice* 14, 4, 412–33

Rock, P, Holdaway, S, 1998, Thinking about criminology: 'Facts are bits of biography', in S Holdaway, P Rock (eds) *Thinking about criminology*, London: University College Press

Rodriguez, D, 2006, *Forced passages: Imprisoned radical intellectuals and the US prison regime*, Minneapolis, MN: University of Minnesota Press

Rodriguez, D, 2014, Goldwater's left hand: Post-raciality and the roots of the post-racial racist state, *Cultural Dynamics* 26, 1

Roedigger, D, 2007, *The wages of whiteness: Race and the making of the American working class*, London: Verso

Rolston, W, 1999, Are the Irish black?, *Race and Class* 41, 1–2

Rolston, W, 2003, Bringing it all back home: Irish emigration and racism, *Race and Class* 455, 2, 39–53

Ross, IR, Richards, SC (eds), 2003, *Convict criminology*, Belmont, CA: Wadsworth

Ross, JI, Darke, S, Aresti, A, Newbold, G, Earle, R, 2014, Developing convict criminology beyond North America, *International Criminal Justice Review* 24, 2, 121–33

Russon, J, 2003, *Human experience*, Albany, NY: SUNY Press

Ryden, W, Marshall, I, 2012, *Reading, writing and the rhetorics of whiteness*, London: Routledge

Sabo, D, Kupers, T, London, W (eds), 2001, *Prison masculinities*, Philadelphia, PA: Temple University Press

Sartre, JP, 2004, *Critique of dialectical reason*, London: Verso

Sayyid, B, 1997, *A fundamental fear: Eurocentrism and the emergence of Islam*, London: Zed

Scotini, M, 2008, Remember revolution: 68 at 40, Nottingham: Nottingham Contemporary, www.nottinghamcontemporary.org/art/remember-revolution-68-40

Sedgwick, E, 1990, *The epistemology of the closet*, Berkeley, CA: University of California Press

Seligman, MEP, 1975, *Helplessness: On depression, development, and death*, San Francisco, CA: WH Freeman

Sennett, R, 1974, *The fall of public man*, Cambridge: Cambridge University Press

Serge, V, 1977, *Men in prison*, London: Writers and Readers

Seshadri-Crooks, K, 2000, *Desiring whiteness: A Lacanian analysis of race*, London: Routledge

Shalev, S, 2009, *Supermax: Controlling risk through solitary confinement*, Cullompton: Willan

Shepherd, J. (2008) 'Medical Ethics?' *Guardian*, 1/7/2008, http://www.guardian.co.uk/education/2008/jul/01/pupilbehaviour.highereducation/print , accessed 16/05/11

Silke, A, 2013, *Prisons, terrorism and extremism: Critical issues in management, radicalisation and reform*, London: Routledge

Simmel, G, 1969, The metropolis and mental life, in R Sennett (ed) *Classic essays on the culture of cities*, New York: Appleton-Century-Crofts

Simon, J, 2007, *Governing through crime: How the war on crime transformed American democracy and created a culture of fear*, Oxford: Oxford University Press

Simon, J, 2014, *Mass incarceration on Trial: A remarkable court decision and the future of prisons in America*, New York: The New Press

Skeggs, B, 2004, *Class, self, culture*, London: Routledge

Smart, C, 1990, Feminist approaches to criminology or postmodern woman meets atavistic man, in L Gelsthorpe, A Morris (eds) *Feminist perspectives in criminology*, Buckingham: Open University Press

Solomos, J, 1993, Constructions of black criminality: Racialisation and criminalisation in perspective, in D Cook, B Hudson (eds) *Racism and criminology*, London: Sage

Spark, M, 1981, *Loitering with intent*, London: Bodley Head

Spivakovsky, C, 2013, *Racialized correctional governance: The mutual construction of race and criminal justice*, Farnham: Ashgate

Squires, P, Lea, J (eds), 2013, *Criminalisation and advanced marginality: Critically exploring the work of Loïc Wacquant*, Bristol: Policy Press

Stacey, C, 2015a, Looking beyond re-offending: Criminal records and poverty, *Criminal Justice Matters* 99, 4–5

Stacey, C. (2015b) Rehabilitation & Destistance vs Disclosure, Criminal records: Learning From Europe, London. Unlock http://www.unlock.org.uk/wp-content/uploads/Rehabilitation-Desistance-vs-Disclosure-Christopher-Stacey-WCMT-report-final.pdf (accessed 5/01/16)

Standing, G. (2014) The Precariat – the new dangerous class, London. Bloomsbury.

Stiegler, B, 1998, *Technics and time: The fault of Epimetheus*, Standford, CA: Stanford University Press

Stiegler B, 2009, *Acting Out*, Stanford, CA: Stanford University Press

Stiegler, B, 2010, *For a new critique of political economy*, Cambridge: Polity Press

Stiegler, B, 2014, *Stupidity and knowledge in the 21st century: Pharmacology of the university*, Cambridge: Polity Press

Sumner, C, 1994, *The sociology of deviance: An obituary*, Buckinghamshire: Open University Press

Sviensson, KP, 2012, Introduction, in KP Sveinsson (ed) *Criminal justice v racial justice: Minority ethnic overrepresentation in the criminal justice system*, London: Runnymede Trust

Sykes, G, 1958, *The society of captives: A study of a maximum security prison*, Princeton, NJ: Princeton University Press

Tannenbaum, F, 1924, *Darker phases of the south*, New York: GP Putnam's Sons

Tannenbaum, F, 1938, *Crime and the community*, New York: Columbia University Press

Tannenbaum, F, 1946, *Slave and citizen: The Negro in the Americas*, New York: Vintage

Taylor, B, 2008, *Travellers and the state*, Manchester: Manchester University Press

Taylor, I, Walton, P, Young, J (eds), 1973, *The new criminology: For a social theory of deviance*, London: Routledge and Kegan Paul

Taylor, I, Walton, P, Young, J (eds), 1975, *Critical criminology*, London: Routledge and Kegan Paul

Thomas, T (1972) Why Can't We Live Together, Miami. Florida. Glades/TK Records.

Thomas, T, 2007, *Criminal records: A database for the criminal justice system and beyond*, Basingstoke: Palgrave

Thomas, WI, Thomas, DS, 1928, *The child in America: Behavior problems and programs*, Boston, MA: Knopf

Thrasher, FM, 1927, *The gang: A study of 1,313 gangs in Chicago*, Chicago, IL: University of Chicago Press

Tifft, L, Sullivan, D, 1980, *The struggle to be human: Crime, criminology and anarchism*, Orkney: Cienfuegos Press

Toch, H, 1998, Hypermasculinity and prison violence: Masculinities and violence, in L Bowker (ed) *Masculinities and violence*, Thousand Oaks, CA: Sage

Tonry, M, 1996, *Malign neglect: Race, crime and punishment in America*, Oxford: Oxford University Press

Tonry, M, 2004, *The future of imprisonment*, Oxford and New York: Oxford University Press

Tosh, J, 1999, *A man's place: Masculinity and the middle-class home in Victorian England*, Yale: Yale University Press

Tronto, J, 1995, Care as a basis for radical political judgements, *Hypatia* 10, 2, 141–9

Tseloni, A, Mailley, J, Farrell, G, Tilley, N, 2010, Exploring the international decline in crime rates, *European Journal of Criminology* 7, 5, 375–94

Tuana, N, 2004, Coming to understand: Orgasm and the epistemology of Ignorance, *Hypatia* 19, 1, 194–232

Tuana, N, 2006, The speculum of ignorance: The women's health movement and epistemologies of ignorance, *Hypatia* 21, 3, 1–19

Tuck, M, 1994, Research and public policy, in A Coote (ed) *Families, children and crime*, London: Institute for Public Policy Research (IPPR)

US News, 2014, Education, http://grad-schools.usnews. rankingsandreviews.com/best-graduate-schools/top-humanities-schools/criminology-rankings

Van Swaanigen, R, 1997, *Critical criminology: Visions from Europe*, London: Sage

Van Swaanigen, R, 2010, Louk Hulsman, in K Hayward, S Maruna, J Mooney (eds) *Fifty key thinkers in criminology*, London: Routledge

Van Zyl Smit, D, 2003, Civil disabilities of former prisoners in a constitutional democracy: Building on the South African experience, *Acta Juridica* 1, 221–37

Wacquant, L, 2002, The curious eclipse of prison ethnography in the age of mass incarceration, *Ethnography* 3, 4, 371–98

Wacquant, L, 2007, *Urban outcasts: A comparative sociology of advanced marginality*, Cambridge: Polity Press

Wacquant, L, 2009a, *Punishing the poor*, Durham, NC: Duke University Press

Wacquant, L, 2009b, *Prisons of poverty*, Minneapolis, MN: University of Minnesota Press

Wacquant, L, 2010a, Class, race, hyperincarceration in revanchist America, *Daedalus* Summer, 74–90

Wacquant, L, 2010b, *Deadly symbiosis: Race and the rise of the penal state*, Cambridge: Polity Press

Wacquant, L, 2014, Marginality, ethnicity and penalty in the neoliberal city: An analytic cartography, *Ethnic and Racial Studies* 37, 10, 1687–711, http://loicwacquant.net/assets/Papers/MARGINALITYETHNICITYPENALITY-Article-ERS.pdf

Waldram, JB, 2007, Everybody has a story: Listening to imprisoned sexual offenders, *Qualitative Health Research* 17, 7, 963–70

Waldram, JB, 2009, 'It's just you and Satan, hanging out at a pre-school': Notions of evil and the rehabilitation of sexual offenders, *Anthropology and Humanism* 34, 2, 219–34

Waldram, JB, 2012, *Hound pound narrative: Sexual offender habilitation and the anthropology of therapeutic intervention*, Berkeley, CA: University of California Press

Waldram, JB, 2015, Writing bad: Prison ethnography and the problem of 'tone', in DH Drake, R Earle, J Sloan (eds) *The Palgrave handbook of prison ethnography*, Palgrave Studies in Prisons and Penology, Basingstoke: Palgrave

Ware, V, Back, L, 2002, *Outside the whale: Color, politics, culture*, Chicago, IL: University of Chicago Press

Warr, J (2016) The prisoner: inside and out, in B Crewe, Y, Jewkes, Y (eds) *The handbook of prisons*, Abingdon: Routledge

Weber, M (2004). *The Vocation Lectures*, tr. by R. LIvingstone, (ed) D. Owen and T. Strong, Illinois: Hackett Books.

Weil, S, 1977, The *Illiad*, poem of might, in G Panichas (ed) *The Simone Weil reader*, New York: David Mackay

Weil, S, 2009, The situation in Germany, in DT McFarland and W Van Ness (eds) *Simone Weil: Formative writings 1929–41*, London: Routledge

Williams, D, Burnett, J, 2012, Interrelated problems of silencing voices and sexual crime: Convict criminology insights for reducing victimisation, *Journal of Prisoners on Prison* 21, 1 and 2, 132–8

Williams, R, 1971, *Orwell*, London: Fontana

Williams, R, 1977, *Marxism and literature*, Oxford: Oxford Paperbacks

Williams, R, 2014, *Keywords: A vocabulary of culture and society*, London: Fourth Estate

Wintz, C, Finkelman, P, 2004, *Encyclopedia of the Harlem renaissance*, New York: Routledge

Yarborough, R., 2010. Becoming 'Hispanic' in the 'New South': Central American immi-grants' racialization experiences in Atlanta, GA, USA. *Geojournal*, 75(3) 249-260

Yeager, M, 2011, Frank Tannebaum: The making of a convict criminologist, *The Prison Journal* 91, 2, 177–97

Yee, M, 1973, *The melancholy history of Soledad Prison: In which a Utopian scheme turns Bedlam*, New York: Harper Collins

Young, M. I. (2005) The Logic of Masculinist Protection: reflections on the current security state, in Friedman, M (ed) *Women and Citizenship: Studies in Feminist Philosophy*, Oxford. Oxford University Press

Young, J, 2007, *The vertigo of late modernity*, London: Sage

Young, J, 2011, *The criminological imagination*, Cambridge: Polity Press

Young, J, Mathews, R, 1992, *Issues in realist criminology*, London: Sage

Young, J, Mathews, R, 1993, *Rethinking criminology: The realist debate*, London: Sage

Index

Note: 'n' following page numbers indicates notes

UNIVERSITY OF WINCHESTER
LIBRARY